Bescherelle
EXERCICES
Anglais

Michèle Malavieille
agrégée de l'Université
professeur au lycée Lakanal (Sceaux)

Mireille Quivy
agrégée de l'Université
enseignante à l'université de Rouen

Wilfrid Rotgé
agrégé de l'Université
professeur de linguistique anglaise
à l'université de Toulouse - Le Mirail

HATIER

© Hatier, Paris, février 1999 - ISBN 2-218-72696-3

Conception graphique : **Massimo Miola** • Mise en page : **Isabelle Quentin**

Mode d'emploi

Les *Exercices Bescherelle* sont le complément indispensable de la *Grammaire anglaise Bescherelle* mais ils peuvent s'utiliser **indépendamment** de celle-ci.

Un outil pour maîtriser la langue anglaise

Conçus dans la même logique et suivant le même plan (mêmes parties, mêmes chapitres) que la *Grammaire anglaise Bescherelle*, les *Exercices Bescherelle* proposent un travail d'**appropriation**, de **consolidation** et de **réflexion** permettant la maîtrise de la langue anglaise.

Un outil complet et progressif

Les *Exercices Bescherelle* sont **variés** et précisément **adaptés** aux points de langue abordés. Tous les points clés y sont explorés.

Ils ne sont pas organisés en niveaux de difficulté afin de ne pas figer la dynamique de l'entraînement. En revanche, une **progression** existe, **du plus simple au plus difficile**, à l'intérieur de chaque exercice et d'un exercice à l'autre dans chaque point de grammaire abordé.

Un outil pour tous les publics

S'adressant à un large public - **lycéens, étudiants, adultes** - les *Exercices Bescherelle* sont **intégralement corrigés.**

Ils peuvent donc être utilisés aussi bien **en autonomie** qu'**en classe** (en travail individuel ou collectif). Il est conseillé de les faire en temps limité et de ne consulter les corrigés que pour valider les réponses.

Une révision préliminaire peut être nécessaire. Il suffit de se reporter pour chaque chapitre des *Exercices Bescherelle* au chapitre correspondant de la *Grammaire anglaise Bescherelle*. Des renvois de pages annoncés par le symbole → permettent des révisions plus ciblées.

Verbe + particule → 14 - 15

Sommaire

1 Le groupe verbal

1 Les verbes à particules et les verbes prépositionnels

Verbe + particule

→ 14-16

1 **Complétez ces phrases avec une particule.**

1. Go .... ! Leave me alone!
2. The plane took .... on time.
3. Don't forget to take your passport .... when you leave.
4. When can I get my money ....?
5. You're cold. Why don't you put .... a cardigan?
6. We usually eat .... on Friday evening.
7. Don't stay here, move ....
8. He says he'll do the kitchen .... when he is on holiday.
9. Has he given .... smoking yet?
10. Do come .... and see us one evening.

2 **Complétez les phrases avec la particule qui convient puis traduisez les verbes ainsi obtenus.**

1. When she said she didn't trust him, he blew .... at her.
2. Could you call .... at the post office on your way home tonight?
3. The match was called .... due to the bad weather conditions.
4. I'll call you .... at six.
5. You'll get into trouble if you carry .... like that!
6. You'll have to cut .... on luxuries if you want to go on that cruise.
7. She is most unpleasant: she keeps cutting .... when others are talking.
8. I ended .... by telling him the whole story...
9. How is he getting .... with his wife now?
10. She is a poor speaker: she can't get her ideas .... to her audience.
11. They seem to be pretty close: they always hang .... together.
12. Can you put us .... for the weekend when we come to London?
13. Don't put .... going to the dentist's if you have a toothache.
14. We'd better hurry: our time is running ....
15. Techno doesn't turn me ....

3 **Remplacez le verbe en italiques par le verbe entre parenthèses plus une particule.**

► The fire-brigade soon *extinguished* the fire. (put) ▷ The fire-brigade soon put the fire out.

1. Five prisoners have *escaped* and are on the run. (break)
2. Several experiments have been *conducted* in that field. (carry)
3. The news *spread* that more people would be made redundant. (get)
4. The exam was easy enough. Most candidates *passed.* (get)
5. His book was *refused* by four publishers. (turn)

6. If you can't *persevere*, then *admit defeat*! (keep) (give)
7. He *entered suddenly* and switched off the television. (burst)
8. Her interest in him seems to have *lost in power*. (wear)
9. He *proved* to be an excellent cook. (turn)
10. If you'll *wait* a second, I'll look for her and tell her you're on the phone. (hang)

Verbes transitifs / verbes intransitifs

→ 13-19

4 **Traduisez.**

1. Il n'a pas encore répondu à ma lettre.
2. Il cherche ses clefs.
3. Il manque de courage.
4. Hier, nous avons attendu un taxi vingt minutes.
5. As-tu téléphoné à Judith ?
6. Je leur demanderai davantage de renseignements.
7. Que penses-tu de ça ?
8. J'ai pensé à ce que tu as dit.
9. Elle se souvient de lui.
10. Est-ce que tu lui fais confiance ?
11. Elle joue merveilleusement du violon.
12. Qu'est-ce que tu regardes comme ça ?
13. Il entra dans la pièce sans frapper.
14. Vous n'avez pas traité le sujet.
15. As-tu besoin d'un dictionnaire ?
16. J'ai assez d'argent pour payer le repas.
17. Nous discuterons de ce sujet plus tard.
18. J'espère des jours meilleurs.
19. Est-ce que tu assisteras à la réunion ?
20. Je ne peux pas t'expliquer ce mot.

2 Be - Have - Do

Be - have

→ 20-29

1 **Remplacez *'s* par *is* ou *has* lorsque c'est possible.**

1. That's what he's just said.
2. He's had a long chat with her at Paul's and it's all sorted out.
3. She's getting married next month.
4. It's got a certain reputation.
5. She thinks she's always right.
6. What's the matter with her? She's always cold.
7. He's agreed to her proposal.
8. It's them again! Let's get out of here!
9. He's said to have married twice.
10. "We've got him. He's agreed. He signed tonight." "It's wonderful. He's the right age, he's got the right contacts, he's worked in America..."

2 **Employez *have* au temps indiqué et à la forme qui convient.**

1. .... you .... a good time? (prétérit)
2. She .... not .... a car. (présent)
3. I .... never .... so much to do. (present perfect)
4. Yesterday they .... dinner at 9. (prétérit)
5. "......... you really .... to go now?" "Yes, I'm afraid I .... to." (présent)
6. I .... not usually .... a drink before dinner. (présent)
7. We had free tickets: we .... not .... to pay. (prétérit)
8. This ring is very dear to me: I .... it for years. (present perfect)
9. We couldn't go out in the rain: we .... not .... an umbrella. (prétérit)
10. We .... plenty of time: we .... not .... to hurry. (présent)

3 **Traduisez.**

1. Il aura quatorze ans en décembre.
2. Tu devrais avoir honte.
3. Il a les yeux bleus.
4. As-tu faim ou soif ?
5. Nous avons reçu beaucoup de visiteurs cet été.
6. Vous en reprendrez ?
7. Vous vous êtes bien amusés ?
8. Elles ont le même âge.
9. J'ai tout ce qu'il me faut.
10. Ça a quelle hauteur ?

"Il y a" / "Il y avait" / "Il y aura"

→ 22

4 **Soulignez les formes qui équivalent à "il y a / il y avait / il y aura..." Puis classez-les dans le tableau proposé.**

1. I'm not new; I've done it for years.
2. Winning is an important word. There is one that achieves what he wanted to do and there are hundreds of thousands that fail.
3. Now they were twenty and they had not seen each other for years.
4. It has been a long time since you came to town.
5. Twenty years ago tonight I dined here with my friend.
6. The building teemed with (*grouillait de*) cats. There were even a couple of dogs... There were many complaints.
7. I found a bag of money 52 years ago. I took that bag and used it to make more money.
8. The school has only been here a hundred years.

- pose l'existence de : ....
- établit un repère dans le révolu : ....
- exprime la durée : ....

5 **Traduisez les phrases de l'exercice 4.**

6 **Traduisez.**

1. Il y a un restaurant indien dans ma rue. J'y ai dîné il y a trois jours.
2. "Quand as-tu vu ta mère pour la dernière fois (*last*) ? – Il y a presque deux ans."
3. Il y a vingt huit ans qu'il est député (*an M.P.*).
4. "Il y a combien de temps que tu as visité Londres ? – Cinq ou six ans."
5. Il y a neuf mille kilomètres de Paris à San Francisco.
6. Il y a huit ans que je le connais.
7. Il y a combien jusqu'au prochain arrêt de bus ?
8. Il y a vingt ans, c'était différent.

Do (does / did) de reprise

→ 29-35

7 **Complétez ces phrases avec *do* (*does* / *don't* / *doesn't*) ou *did* (*didn't*).**

1. "I punched him in the nose once or twice, I think." "You think?" "I guess I ...."
2. "So you like that, ... you?" "Well, yes," she answered. "I must say I ...."
3. He inquired whether they had enjoyed themselves. "Yes, we .... ," Grace replied.
4. "I overheard you talking about those books." "Oh? You ...., ... you?"
5. "You knew all the time she was ill, ... you?"
6. "Would you like me to explain?" "Please ...."
7. You never know what to expect from these sorts of things, ... you?
8. "You gave him the address, ... you?"
9. "I don't suppose you phoned him, ... you?"
10. "What right have they got to send me this?" "I don't know, I really ...."

8 Traduisez.

1. Je te l'ai dit, non ?
2. Vous ne connaissez pas l'homme, moi oui.
3. "Je pourrais obtenir un meilleur travail. – J'en doute. – Ah oui ? Pourquoi ?"
4. "Il vit ici maintenant. – Ah oui, c'est vrai ? Je ne savais pas."
5. "Il m'a dit quelque chose sur toi. – Il a fait ça ? Et qu'est-ce que c'était ?"
6. Je ne comprends pas pourquoi il est venu si tôt. Et toi ?
7. "Je t'avais dit d'utiliser l'ordinateur. – C'est ce que j'ai fait !"
8. Nous savons où c'est. Et vous ?

3 Le présent

Formes du présent simple et du présent en be + V-ing → 36-39

1 **Mettez les verbes suivants à la troisième personne du singulier du présent, forme affirmative.**

run • work • pay • lie • cry • catch • laugh • go • hurry • pass • relax

2 **Mettez ces phrases à la forme interrogative.**

1. She gets up at 6. What time .... ?
2. Yes, it's raining very hard. .... ?
3. I'm reading *Dark Water*. What .... ?
4. Yes, she agrees with you. .... ?
5. No, I don't like sweets. .... ?
6. He's coming back tomorrow. When .... ?
7. She leaves home at 7 every day. When .... ?
8. They do nothing. What .... ?
9. Yes, she knows him. .... ?
10. I'm waiting for my change. What .... ?

Valeur de be + V-ing → 37-43

3 **Mettez le verbe entre parenthèses au présent simple ou en *be* + V-*ing*.**

1. Did I hear you alright or (dream / I)?
2. I hardly ever (dream) of him and yet I (love) him.
3. You can't see her now. She (have) a bath.
4. You (look) sad. What (think / you) about?
5. "(write / you) to him tonight?" "Yes, I always (write) to him on June 17th."
6. This film (come) to the local cinema next week. (want / you) to see it?
7. Mark, whose forty fourth birthday (come up), (think) of himself as a lucky man.
8. When people (say) the subway (frighten) them they (not be) silly.
9. "They (not have) cars like we (do), (do / they)?" said my mother.
I said, "What (talk / you) about, Mom, of course the British (have) cars."
"What about the food? Should I bring some with me?"
"Mom, you (come) to London, you (not trek) through Katmandu."
10. "You (look) so young!" "I'm twenty two." "Then this year in America – (look / you) for work there?" "I (actually not look) for anything. I (pass through)."
11. Before he (leave) the office in the evening, Patrick always asks, "(come / anyone) for a drink?"
12. He (give up) trying to drill the safe open and he (start) looking through his satchel for something. It (seem) that what he (look for) is a little bottle of explosive.

4 **Soulignez les verbes au présent puis classez-les dans le tableau.**

1. I am just going round the corner. Your tea is ready. Don't feed the cat.
2. "Where do you shop?" "Sainsbury's."
3. We begin the journey home. The snow is falling heavily. The temperature is dropping.
4. "It's a pity you don't like her. You don't, do you?" "Why do you ask?" "My intuition," said her daughter.
5. "We're expecting great things of you, Mr Perry." "Thank you, Mr Nolan."
6. He sits on his bar-stool and I reckon he's thinking the same things I'm thinking.
7. Gus ties his laces, rises, yawns and begins to walk slowly to the door. He stops, looks down, and shakes his foot.
8. What I'm saying is this: I don't want Jane heading for a nervous breakdown.
9. "I really am sorry. I'm always doing this." "Oh, it doesn't matter."
10. Nobody in this house is speaking to you ever again.
11. Don't talk to me. I don't care. It doesn't bother me. I don't know why you're all being so unsociable.
12. "You say 'bloody'," she said to Larry.
"You say it all the time."
"No, I don't."
"Come off it. You're always saying 'bloody this' and 'bloody that.'"

Le **présent simple** est utilisé pour :
- énoncer une caractéristique du sujet : ....
- relater un film d'actions successives : ....
- décrire une habitude : ....

Le **présent en *be* + V-*ing*** est utilisé pour :
- montrer l'événement à un moment de son déroulement : ....
- insister sur un fait ou une action : ....
- exprimer un point de vue dépréciatif : ....
- annoncer la réalisation d'une action déjà envisagée : ....

5 **Traduisez.**

1. Je ne fais pas la cuisine aujourd'hui.
2. Je pense déménager (*move*) à Londres.
3. Ce que je suis en train d'essayer de dire, c'est que tu ne peux pas revenir ici.
4. Si je ne fais pas ça maintenant, ce ne sera pas prêt ce soir.
5. Vous avez tous les deux besoin d'une coupure. Pourquoi ne partez-vous pas ?
6. J'ai pensé qu'il valait mieux que je te le dise : je pars. J'ai envie de changer.
7. "Ta mère est d'accord ? – Oui."
8. "C'est Patrick. Comment ça va ? – Patrick ! – J'espère que je ne vous dérange pas."
9. "On s'occupera de lui, ne t'inquiète pas. – Tu veux me dire (*tell*) qu'il va mal ?"
10. Chaque soir, il raconte une histoire aux gosses et puis il va au lit.

4 Le prétérit

Formes du prétérit simple

→ 44-45

1 **Mettez le verbe entre parenthèses au prétérit simple. Attention aux verbes irréguliers (+ = forme affirmative, – = forme négative, ? = forme interrogative).**

1.	+	(see)	I .... your sister yesterday.
2.	+	(carry)	They .... a great amount of cash.
3.	?	(fly)	.... you .... to New York?
4.	+	(teach)	She .... English for two years.
5.	–	(think)	She .... about it.
6.	+	(think)	I .... it would make you happy.
7.	?	(forgive)	.... he .... her?
8.	+	(lose)	He .... his key.
9.	+	(send)	I .... the letter yesterday.
10.	?	(send)	Why .... you .... it to the laundry?
11.	–	(sleep)	He .... well.
12.	–	(catch)	They .... the thief.
13.	+	(lay)	He .... his briefcase on the table.
14.	?	(lie)	Why .... you ....? You could have told the truth!
15.	+	(lie)	He .... in bed, thinking of nothing.
16.	+	(fall)	He .... downstairs.
17.	+	(feel)	She .... very happy indeed.
18.	?	(win)	.... they .... ?
19.	+	(strike)	He .... the first blow.
20.	+	(bring)	He .... me nice flowers.
21.	?	(buy)	How many .... they .... ?
22.	+	(mean)	It .... she could not go.
23.	?	(meet)	Where .... you .... her?
24.	+	(pay)	He .... attention.
25.	+	(lead)	She .... them into the living room.

Emploi du prétérit simple

→ 45-50

2 **Indiquez la valeur du prétérit dans les énoncés suivants : renvoi au révolu (R.R.), discours indirect (D.I.), non réel (N.R.). Puis traduisez.**

1. When I **was** eighteen I **decided** to study medicine.
2. “What should I say if I **was asked** when I last **saw** him?”
3. Sitting next to her, Adam **shook** his head. He **was** tall, dark. She **thought** he **looked** like one of those perfect men in magazine advertisements.
4. He **talked** to her as if she **were** a baby.
5. What would happen if I **went**?
6. She **felt** vexed. Why **didn't** those thoughts **stay** hidden at the back of her mind?

7. "You think it's a good idea? It seems..." How **did** it **seem**? He **wondered**.
8. She **knocked off** work early, **said** she **had** a headache, **packed up** and **hit** the road.
9. It would be best if you **discussed** this with her.
10. In the days following the funeral, her movements **slowed down**, as if she **were sleepwalking** and any movement **seemed** to take a lot of effort.
11. I'd much rather you **didn't tell** him.
12. If only I **was** their age and **knew** what I know now.

Prétérit simple ou prétérit en be + V-ing

→ 44-54

3 **Mettez le verbe entre parenthèses au prétérit simple ou au prétérit en *be* + V-*ing*.**

1. I (think) while you are in the village you might have a word with Mr Blank.
2. Shortly before nightfall, a group of campers (enjoy) a barbecue near Ayers Rock. Suddenly, there (be) a shout.
3. Watches? Rings? Beck (not know) what she (talk) about and when she (persist) he (run) off to tell a policeman that a strange lady (annoy) him.
4. "What's going on here?" "That's precisely what I (ask)."
5. Something strange (happen) to me last night: I (go) home on foot and all the time I (have) the strange impression that someone (follow) me. I (turn) around several times but I (never see) anybody.
6. What (do/you) when he (come) in?

4 **Mettez le verbe entre parenthèses au prétérit simple ou au prétérit en *be* + V-*ing*.**

1. *Mr James S. (kill) his wife in a dream yesterday night. He (dream) that his daughter who (sleep) in the same room (be attacked) by assassins and he (fire) on them, with the result that he (kill) his wife.*

Yesterday Mr S., his wife and their two daughters (go) to bed as usual about 10. Towards midnight Mr S. (think) he (hear) the window open. Turning over, he (see) two masked men enter the room with knives. One (go) and (stand) over the daughter. In frantic terror Mr S. (fire) the pistol which he (clutch) in his hand beneath the pillow. Switching on the light he (see) that blood (trickle) from his wife's head. He then (realize) he had been dreaming but his wife (be) dead.

The Times, 27. 11. 1919.

2. "I (see) the vet (*le vétérinaire*) ride to the pub..." "What on?" "On his bike." "I (think) he (have) a scooter." "That's right. He (ride) his scooter when he (meet) the rep (*le représentant*)." "Was he a man with a mac?" "Yes, with a mac and specs." "I (see) him then." "As I (say), the vet (meet) the rep and they (go) into the pub with the ref (*l'arbitre*)..." "So there was the ref and the vet and the rep, so what?" "They (talk) of rugger." "Rubbish, there's nothing like soccer!" "Right as I (say) they (talk); suddenly I (see) a woman with a pram..." "Where (come / she) from?" "She (come) out of the hairdresser with a new perm." "So what?" "So she (cry), 'Look! The vet's scooter's gone' and gone it (be)! At full revs (*à toute vitesse*)! A young man had gone off with it!"

E. Lemercier, *36 Sketches in Everyday English*.

Traduction de l'imparfait

→ 53-54

5 **Traduisez.**

1. Elle avait 28 ans et elle allait conquérir le monde.
2. Elle ne savait pas ce qu'ils cherchaient.
3. Il demanda si elle savait à qui appartenaient les clefs.
4. Il ne voulait pas seulement lui plaire.
5. Les enfants n'écoutaient pas, ils étaient trop occupés à regarder le match.
6. Ceci l'intriguait (*puzzle*). Ils atteignirent la plage : tout le monde profitait du beau temps, beaucoup de gens se baignaient.
7. Tous les soirs il allait la voir chez elle; il lui parlait de sa journée de travail; elle faisait semblant d'écouter.
8. C'était une belle matinée. Elle regarda autour d'elle : la rosée (*the dew*) brillait sur l'herbe, les oiseaux chantaient.
9. Lorsque les vagues déferlaient (*break*), Jimmy était toujours à la plage. Il aimait faire du surf.
10. Et à présent la femme se baissait et lâchait (*release*) le chien. Comme s'il obéissait à un ordre (*obey some command*), il se glissa (*slip*) dans les buissons.

SYNTHÈSE

Prétérit ou present perfect ?

1 **Relevez les verbes au prétérit, puis les verbes au present perfect. Soulignez les indices qui justifient l'emploi de l'un ou l'autre temps.**

Carol Shields does not write about gangsters or spies. She once said: "I am interested in reality."
Gradually, this modest part-time academic, mother of five children, has become one of Canada's best-known novelists. She was born in Illinois in 1935, she attended the University of Ottawa and settled in Canada in 1957. She has lived there since that date.
"I guess I always wanted to be a writer," she says, "but it seemed impossible, like being a movie star."
She was awarded a Pullitzer Prize for *The Stone Diaries* which was published in 1993. *Larry's Party,* her latest novel, is likely to be widely successful. "I wanted to write about a man," she says, "I have written about men before but not, I think, very thoroughly or very well."
Carol Shields, in *Larry's Party* has written a novel that examines a cultural revolution. "I think the biggest change of the millennium is the emergence of women as whole people. This is what feminism has always meant to me, just that women are wholly human. Before they were half beings. This change has had a tremendous impact on men – they have had to redefine what it means to be masculine."

Adapted from *The Good Book Guide*, October 1998.

2 **Mettez le verbe entre parenthèses au prétérit ou au present perfect.**

1. (taste / you) this new snack yet? It's delicious.
2. It wasn't the Americans who (invent) ice-cream. In 200 B.C. Chinese peasants (mix) snow with milk and rice and they (teach) the art of ice-cream making to the Indians. Ice-cream (become) now a part of the staple diet all over the world.
3. An eleven-year old boy (be electrocuted) at a sea-side amusement arcade. His body (be found) behind a machine. Police say that he (touch) the wires at the back of the machine and (be electrocuted)
4. It just (happen) when we (meet) at a club. We (swap : *échanger*) telephone numbers but I (not hear) from her since and she (not hear) from me.
5. Charleston, the city that (give) its name to a dance (step) into the limelight again.
6. The general tendency of industrialisation (be) to replace human skill by the skill of machines.
7. "Well, friends," the captain (say), "it seems we (make) it."
8. "Is your eyesight good?"
"I (never have) to wear spectacles."
"So, you have no doubt that the man you (see) that night is the prisoner?"

3 **Mettez le verbe entre parenthèses au prétérit ou au present perfect.**

1. Between 1914 and 1991 the world (change) more profoundly and more violently than at any time in history.

The history of the 20 years after 1973 is that of a world which (lose) its bearings and (slide) into instability and crisis.

2. "Bill Clinton says he (create) 11 million new jobs since he (become) president", a police officer in Annapolis, Maryland, (tell) me sarcastically in the autumn of 1996. "Sure he has. I have four of them."

Gavin Esler, *The United States of Anger.*

3. The members of the scientific mission from Madrid (complete) their examination of the skeleton of the Dinosaur discovered near Tetuan. They (come) to the conclusion that the remains are not those of a Dinosaur at all. The mysterious "reptile" is a hay-making machine which (belong) to a Spanish farmer who (abandon) his property in 1917 during the Rifi war. The agricultural machinery (be enveloped) in a landslip caused by the heavy rains of that winter.

The Times, 30. 1. 1930.

5 Le present perfect

Formes du present perfect

→ 55-56 et 61

1 **Mettez le verbe entre parenthèses au present perfect simple (+ : forme affirmative, – : forme négative, ? : forme interrogative).**

1.	?	(be)	Where .... you ....?
2.	+	(catch)	She .... a mouse.
3.	–	(hear)	I .... of him lately.
4.	+	(forget)	He ....
5.	+	(go)	They .... just .... out.
6.	+	(spend)	She .... a lot of money.
7.	?	(speak)	.... you .... to him yet?
8.	?	(think)	.... you .... about it?
9.	+	(weep)	She .... many tears.
10.	–	(pay)	We .... the telephone bill yet.
11.	+	(ride)	I .... never .... a camel.
12.	+	(teach)	He .... physics for ten years.
13.	?	(win)	.... you ....?
14.	–	(meet)	They .... yet.
15.	?	(read)	.... you .... her latest novel?

2 **Mettez le verbe entre parenthèses au present perfect en *be* + V-*ing* (+ : forme affirmative, – : forme négative, ? : forme interrogative).**

1.	+	(read)	I ....
2.	?	(smoke)	.... you ....?
3.	+	(fish)	They .... for hours.
4.	+	(wait)	We .... for hours.
5.	?	(look)	How long .... they .... for him?
6.	?	(do)	What .... you ....?
7.	+	(sleep)	He .... for ten hours, it's time he woke up.
8.	?	(wear)	How long .... you .... glasses?
9.	+	(shop)	I .... all day, my feet are dropping off.
10.	+	(ask)	I .... you to mend the floor for six weeks.

For ou since ?

→ 59-61

3 **Complétez les phrases suivantes avec *for* ou *since*. Puis traduisez.**

1. I've known him .... eight years.
2. He travelled in Australia .... six months.
3. It has been a long time .... he played this sonata.
4. Have they actually been here .... Monday?
5. I have not seen them .... the birth of their son.
6. Can I leave these here .... a few hours?

7. .... when have you been watching TV?
8. She's been married .... two years.
9. It's twenty years .... she died.
10. I'll love him .... ever.

4 **Employez *for* ou *since* et mettez le verbe entre parenthèses au temps qui convient : present perfect simple ou en *be* + *V-ing*, past perfect simple ou en *be* + V-*ing*.**

1. I (be stuck) .... at the same career grade .... seven years.
2. He (be known) .... as Chubby .... a teenager. No one can remember the time when he was called by his real name.
3. This statue is probably the most startling thing to (be seen) .... the founding of Oxford University.
4. It (rain) .... ten days when I arrived in Edinburgh.
5. .... 1990 our team (win) .... the world championship five times.
6. The proportion of lone-parent families (triple) .... 1971.
7. The woman (wander) .... round the car showroom .... nearly an hour before a salesman at last offered to help.
8. Consider what (happen) .... to him .... he (turn) .... twenty five last August.
9. .... July 1st large numbers of Californian teenagers (have) .... a hard time. The reason: all those obtaining their driving licences after that date (be prohibited) .... a year from driving at night unless accompanied by someone over twenty five.

5 **Traduisez.**

1. Il est réveillé depuis trois heures. (Cela fait trois heures...)
2. Il est réveillé depuis trois heures de l'après-midi.
3. Il est en mer (*at sea*) depuis plus de six semaines.
4. Elle est professeur d'économie politique à Oxford depuis 1991.
5. Nous ne sommes pas payés depuis cinq semaines.
6. "Depuis combien de temps faites-vous cela ? – Depuis que j'ai quitté l'université, il y a neuf ans."
7. Toute une année s'est écoulée depuis son retour.
8. J'essaie d'ouvrir cette porte depuis 45 minutes.
9. Son roman est un best seller depuis presque un an.
10. Le jardin était à l'abandon (*be neglected*) depuis des années quand nous l'avons acheté.

Present perfect simple ou en be + V-ing ? → 62-65

6 **Traduisez.**

1. Cela fait deux heures que tu téléphones. Tu n'as pas bientôt (*nearly*) fini ?
2. "Tu as l'air exténuée (*exhausted*). — Oui, j'ai fait du jogging et cela fait des années que je n'ai pas couru."
3. Qu'est-ce que tu fabriquais ? Ça fait des heures que je t'attends.
4. Tu as déjà fait ton travail (*homework*) ? Moi, je travaille depuis des heures et je n'ai pas encore fini.

7 Mettez le verbe entre parenthèses au temps qui convient.

1. He (sleep) since 10 o'clock; it's time he woke up!
2. He (sleep) through the alarm clock, that's why he's so late.
3. This is the most comfortable bed I (ever sleep) in.
4. I (teach) hundreds of students but I (never meet) such a hopeless group.
5. I (teach) for thirty years, so don't think you can teach an old dog new tricks!
6. "(smoke / you) today?" "Yes, four or five cigarettes."
7. The room smells. (smoke / you)?
8. He (paint) the ceiling, that's why the room looks so bright now.
9. "Her clothes are covered in paint." "Of course, she (paint)."
10. He (drink) two pints of beer. He shouldn't drive.

8 Mettez le verbe entre parenthèses au temps qui convient.

1. What happened to your hair? What (do / you) with yourself?
2. I (not laugh) so much in ages.
3. "I (try) to finish this exercise for hours. I wish you'd stop talking." "I (hardly say) anything."
4. "I (never see) you crying before." "It (happen) for ages." "I didn't know. How awful!"
5. The peanut probably originated in Brazil although no fossils (be found) to prove this. But as long as people (make) pottery in South America, that is for about 3,500 years, they (make) jars decorated with peanuts. There was a lull in the 60s but over the past three years the trade (grow) again.

SYNTHÈSE

Présent ou present perfect ?

1 **Complétez les phrases en employant le verbe entre parenthèses au temps qui convient : présent simple ou en *be* + V-*ing*, present perfect simple ou en *be* + V-*ing*.**

1. “I (go) out. (want / you) anything?”
2. “Pleased to meet you, Sandy. Where (come / you) from?” “I (come) from Maryville. “How long (be / you) here?” “I’ve just only arrived.”
3. (know / he) what we (talk) about?
4. What (plot / you) four?
5. The bus (leave) at half past ten.
6. “Your report is a disgrace” “It’s not fair. I (try) hard, really.”
7. He (run) restaurant for more than twenty years.
8. It’s the first time she (kiss) him.
9. “Wake up! It’s the day I (wait) for. Come on, get up!” “What is it? I (sleep)!”
10. The jeans market (shrink). Jeans sales (slump) by more than 3 million pairs in the year to May. Yet, denim (remain) fashionable – as long as it’s used for anything but jeans. Whether it (be) hip or nostalgic its appeal is universal.

2 **Traduisez.**

1. Que se passe-t-il lorsque les portes sont fermées ?
2. Qu’est-ce que c’est que tout ce bruit ? Que se passe-t-il ?
3. “Tu as entendu le téléphone ? – Oui, j’arrive.”
4. J’utilise ce stylo depuis des années.
5. Il a acheté son billet ce matin : il prend l’avion pour Londres cet après-midi.
6. C’est la première fois que je suis loin d’elle.
7. Tu dors tout le temps !
8. Cela fait combien de temps qu’il est assis là ?
9. C’est un problème qui nous menace (*creep up on*) depuis des années.
10. Tu as travaillé tout ce temps-là ?

3 **Le passé composé : prétérit ou present perfect ? Traduisez.**

1. Et la nuit dernière, tu as réussi à dormir ?
2. Tu n’as pas écouté ce qu’il a dit.
3. Nous y sommes allés il y a trois ans.
4. “Combien de comédies Shakespeare a-t-il écrit ? – Je ne sais pas, mais il les a écrites quand il était jeune.”
5. J’ai marché trop vite, c’est pourquoi je suis fatiguée.
6. Tu as pris combien de cachets (*tablets*) ?
7. Tu n’es pas revenu à la maison une seule fois en cinq ans.
8. “Pourquoi as-tu accepté ? – Je n’ai pas pu dire non.”
9. Qu’est-ce que tu as fait à ce couteau ? La lame (*the blade*) est tordue (*twisted*).
10. “Nous allions commencer sans toi. – Désolée, je me suis perdue.”

4 Choisissez la forme verbale appropriée.

is working • works • has worked • worked • has been working

1. Il **travaille** quarante heures par semaine.
2. Il **a** beaucoup **travaillé** la semaine dernière.
3. Elle est fatiguée, cela fait trois heures qu'elle **travaille.**
4. Elle **travaille** depuis cinq ans dans cette usine.
5. Tais-toi, il **travaille.**

has never worked • does not work • did not work

6. Ça ne **marche** pas.
7. Ça ne **marchait** pas il y a deux semaines.
8. Ça n'**a** jamais **marché.**

wrote • has written • writes • has been writing

9. Il **a écrit** un article sur ce sujet.
10. Il y a quatre ans, il **a écrit** un article sur ce sujet.
11. Cela fait dix ans qu'il **écrit** pour *The Economist.*
12. Il **écrit** pour *The Economist.*

6 Le past perfect

1 Mettez le verbe entre parenthèses au prétérit ou au past perfect.

1. "Thank you very much," he said, astonished. He (never see) her so generous.
2. The next day she (move) away, as she (plan) to.
3. They wondered where she (go).
4. Sometimes they (talk) about places they (visit) together. They (never seem) to remember the same things.
5. When she (cry) for half an hour she (begin) to feel better.
6. For three weeks she (behave) as if nothing (change).
7. She thought perhaps he (forget).
8. When he came back, she (be) puzzled and a little hurt. (forget / he)?
9. She (take) the news as calmy as if she (expect) it.

2 Mettez le verbe donné entre parenthèses au prétérit ou au past perfect.

1. A Chicago judge today (grant) divorce to Mr R. on the grounds of his wife's silence. The plaintiff (*le plaignant*) (inform) the Court that, although his wife (live) in his house, she (not speak) to him for eighteen years. He (declare) that it (be) like living with a ghost. He (consult) physicians in the effort to get her to talk but it (be) impossible to surprise her into uttering a word.

The Times, 7. 10. 1922.

2. Through the arrest of three former prisoners of the San Quentin prison in California who (be released) on parole at various times last year, it (become) known today that counterfeit $ 10 bank notes, with which they (be supplied) (be manufactured) on the prison's own printing presses. In examining the men's prison records, the Secret Service (find) that all three (have) access to the printing shop while they were serving their terms.

The Times, 13. 2. 1936.

3. I (go) back to Oxford recently. I (not be) back since we all (leave), almost twenty years ago. I (be) surprised to see how little the city (change). Although there (be) new buildings everywhere and the main crossroads (be widened), the main landmarks (remain) in place.

3 Complétez avec le verbe entre parenthèses conjugué au temps qui convient : prétérit simple ou en *be* + V-*ing*, past perfect simple ou en *be* + V-*ing*.

1. It happened one Saturday morning: I (go) down to see if there (be) any post for me. I (pass) Wanda on the stairs. She (smile) with her letters in her hands. For me, there (be) a letter from my cousin. I (stand), beside the hall-stand, opening it. Suddenly from Wanda's room (come) a long, loud cry.
2. He (stop) reading and (stare) at the wall across from his desk. The wall (need) painting. It (need) painting for years.
3. She (stand) in the doorway when he (begin) to speak: she (not have) time even to take off her coat.

4. On the third morning she (look) out of her bedroom window and (sniff) the air happily. It (be) a gentle grey morning with a smell of soft wet earth. The kind of smell that she (miss) for the past two years and a half. Wonderful to be home again, wonderful to be here in her own little bedroom which she (think) of so often when she (be) overseas.
5. Brian Blessed (cheat) death when his plane (crash-land) in a Venezuelan rain forest. The 61-year-old actor, who (film) *The Lost World* for BBC TV (have) to swim through a swamp (*un marécage*) for fear the plane would explode.

4 **Complétez avec le verbe entre parenthèses conjugué au temps qui convient : prétérit simple ou en *be* +V-*ing*, past perfect simple ou en *be* + V-*ing*.**

1. She (push) open the door. Women (sit) at the table. She (see) her mother among them. In five years her hair (go) grey and she (look) very old. Everyone (stop) what they (do)
2. "What (happen)?" "A massive heart attack. He (have) two or three warnings before but..." "Where (be / he)?" "He (say) he (not feel) great. Yesterday morning. (Be / it) yesterday or the day before? Anyway, he (feel) sickish and (have) a bit of pain across here." She (touch) her chest. "And he (have) these pains in the upper arm. I (tell) him to take his tablets. And off he (go) to open the bar. The next time I (see) him he (be) dead."

Bernard MacLaverty, *Grace Notes.*

Maîtriser les formes verbales

1 **Complétez les phrases avec la forme verbale appropriée : prétérit ou participe passé.**

1. She (teach) English for two years and then decided to immigrate to Australia. There, she (meet) a surfer and (fall) in love with him.
2. When I was a kid I (read) a chapter of that book every night.
3. I have (know) him for years.
4. I (think) you had (forget) him.
5. He (lay) his attaché case on the desk and (leave).
6. I have never (ride) a camel.
7. She often (lie down) after lunch.
8. He (fall) downstairs and (break) his arm.
9. Have you (run)?
10. He has (catch) a cold.

2 **Traduisez.**

1. Combien d'argent a-t-il perdu? *How much money did he ....?*
2. As-tu compris ? *Have you ....?*
3. Que vas-tu choisir ? *What are you going to ....?*
4. Est-ce que la cloche a sonné ? *Has the bell ....?*
5. Il m'a apporté des fleurs. *He has .... me flowers.*
6. Il n'en a pas pensé grand'chose. *He .... much of it.*
7. Il se mit aussitôt au travail. *He .... to work at once.*
8. À quelle heure le soleil se lève-t-il ? *What time .... ?*
9. Est-ce que tu as retrouvé ton porte-monnaie ? *Have you .... your wallet?*
10. Qui a écrit cette lettre ? *Who .... ?*

3 **Conjuguez le verbe entre parenthèses au temps et à la forme indiqués (+ : forme affirmative, – : forme négative, ? : forme interrogative).**

1. Every time someone (**tell** / présent / **+**) .... me the world (**go** / présent en *be* + V-*ing* / **+**) .... to end I simply (**believe** / présent / –) .... it.
2. "What experience (**have** / present perfect / **?**) .... you .... and (**have** / present / **?**) .... you .... references ?" "I (never **do** / present perfect / **+**) .... anything quite like this before but I (**keep** / present perfect / **+**) .... house for my mother for quite a time and I (**do** / present perfect / **+**) .... quite a lot of cooking for dinner parties.
3. "I wish you (**live** / prétérit / –) .... in such a mess. And by the way where are all the books I (**bring** / prétérit / **+**) .... you last time I (**come** / prétérit / **+**) ....?
4. I wish everything (**become** / prétérit en *be* + V-*ing* / –) .... so complicated.
5. We (**have** / présent en *be* + V-*ing* / **+**) .... a wonderful time here. Why (you / **come** / présent / **interro-négatif**) .... over and spend the weekend with us?

4 **Conjuguez le verbe entre parenthèses au temps et à la forme indiqués (+ : forme affirmative, – : forme négative, ? : forme interrogative).**

1. (you / **know** / présent / **?**) .... what I (**say** / present perfect en *be* + V-*ing* / **+**) .... ? (you / **understand** / présent / **?**) .... ?
2. I (**tell** / present perfect / **+**) .... you what you live for. You (**pay** / prétérit en *be* + V-*ing* / –) .... attention. You live for the sake of living.
3. Miss M. was 82 when she (**die** / prétérit / **+**).........
4. I (**see** / prétérit / **+**) .... at once he (**fight** / past perfect en *be* + V-*ing* / **+**) .... for he had a black eye.
5. If I (**know** / past perfect / **+**) .... I never would have gone.
6. People (**say** / present perfect en *be* + V-*ing* / **+**) .... for years that the South-west is the new frontier in America. It certainly (**be** / present perfect / **+**) .... true for me.
7. They (**pick up** / prétérit / **+**) .... a hitchhiker. He (**carry** / prétérit en *be* + V-*ing* / **+**) .... a sack of tomatoes. They never (**see** / past perfect / **+**) .... a man so happy to get a ride.
8. "It's time you (**turn** / prétérit / **+**) .... out your light and (**go** / prétérit / **+**) .... to sleep." "I (**finish** / present perfect / –) .... my English yet." "What ? I bet you (**work** / present perfect en *be* + V-*ing* / –) .... You (**read** / present perfect en *be* + V-*ing* / **+**) .... that Sears Roebuck catalogue. That's what you (**do** / present perfect en *be* + V-*ing* / **+**)......... "
9. If I (**stay** / past perfect en *be* + V-*ing* / **+**) .... for a long time, he wouldn't have been so friendly.
10. In 1997 they told him he (**go** / prétérit en *be* + V-*ing* / **+**) .... blind.

7 Le passif

Formes du passif → 73

1 **Employez le verbe entre parenthèses à l'actif ou au passif, au temps demandé.**

Présent

1. In the United States, most schools (start) at 8 every morning and classes (not finish) until 3 or 4 in the afternoon.
2. Many sports that in other countries (offer) by private clubs are available to American students at no cost.
3. Each year the SAT (*Scholastic Aptitude Test*) (take) by more than 2 million students.

Présent en *be* + V-*ing*

4. "Gifted children throughout Britain (neglect) by schools," the director of the National Association for gifted children recently declared. The association (press) the education minister to publish a report on the subject. It is also concerned that gifted children (overlook). Many parents of such children (opt) for private education.

Prétérit

5. This store (build) in 1899. It (remodel) in 1904 after it (partially destroy) by a fire. The north portion (acquire) in 1906. The first owner's son (operate) the business until 1977 when it (sell).
6. The greatest tragedy of the Gold Rush (occur) in 1898 when over 60 men (kill) in a snowslide. They (carry) back down the trail and (bury) near Dyea.

Present perfect

7. These researchers (spend) years studying children who are exceptionally gifted in mathematics.
8. This song (record) in almost every country on the planet.
9. English (largely replace) French as the language of diplomacy.
10. It (often say) that the best national anthems (write) by amateur musicians.
11. For many Burmese tribes life (not change) for centuries.

Modal + verbe à l'actif ou au passif ?

12. Means of purifying the air will (find) before life becomes unlivable.
13. Science will (come) up with a solution.
14. This may (easier say) than (do).
15. If you start at midday you may well (not close) the book until midnight.
16. For an extra £ 1 we will (send) your parcel by 1st class post. For an extra £ 10 your parcel will (send) "next day delivery" but orders must (place) by 1 p.m.
17. Our brochure will (give) more detailed information than can (include) here.
18. Can the suburbs (blame) for draining the life out of our cities?
19. How can we (make) our cities more civilised?
20. Children should (teach) to speak the truth.

2 **Soulignez les formes passives, puis traduisez-les.**

1. The concert was sponsored by the European Broadcasting Union and was being transmitted live to about twenty countries.
2. Things are simple or complex according to how much attention is paid to them.
3. For the past twenty years I have been a nurse manager of Ward 6 where children with chronic diseases are cared for. Three months ago I was asked to take over an additional ward.
4. Hotels and guesthouses are spread all over the island.
5. The baby must be in bed. And asleep. The washing must be done. And the dishes and God knows what.
6. This word is seldom used in contemporary English.
7. These nests (*ces nids*) are collected at great risk and are to be sold at £ 1,000 a kilogram for birds-nest soup.
8. There remains lots of things to be done.
9. She was born in 1990.
10. Children need to be played with and talked to.

Emplois du passif ➜ 73-78

3 **Transposez ces phrases au passif en prenant pour sujet l'élément en gras.**

▶ They have changed **the date**. ▷ The date has been changed.

1. Millions of viewers will watch **our programme**.
2. We must make **them** acceptable.
3. The Royal Ocean Racing Club instituted **the Admiral's Cup** in 1957.
4. He rarely punished anyone but everyone obeyed **him**.
5. The last time the Cutty Sark carried tea from China was in 1877 and by then the steamers were bringing back **most of the tea**.
6. His father had told **him** about them.
7. The president will greet **those who arrive first**.
8. Scientists at the University of Ottawa have carried out **several experiments in that field**.
9. In the modern world technology has replaced **magic**.
10. Who wrote **it**?

4 **Transposez ces phrases au passif lorsque c'est souhaitable pour mettre l'objet de l'action en valeur.**

1. People tell me there will be a delay of six weeks.
2. A visitor will bring you good news.
3. They will open the park gates at 5 a.m. They usually lock them at night.
4. The inhabitants of the village gave money and young people offered to work.
5. Thieves were regularly stealing goods from his shop. So he set a trap.
6. The ball hit the batsman on the leg, on his trouser pocket.
7. They had announced the news of the strike on April 30th.
8. A group of nature lovers are trying to persuade the paint manufacturers not to continue making paint which contains insecticide.
9. If people painted every house with insecticide paint, it would seriously disturb the balance of nature.

5 **Répondez aux énoncés en employant une forme active ou passive du verbe donné conjugué au temps qui convient.**

▶ Why didn't she come? (she / not invite) ▷ She was not invited.

1. Why couldn't she get into the pub? (People under 16 / not admit)
2. Is this house very old? (Yes, it / build in 1880)
3. Why are you so late? (The plane / delay)
4. He's a dangerous maniac. (He ought to / lock up)
5. Why is he so optimistic? (He is sure he can / solve the problem)
6. Is it a formal occasion? (Yes, evening dress / wear)
7. He should be sentenced for life. (I / not agree)
8. Why is she so upset? (She / not offer the job)
9. Why is he so happy? (His colleagues / give him a TV set when he retired)
10. Do you know William Turner? (Yes, he was an English painter / recognize as a revolutionary genius / make his name with painting seascapes / leave some 300 paintings)

6 **Transformez ces phrases suivant le modèle :**

▶ It is said that he drinks champagne at breakfast. ▷ He is said to drink champagne at breakfast.

1. It is acknowledged that education is the prime purpose of maintaining the national museums.
2. It is considered that Frank Lloyd Wright was the greatest American architect of the 20th century.
3. It is known that Chicago is the birthplace of the first skyscrapers.
4. It is understood that the man, who will be questioned by police today, has been a member of the Gun Club for the last five years.
5. It was reported later that he is dismayed at the circumstances in which he was interviewed.
6. It is believed that she paid £350 to get a ticket.
7. It is believed that the couple suffered domestic problems recently.
8. It is expected that this gold nugget will fetch around £ 200,000 at auction.

7 **Complétez ces phrases en utilisant les verbes proposés à la forme et au temps voulus.**

put an end to • lose sight of • guess at • discriminate against • look into • disapprove of • look after • refer to • apply for • shout down

1. In some countries ethnic minorities .... still ....
2. Those children are untidy. They .... not properly ....
3. A visa has to .... six months before departure.
4. Yesterday at the meeting he .... by the crowd.
5. They have signed an agreement: at long last (*enfin*) the conflict ....
6. "What of his complaint?" "It .... but it's likely to last for a while."
7. She .... two years ago and nobody has heard of her ever since.
8. Western- style values and culture .... by the New Age Movement.
9. There were 40 people employed but details of the construction can only ....
10. The two towers of the Marina City in Chicago are often .... as the "Corn Cobs".

8 Le renvoi à l'avenir

1 **Choisissez l'expression appropriée afin de compléter ces phrases.**

1. There's something ominous about being 65 years old. Suddenly, old age is not a phenomenon which .... ; it has occurred.
   • is occurring • will occur • is going to occur
2. "The day .... ," he prophesied, "when you .... you aren't as smart as you think you are."
   • will come / are going to find out • is going to come / find out
   • is going to come / will find out
3. "So, we're all going now, and what about Uncle Jim? .... he .... too?" she asked.
   • is he going to come • is he about to come • is he coming
4. "No, he .... at the farm.
   • will stay • is staying • is going to stay
5. He .... the place going."
   • 'll keep • is keeping • is going to keep
6. I .... you before Thursday but if you can't make it, can you call me up?
   • 'll probably see • am probably going to see • am probably seeing
7. I .... anything you ....
   • am going to sell / are buying • 'll sell / will buy • will sell / are going to buy
8. I'm warning you. You .... out of a job if you don't wake up!
   • will be • are • are going to be

2 **Traduisez.**

1. Nous saurons ce soir.
2. Il part dans quelques jours.
3. C'est facile, je vais te montrer.
4. "Qu'est-ce que vous voulez boire ? – Je prendrai du thé."
5. J'y croirai lorsque je le verrai.
6. "Est-ce-que tu peux venir dimanche ? – Désolée, je ne peux pas, je vais au théâtre."
7. Il n'a pas l'intention de prendre sa retraite (*retire*) maintenant, il a trop à faire.
8. Bon, je vais vous dire ce que nous allons faire.
9. Le spectacle va commencer.
10. Je ne vais pas regarder le match, j'ai du travail.

3 **Complétez les phrases en employant *will* + V, *will have* + participe passé ou *will be* + V-*ing*.**

1. By the end of the month around 800,000 people (see) the Sensational exhibition.
2. "Having this exhibition at Gatwick Airport is fantastic because it (reach) all sorts of people," the organizer said.

3. “What I’d do without you... You make everything bearable.” “There, there, it’s over now. I assure you we (go) home tomorrow.”
4. This was one of the most popular programmes on television. “They (discuss) this story line in every pub, office, and factory in Britain tomorrow,” he said.
5. It could take 5 weeks to defrost the instruments but Dr Richard Harrison is confident that they (survive) at the end of that period.
6. I wanted to know. When (move out / you)?
7. Shopping with Eurostar is so easy that you (want) to repeat the experience, we can guarantee it.
8. It made me think how lovely it would be if you could preserve your memories in a book so that you (leave) your mark in the world.
9. I could give you some money for the time and trouble you (spend) on our project.
10. With our new facial cream your complexion (look) smoother in one day, seem younger in just one week.
11. In the time it takes you to read this paragraph another three vulnerable youngsters (lose) their lives.
12. You (not find) this Swedish hotel in summer. It (melt away): situated 100 miles north of the Arctic Circle the Ice Hotel is rebuilt each year and open from November to March.

9 Les modaux

Les degrés de certitude

→ 87-90

1 **Soulignez les modaux puis classez les phrases du plus au moins certain.**

1. It might be a good idea.
2. There must have been someone beside them to drive the car.
3. I thought you might like to see the children before they went to bed.
4. She may have been responsible for the accident.
5. He could very well win a thousand dollars.
6. The phone rang. "That'll be for me," he said.
7. He might become famous one day.
8. There must be better songs to sing than this.
9. He can't be dead!
10. She should be back in a few minutes.
11. It couldn't happen again.

• quasi certain : .... • probable : .... • possible : .... • incertain : ....
• imaginable : .... • difficilement imaginable : .... • impossible : ....

2 **Traduisez les phrases de l'exercice 1.**

3 **Reformulez les phrases en employant un modal.**

1. You are certainly joking.
I am sure he was lying.
2. You will probably be surprised.
Maybe he gave her a diamond ring.
3. Perhaps we'll never see each other again.
I don't know where she is. Perhaps she is waiting for us at the airport.
4. I am sure she is not as old as you say she is.
I am sure she's not sleeping, not at this time of day!
I am sure I have not lost his address.
5. I suppose he speaks English fluently: he has lived for three years in London.
They are almost certain to have arrived now.

4 **Traduisez.**

1. Il se pourrait qu'elle devienne vétérinaire (*a vet*).
2. Il doit y avoir une autre solution.
3. "Tu penses qu'il pourrait être absent (*be gone*) un mois ? – Ça se pourrait."
4. Il se peut qu'elle n'aime pas cette idée.
5. Il doit avoir trois ou quatre ans de moins qu'elle.
6. Ça a dû se passer juste avant la guerre.
7. Ça pourrait être très embarrassant (*embarrassing*) si on nous voyait ensemble.
8. On aurait pu croire qu'il était ivre.
9. Pourquoi as-tu jeté ces vêtements ? Quelqu'un aurait pu en vouloir.

 → 91-96

5 **Complétez les phrases en utilisant *can* (*can't*), *could* (*couldn't*), *will* ou *would* puis traduisez-les.**

1. I wish I .... stay here for ever.
2. I can explain if you .... only listen.
3. Interflora has launched a website so that you .... send flowers from work without even picking up the phone.
4. This classic white shirt .... stand the test of time.
5. You .... buy anything here, from oysters to cigars!
6. Bears are mostly vegetarian, but they .... eat whatever meat they .... catch or find.
7. What I .... stand is the thought of him lying and lying for all those years.
8. .... you do me a favour?
9. James Dean was her hero at that time. She .... save every photograph from the magazines and she fixed them to the walls of her bedroom.
10. Come with me, ... you?

6 **Complétez les phrases en utilisant *can* (*can't*), *could* (*couldn't*), *will* ou *would* puis traduisez-les.**

1. "I .... remember the address." " .... you even remember the street?"
2. "He says you're foolish to take such a risk." "He .... ! He's always finding fault with me!"
3. When I was a child I .... understand adults, and now that I am an adult I .... understand children.
4. They .... have us believe that the situation is improving but the plain fact is that it's getting worse.
5. .... you be so kind as to lend me your laptop?
6. He said it was perfectly obvious, as far as he .... see.
7. If only he .... have spent the night here!
8. When the car started he said, "Wonders .... never cease."
9. I had an alarm clock which was set for nine o'clock, but invariably every morning I .... wake up before then.
10. I had not heard of them for as long as I .... remember but I knew they were still alive.

7 **Modal + V ou modal + *have* + participe passé ? Traduisez.**

1. Je ne pourrais pas le quitter. Où irais-je ?
2. Je n'aurais pas pu le quitter. Où serais-je allée ?
3. Tu devrais lui parler parce que tu peux répondre à ses questions.
4. Tu aurais dû lui parler parce que tu aurais pu répondre à ses questions.
5. Elle préférerait que tu écrives en anglais.
6. Elle aurait préféré que tu écrives en anglais.
7. Certainement les choses pouvaient s'améliorer, la vie pouvait être meilleure.
8. Certainement les choses auraient pu s'améliorer, la vie aurait pu être meilleure.
9. Tu n'aurais rien à perdre et tu pourrais peut-être avoir beaucoup à gagner.
10. Tu n'aurais rien eu à perdre et tu aurais peut-être eu beaucoup à gagner.

8 **Modal + V ou modal + *be* + V-*ing* ? Complétez les phrases avec la forme appropriée du verbe entre parenthèses.**

1. Rome wasn't built in a day. You must (take) time.
2. "Where is she?" "I think she's upstairs. She must (read)."
3. He wondered what he was doing here when he should (ride) far away from San Francisco.
4. What about a glass of champagne? I really think we should (celebrate).
5. You can always (tell) a person by their shopping.
6. They can't (have) lunch at this time of day!
7. "I wonder where she is." "She could (play) tennis."
8. I couldn't (hear) what they were saying.
9. She doesn't want to be disturbed: she might (work) at the moment.
10. Might I (suggest) a nice dry white wine?

9 **Infinitif, *be* + V-*ing* ou *have* + participe passé du verbe ? Employez le verbe entre parenthèses à la forme qui convient.**

1. "Mr Parkins?" I asked. "The same," he said. "And you must (be) Mr Banks. I'm honoured to meet you, sir."
2. "You say they stopped you at the frontier. That must (be) rather frightening." "So it was."
3. "Can I do anything?" "Yes, we're running out of glasses already. Everyone must (leave) them around." "I'll go round and see what I can find and wash some."
4. "Shall we go back?" "Go back?" "Yes, something may (go) wrong if we don't."
5. Mrs Parker said that during a quarrel, her husband emptied a bowl of cold potatoes over her head. "Didn't he?" I asked. "He may (do) it or not. That's not the point."
6. If she had only had half your beauty and character, I might (love) her.
7. If you're going to be in town we might (have) coffee together.

10 **Infinitif, *be* + V-*ing* ou *have* + participe passé du verbe? Employez le verbe entre parenthèses à la forme qui convient.**

1. "Where did you go?" "I posted that letter to Hans." "Couldn't it (wait) until the morning?"
2. "What do you think of him as a student?" "I had to give him a B. He could (do) better but he got rattled."
3. "I wish he'd raised his voice when answering the questions," she said. "I don't know why he wouldn't (speak up)." "It wouldn't (change) the facts," said Morris. "It might (help) convince them that what he said was true."
4. These women are paid so little that they can't possibly (do) it for the money.
5. I'm afraid I can't (explain) it to you now.
6. I searched for my wallet but I couldn't (find) it. Could I (drop) it on the train?
7. That afternoon he scrubbed the house as if it hadn't been cleaned for ages. I couldn't (believe) my eyes. You must (think) I was pretty stupid not to have stopped him.
8. "You knew I was here? You should (call) me."
9. "I'd like to see your house." "You should (come) to dinner. I was going to ask you to dinner with the Clarks."
10. I shouldn't (come). What would my mother say if she knew?"

Une pression est exercée sur le sujet → 96-102

11 **Soulignez les modaux, classez-les dans le tableau selon leur valeur. Puis traduisez les phrases.**

Emplois fréquents

1. Left lane must turn left.
2. Can I leave my stuff here?
3. Could I speak to you, Sir?
4. I think you should see a doctor.
5. He shouldn't have talked to you about that.
6. May I remind you that all this is being done for your benefit?
7. Shall I take that plate?
8. You must not tell lies.
9. If you're under 17, you can't drive a car in Britain.
10. You can both go. I don't need you.

Emplois moins fréquents

11. Thou shalt not steal.
12. Might I speak to you for a moment?
13. Each voter may vote for one candidate.
14. He refuses to go? I tell you he shall go.
15. Two parallel white lines mean that you may not overtake.
16. You might have a word with him on that subject.

- contraindre / donner un ordre : ....
- interdire : ....
- offrir / suggérer de : ....
- donner un conseil : ....
- accorder une permission : ....
- demander une permission : ....
- refuser une permission : ....

12 **Traduisez.**

1. J'ai faim. Je peux avoir quelque chose à manger (*a snack*) ?
2. Vous devez obéir à la loi.
3. Tu peux m'emprunter mon journal si tu veux.
4. Puis-je voir votre passeport s'il vous plaît ?
5. Désirez-vous que je vous aide ?
6. Tu n'aurais pas dû boire autant.
7. Ils devraient être au lit, pas en train de regarder la télévision.
8. Il est interdit de nourrir les animaux. (*Visitors...*)
9. Pourrais-je vous donner un conseil ?
10. Est-ce que je pourrais me servir de votre téléphone ?
11. Il fallait me le dire !
12. Il ne faut pas y toucher.

Le conditionnel

➜ 105-107

13 **Complétez ces phrases en mettant le verbe entre parenthèses à la forme appropriée du conditionnel.**

1. What (do / you) if I left you?
2. If I were you, I (not worry) about the future.
3. What (tell / he) her if she had asked?
4. They (be) glad if you could come.
5. Supposing it rained that (not be) much fun.
6. If she had followed his advice she (may succeed).
7. I'm thirsty: I (can do) with a cup of tea.
8. It's up to you but I (not accept) his invitation.
9. I (imagine) you were glad to hear from him.
10. She thought she (cannot live) without him.

Les emplois non conditionnels de should

➜ 107-109

14 **Traduisez.**

1. Il est étrange qu'il ne soit pas là.
2. Au cas où il demanderait, dis-lui que je reviendrai mercredi.
3. Que suggérez-vous que je prenne ?
4. C'est drôle que tu dises ça.
5. Il est important que vous écoutiez attentivement.
6. Ils ont insisté pour que nous dinions avec eux.
7. Si jamais vous changez d'avis, faites-le moi savoir.
8. Il est absurde qu'elle soit payée moins que lui.
9. Je lui ai donné une carte de peur qu'elle ne se perde.
10. Il a suggéré qu'elle vende sa voiture.

Should ou would ?

➜ 88, 93-98 et 105-109

15 ***Should* ou *would* ? Complétez les phrases suivantes.**

1. What .... I say? How am I going to put it?
2. My life was over and it .... never come back.
3. When I asked her why she married Bob she .... say she had no choice.
4. She used to say we .... make the most of what we had.
5. There were five bedrooms, and it was only natural that Charlie .... have the biggest.
6. She could do something better. I wish you .... talk to her about going to university.
7. I suppose I thought it .... always go on like that. I don't remember thinking about the future at all.
8. "Do you think this is the place?" "Yes, it .... be just here."
9. .... you help me with this?
10. She was a very patient cat. She .... sit for hours, bird watching.

16 ***Should* ou *would* ? Complétez les phrases suivantes.**

1. I dread to think what your poor father .... have thought.
2. "Don't you get bored?" "Why .... I get bored?" "With nothing to do." "I have a thousand things to do."
3. "What .... you like first? The good news or the bad news?"
4. "I was thinking, maybe I .... change my name?" "What .... you change it to?"
5. I called the police right away. They .... be here by now.
6. I don't know why this .... have happened to me.
7. If only things .... stop happening, but they never do, don't you agree?
8. "How long until supper?" "About half an hour. Your father .... be home by then."
9. "Shall we meet at five, at the library?" "That .... be fine."
10. It wasn't my fault if I was late. The car ....n't start.
11. You won't tell anyone, will you? It .... be so embarrassing.

10 Autres façons d'exprimer la modalité

1 **Complétez les phrases en employant *can, can't* ou *be (un)able to* à la forme qui convient.**

1. I carry more secrets than you .... imagine.
2. For the first two years I saved so that we .... buy the house of our dreams.
3. Neither of them asked me why. If they had I .... have answered.
4. Do you think you'll .... fix it?
5. He told her she .... keep the letter if she wanted to.
6. Now you .... see why I am worried.
7. Have you ever dreamt that you .... make an emergency phone call?
8. He seemed to know whom he .... pick on (*harceler*) and whom he ....
9. Yesterday I .... drive 500 miles although the weather was terrible.
10. Her first name was India. She .... never .... get used to it.

2 **Complétez ces phrases en employant *would, used to* ou *be used to* à la forme qui convient.**

1. When she wanted something she .... have to ask and I .... see if we could afford it.
2. He .... be President of the Rotary Club in Winchester.
3. She no longer worried: she .... now .... waking suddenly in the night sometimes from alarming dreams, sometimes from nothing.
4. He .... throw a tantrum (*piquer une crise*) if his cup of tea wasn't waiting for him at 10.
5. This is exactly how I .... feel when you were little.
6. "Do you know them?" "Yes they're friends of my parents'. I .... play with their son in the paddling pool."
7. When he consented to eat normally he .... order the same dinner day after day.
8. He doesn't feel lonely: he .... spending hours alone, watching the sea, writing poetry.
9. There .... be an important fruit and vegetable market in Covent Garden.

3 ***Ought to, had better* ou *should* ? Traduisez.**

1. Il ferait mieux de ne pas conduire.
2. Tu ne devrais pas prêter attention (*take notice of*) à ce qu'il te dit.
3. Je crois qu'il vaudrait mieux que je parte. J'ai besoin d'être seul.
4. "Il devrait dormir maintenant. – Vous pensez qu'il va s'en sortir (*be alright*) ? – Il est seulement choqué (*be in a shock*). Quelques heures de repos devraient (normalement) tout arranger (*take care of it*).

5. Je décidai qu'il valait mieux que je sois présent lorsqu'elle le rencontrerait.
6. J'ai encore la grippe. Je devrais être à la maison au lit.
7. Il vaudrait mieux que tu réfléchisses bien à ce que tu vas faire.
8. C'est un scandale (*a disgrace*). Il devrait y avoir une pancarte (*a notice*).
9. C'était une enfant. Elle n'aurait pas dû connaître ce genre de chose.
10. J'aurais dû prendre un taxi au lieu de rentrer à pied.

4 Complétez avec *must*, *must not*, *have to* ou *don't have to*.

1. She will be hard to deal with, even to speak to at first. He .... be prepared for this.
2. Turn the radio down, please, so you can hear what I .... say.
3. She .... cry again, it will only exhaust her and besides, it's useless.
4. These arguments .... convince her, since they are true.
5. "I'll drive you home." "You .... do that. I can walk."
6. I can't go but it .... let it stop you if that's really what you want.
7. I just .... do what I can with what I am, which is what everyone .... do.
8. Anyway, you .... admit that it was pretty funny.
9. You'll .... wait here until we get this checked by a doctor.
10. "How was your vacation?" "Oh nice – I don't know – disappointing." "Oh? You .... tell me about it."
11. She glanced at the clock. "You .... go," she stated, "right away."
12. You .... absolutely go to bed, with a fever like that.
13. If you didn't go to that concert, I wish you'd tell me. You .... lie to me, baby.
14. "Have you anything planned today?" "I .... go into University this morning."
15. Jane? Well, you .... admit she's in a difficult position. What would you do in her position?
16. You .... go on with it if you don't want to.
17. The race isn't won yet, I know I .... concentrate but I .... get too tense.
18. He runs to work. He .... worry about traffic jams.
19. Commercials are very good television: they .... be.
20. I am afraid you .... take the decision yourself: either you stay or you leave and face the resulting difficulties.

5 Employez *need* à la forme qui convient.

1. You .... not drive so fast: we have plenty of time.
2. She is well again: .... she .... to take more pills?
3. They .... not worry: they will succeed.
4. You .... not write to her: she will be here tomorrow.
5. There's plenty of food in the fridge: I .... to go shopping.

6 Traduisez en employant *need*.

1. Tu n'avais pas besoin de conduire vite : nous avions tout notre temps.
2. Elle allait bien : il n'était pas nécessaire qu'elle continue à prendre des pillules.
3. Ce n'était pas la peine qu'ils s'inquiètent : ils réussiraient.
4. Tu n'avais pas besoin de lui écrire.
5. Il y avait largement assez de provisions dans le frigidaire : je n'avais pas besoin d'aller faire des courses.

7 Les équivalents de “devoir”. Traduisez ces phrases.

1. Je dois dire que j’ai été plutôt surprise.
2. Il ne voit pas très bien : il doit porter des lunettes.
3. Tu devras t’y habituer.
4. Pourquoi doivent-ils lui obéir ?
5. Il devait mourir quatre ans plus tard.
6. Il a dû manquer son train.
7. Tu dois faire comme on te dit.
8. Ils doivent se marier dans deux mois.
9. Tu dois avoir hâte de le revoir.
10. Il devait être en Angleterre lorsque l’accident s’est produit.

11 Le subjonctif et l'impératif

1 Traduisez.

1. C'est drôle que tu dises ça. *It is funny that ....*
2. Elle a insisté pour que je reste. *She insisted that ....*
3. Il a suggéré que nous nous arrêtions. *He suggested that ....*
4. Si tel est le cas, il partira. *If .... he will go.*
5. Quoiqu'il advienne, il ne changera pas d'avis. .... *he will not change his mind.*
6. Si j'étais à votre place, je prendrais rendez-vous. *If .... I would take an appointement.*
7. À tes souhaits ! (*God*) ....
8. Il est essentiel qu'il soit préparé à ça. *It is essential that ....*
9. Si besoin est, je peux faire une photocopie. *If .... I can photocopy it.*
10. Son excuse, pour ainsi dire, ressemblait à une insulte. *His apology, ...,* *sounded like an insult.*

2 Traduisez.

1. Reviens !
2. Demandons-lui !
3. Ne cours pas !
4. Sois sage !
5. Je t'en prie, fais attention !
6. Ne nous plaignons pas.
7. Fais ce qu'on te dit.
8. Qu'ils ne s'en aillent pas !
9. Laisse-le tranquille.
10. Tu veux bien écouter ?

12 Les reprises elliptiques

1 Traduisez les réponses ou questions brèves.

1. "Has he changed?" *"Oh, oui !"*
2. "Did you know her?" *"Non."*
3. "She loves him." *"Oui."*
4. "So, you won't come." *"Mais si!"*
5. "Who spoke first?" *"Simon."*
6. "They have found it." *"Ah, oui ?"*
7. "Are you kidding?" *"Non."*
8. "He lives in Ireland." *"Ah, oui ?"*
9. "Is it open to the public?" *"Je ne pense pas."*
10. "Will you join us?" *"J'aimerais beaucoup."*
11. "Can I go too?" *"Tu n'as pas le droit."*
12. "He has forgotten her." *"J'ai bien peur que oui."*
13. "She caught the train in time." *"Oui, je pense."*
14. "She can manage alone." *"Bien sûr que oui."*
15. "They had to take a taxi." *"Ah, oui ?"*
16. "Has he telephoned yet?" *"J'ai bien peur que non."*
17. "She rang about an hour ago." *"Ah, oui ?"*
18. " Why are you standing here?" *"Parce qu'on nous l'a dit."*
19. "You ought to tell him." *"Je ne sais pas comment."*
20. "You're the only one who can persuade him." *"Ah, oui ?"*

2 Traduisez les réponses en anglais en employant *so*, *neither*, *but*...

1. "She plays the violin beautifully." *"Lui aussi."*
2. "He knew all about it." *"Eux non."*
3. "I entirely agree with him." *"Moi pas."*
4. "It looks like rain." *"C'est vrai."*
5. "I've never felt so exhausted." *"Moi non plus."*
6. "Peter is not here today." *"Effectivement."*
7. "I'll be at the meeting." *"Moi aussi."*
8. "I've no idea where we are going." *"Moi non plus."*
9. "He didn't remember the trip was cancelled." *"Moi non plus."*
10. "She'd love to go to Canada." *"Lui aussi."*

3 Complétez les phrases par un question tag.

1. She is twelve, ...?
2. They aren't tired, ...?
3. You spoke to me, ...?
4. They won't like it, ...?
5. Everybody laughed, ...?
6. You seldom see her, ...?
7. None could do it, ...?
8. Let's go, ...?
9. There was a lot of noise, ...?
10. You will come, ...?

2 Le groupe nominal

1 Le genre et le nombre du nom

Le genre du nom

→ 135-136

1 **Donnez le féminin des noms suivants.**

man • father • uncle • nephew • husband • lion • bull • fox • dog • boy-friend • male • bear • actor • waiter • tom-cat • god • barman • horse • son-in-law • pig

2 **Chassez l'intrus.**

1. nurse • man • bear • he-goat
2. waitress • she-bear • actress • lioness
3. ship • actor • lion • boy
4. cat • goat • dog • bitch
5. chairperson • friend • spokesman • baby
6. aunt • niece • teacher • sister

Le nombre du nom

→ 136-144

3 **Classez les noms suivants en trois groupes, en fonction de la prononciation de leur pluriel : /z/, /s/ ou /iz/.**

self • idea • wish • group • peach • office • kid • member • church • book • tomato • ear • neck • chief • corporation • bachelor • unit • system

4 **Relevez les noms pluriels de ce texte et classez-les en fonction de leur prononciation : /z/, /s/ ou /iz/.**

Invasion of the snails

They came out of their shells, they saw, and they're conquering the gardens of Britain. Snails – in numbers never witnessed before – are on the march, making a meal of the nation's herbaceous borders and turning the lawns and paths into crunchy obstacle courses.

The sheer size of the invasion has prompted unprecedented demand for pest pellets from gardeners who fear for their bedding plants, flowers – roses, carnations, dahlias – vegetables and fruit – tomatoes, salads, carrots, strawberries. Although snails are the most noticeable pests in the garden, slugs are a far bigger problem.

Adapted from *Daily Mail*, 7. 7. 1998.

5 **Mettez au pluriel les noms suivants (assurez-vous que leur sens vous est connu).**

brush • chief • crossroads • photo • path • species • ghetto • criterion • thief • crisis • loaf • brother • potato • medium • leaf • analysis • wolf • phenomenon • aircraft • tooth

6 **Écrivez en toutes lettres les acronymes suivants puis mettez-les au pluriel chaque fois que c'est possible.**

AC / DC • C. D. • C. I. A. • C. V. • G. P. • D. J. • I. C. B. M. • K. K. K. • L. A. • M. C. P. • M. P. • N. A. T. O. • T. U. • U. F. O. • V. C. R.

7 **Mettez au pluriel les noms suivants.**

man • child • louse • foot • ox • mouse • tooth • goose • axis • thesis • stimulus • cherub • campus • tableau • innuendo

8 **Mettez au pluriel les noms suivants quand cela est possible. Justifiez vos choix.**

► *story* ▷ *stories* (consonne + y ▷ consonne + ies au pluriel ; nom dénombrable)

► *cash* ▷ pas de pluriel (nom indénombrable)

grass • leaf • staff • illness • youth • dish • box • porch • robbery • business • kingdom • silence

9 **Mettez les noms composés suivants au pluriel (vérifiez leur sens).**

a son-in-law • a goods-train • a man-servant • a tooth-brush • a man-eater • a woman-hater • a passer-by • a grown-up • a woman doctor • a sit-in • a university-degree • a step-father

10 **Chassez l'intrus.**

1. tomato • hero • potato • photo
2. lady • anxiety • boy • baby
3. leaf • cliff • calf • shelf
4. book • foot • tooth • goose
5. fish • trout • salmon • plaice
6. aircraft • deer • sheep • mouse
7. army • cast • crowd • people
8. cattle • rubbish • management • vermin
9. news • means • species • barracks
10. scales • physics • jeans • stairs

11 **Soulignez les noms qui peuvent venir compléter la phrase : *I would like to have another...***

knife • advice • family • luggage • drink • information • fish • fruit • jeans • wages • water • try

12 **Associez les mots indénombrables suivants aux expressions utilisées pour désigner un élément de ce qu'ils représentent.**

► scissors / a pair of ▷ a pair of scissors

mots indénombrables

grass • compasses • luck • cattle • toast • lightning • thunder • jeans • sugar • snow

expressions utilisées pour désigner un élément

a slice of • a blade of • a pair of • a stroke of • a flake of • a lump of • a head of • a flash of • a crash of

13 Expliquez la différence de sens entre :

1. my brothers **et** my brethren
2. two pennies **et** two pence
3. fruits **et** fruit
4. darts are... **et** darts is...
5. draughts are... **et** draughts is...
6. the customs are... **et** the customs is...
7. two compasses **et** two pairs of compasses

14 **Tous les noms qui suivent comportent un *-s* final. Classez-les en trois catégories : ceux qui admettent un verbe au singulier, ceux qui admettent un verbe au pluriel, ceux qui admettent les deux accords.**

measles • glasses • athletics • savings • politics • barracks • clothes • headquarters • outskirts • news • funds • billiards • shorts • spectacles • remains

15 **Choisissez le bon verbe.**

1. A number of people (has /have) complained about the noise made by aircraft taking off.
2. I think ten pounds (is /are) too much to pay for such a little thing.
3. She picked up her belongings, which (was /were) lying on the floor, and left.
4. The deer that (lives /live) in my forest (is /are) dear to me.
5. The hotel staff (does /do) not like the new manager's wife.
6. More than one house (has /have) been broken into during the holidays.
7. Two weeks (was /were) not enough holiday to recover from a year's stress.
8. The police (think /thinks) that one of the witnesses (is /are) lying.
9. A number of the workers (has /have) decided to ask for a rise.
10. Bacon and eggs (is /are) what the English often (has /have) for breakfast.

16 **Mettez le verbe entre parenthèses à la forme voulue.**

1. Mathematics (have) always been my favourite subject.
2. The salmon (swim) up this river to lay eggs.
3. Look! The cattle (be) grazing in the meadow.
4. My family (gather) at Christmas every year.
5. The management (be) having talks with the workers.
6. The school's staff (be) renewed last year.
7. Vermin (live) on people's or animals' bodies.
8. The crew (be) now waiting for instructions from the captain.
9. Yesterday, police (be) rushed to the scene of the accident.
10. The news (be) alarming.

17 **Tous ces noms de pays finissent par un *-s*. Rangez-les en deux catégories : ceux qui admettent un verbe au singulier, ceux qui admettent un verbe au pluriel.**

the Bahamas • Barbados • Cyprus • Honduras • Laos • the Netherlands • the Philippines • the Seychelles • Wales • the United States of America • the West Indies

Dites ce qui caractérise ceux qui admettent un verbe au pluriel.

18 **Transformez ces phrases en mettant les noms au pluriel à chaque fois que c'est possible (attention à l'accord du verbe).**

Perhaps it was the old woman's long illness that had got her in the habit of staying at home every night when she was young.
By ten o'clock, she was always back with her dog in her flat.
Almost every woman she knew had a husband, a sister or a friend of long standing with whom she could stay.
She had never been able to afford a maid.
She liked fishing trout, which is a rather difficult thing to do.

19 **Traduisez.**

1. Essaie de ne pas oublier tes bagages à l'aéroport !
2. Tu devrais suivre mes conseils.
3. Je ne trouve pas mon pantalon.
4. J'ai acheté de nouveaux meubles pour mon appartement.
5. Kicking John a été le meilleur gardien de but de la coupe du monde.

20 **Traduisez.**

1. Le quartier général des partis politiques est protégé par la police.
2. Le public n'a pas encore été informé des dernières nouvelles.
3. La caserne a été détruite par l'armée.
4. Les spectateurs étaient si contents qu'ils ont applaudi les acteurs au milieu de la pièce.
5. Dix policiers ont été blessés dans les émeutes.
6. Les bagages sont examinés à la douane.
7. Les membres de ma famille sont blonds aux yeux bleus.
8. Le gouvernement américain a décidé d'amplifier sa lutte contre le terrorisme.
9. Je n'ai pas trouvé de meilleur moyen de le faire.
10. Deux avions se sont écrasés après avoir décollé (*take-off*).

2 Les déterminants du nom

Le déterminant Ø

→ 147-152

1 **Traduisez.**

1. L'homme et la femme sont supposés égaux.
2. Le courage, l'amour, la générosité sont des valeurs rares.
3. La vitesse peut tuer, la drogue aussi.
4. Si vous mettez trop d'huile dans la poêle, elle risque de prendre feu.
5. Je devrai y aller en voiture ou en avion vu que les conducteurs de train (*traindrivers*) sont en grève (*be on strike*).
6. L'hôpital est entre l'école et l'église : je me souviens être allée à l'école et à l'église ici, mais pas à l'hôpital.
7. J'aime les livres, même si je ne les lis pas.
8. Qu'as-tu mangé au petit-déjeuner?
9. Le bleu et l'orange sont mes couleurs favorites.
10. Tout le monde devrait parler l'anglais de nos jours.

2 **Traduisez.**

1. Des maladies comme le cancer, le SIDA, l'hépatite (*hepatitis*) seront peut-être un jour de mauvais souvenirs.
2. Les jours sont beaucoup plus courts en hiver qu'au printemps.
3. Le squash est très fatigant mais très relaxant en même temps.
4. Tu veux boire quelque chose ? J'ai du whisky, du gin ou du jus d'orange, pas de champagne, désolé !
5. J'ai dû rester quinze jours au lit à cause d'un mauvais rhume.
6. J'ai en assez de la télévision.
7. Je ne connais personne vivant en Amérique du Nord ou en Australie.
8. L'Éverest m'a toujours fascinée.
9. Vous traversez Regent Street, vous vous dirigez (*find one's way to*) vers le palais de Buckingham et là vous verrez peut-être l'un des membres de la famille royale.
10. Le président McKingates a décidé d'éradiquer le terrorisme international.

3 **Classez ces groupes nominaux en français selon qu'ils ont une valeur générique ou spécifique.**

1. L'apéritif, c'est la prière du soir des Français.
2. L'amour est aussi une affection de la peau.
3. Les miroirs sont des glaces qui ne fondent pas.

Paul Morand

4. L'art, c'est la science faite claire.
5. La vérité est trop nue, elle n'excite pas les hommes.
6. Le style est une façon très simple de dire des choses compliquées.
7. Le génie est l'extrême pointe du sens pratique.
8. La lune est le soleil des statues.

9. La frivolité est un crime en cela qu'elle singe la légèreté.
10. L'enfance sait ce qu'elle veut. Elle veut sortir de l'enfance.

Jean Cocteau

Valeur générique : ....
Valeur spécifique : ....

4 **Traduisez en anglais les groupes nominaux français que vous venez de classer.**

5 **Donnez l'équivalent en français des proverbes suivants.**

1. Speech is silver, but silence is golden.
2. Appearances are deceptive.
3. Appetite comes with eating.
4. Attack is the best form of defence.
5. Charity begins at home.
6. Cold hands, warm heart.
7. Extremes meet.
8. While there's life, there's hope.
9. If you want peace, prepare for war.
10. Time works wonders.

6 **Que pouvez-vous dire des phrases ci-dessus pour justifier l'emploi de Ø ?**

7 **Complétez sur le modèle : *Green is a mixture of blue and yellow...***

1. Orange is a mixture of ....
2. Dark green is a mixture of ....
3. Light blue is a mixture of ....
4. Brown is a mixture of ....
5. Grey is a mixture of ....
6. Purple is a mixture of ....
7. Navy blue is a mixture of ....
8. Pink is a mixture of ....
9. Light yellow is a mixture of ....
10. Beige is a mixture of ....

8 **Expliquez la présence de l'article Ø dans les groupes nominaux soulignés.**

In <u>warm weather</u>, she walked around the little lake near her apartment with <u>Lex</u> on a string. Sometimes she smiled at other people walking around the lake with <u>dogs</u> at <u>night</u>. It was nice the way dogs made <u>things</u> friendly. It was nice the way <u>people</u> with dogs smiled at her because she had a dog, too. But wasn't it dangerous to talk to <u>strange people</u> in <u>parks</u>, <u>dog</u> or no <u>dog</u>?

9 **Formez les noms de langue à partir des noms de pays suivants.**

1. .... is the language spoken in America.
2. .... is the language spoken in Ireland.
3. .... is the language spoken in Norway.
4. .... is the language spoken in Portugal.
5. .... is the language spoken in Wales.

10 **Dites de quels pays sont originaires les personnes mentionnées dans cet extrait d'un poème d'Ogden Nash et quelle langue ils parlent.**

► the Spaniards ▷ The Spaniards come from Spain and speak Spanish.

There came the Spaniards,
There came the Greeks,
There came the Pilgrims in leather breeks.
There came the Dutch
And the Poles and Swedes,
The Persians too
And perhaps the Medes,
The Letts,the Laps and the Lithuanians,
Regal Russians and ripe Roumanians.
There came the French
And there came the Finns,
And the Japanese
With their friendly grins.
The Tartars came,
And the terrible Turks -
In a word, humanity shot the works
And the country that should have been Cathay
Decided to be
The USA.

Poems by Ogden Nash © 1933, 1961 by Ogden Nash.

11 **Soulignez les noms de pays ou d'entités géographiques qui ne sont pas précédés de l'article Ø mais de l'article *the*. Dites pourquoi. (Vérifiez que vous savez les situer !)**

Africa • Transvaal • Atlantic • Bahamas • Belgium • Ben Nevis • Canada • Congo • Cuba • Ethiopia • Netherlands • Irish Republic • Ivory Coast • Mediterranean • New Zealand • Seychelles • Sweden • United Kingdom • Ukraine • United Arab Emirates

12 **Imaginez un vol direct entre New York et Los Angeles. Quels seraient, dans l'ordre, les États survolés? Donnez leurs abréviations entre parenthèses.**

If I flew from New York to Los Angeles, I would fly over ...., then........., then ...., etc.

Dans les phrases que vous avez produites, quel article utilisez-vous ? Pourquoi ?

13 **Imaginez un vol entre Manchester et Londres, énumérez les Comtés survolés.**

When I flew from London to Manchester, I flew over ...., then ...., then ...., etc.

Dans les phrases que vous avez produites, quel article utilisez-vous ? Pourquoi ?

14 **Localisez les entités géographiques suivantes en les faisant précéder d'un article si besoin est.**

(the / Ø) Rocky mountains • (the / Ø) Lake Winnipeg • (the / Ø) St George's Channel • (the / Ø) Belfast • (the / Ø) New Zealand • (the / Ø) Melbourne • (the / Ø) Soweto • (the / Ø) Kalahari desert • (the / Ø) Mount Etna • (the / Ø) Isle of Wight

L'article a / an

→ 152-157

15 *A* ou *an* ?

1. honest proposal 2. one-way ticket 3. honour 4. heroic action 5. hour 6. university 7. heir to the Crown 8. historical landmark 9. European 10. honourable master

16 **Donnez le singulier des mots et groupes de mots suivants en les faisant précéder de *a* / *an*.**

IOUs (*reconnaissances de dettes*) • useful advice • expensive clothes • CD players • honest information

17 **Quantifiez les mots suivants à l'aide d'un dénombreur : *a* / *an* + nom + *of*...**

► advice ▷ a piece of advice

bread • cake • chalk • chocolate • evidence • ice • paper • rice • snow • soap

18 **Quantifiez les mots suivants à l'aide d'un dénombreur : *a* / *an* + nom + *of*...**

cloth • dust • earth • glass • laughter • rain • rock • smoke • transport • weather

19 **Observez l'emploi de *a* / *an* dans ces proverbes et leur traduction.**

A barking dog never bites. *Chien qui aboie ne mord pas.*
A bird in the hand is worth two in the bush. *Mieux vaut tenir que courir.*
There is an exception to every rule. *Il n'y a pas de règle sans exception.*
A fault confessed is half redressed. *Faute avouée est à moitié pardonnée.*
A friend in need is a friend indeed. *C'est dans le besoin qu'on reconnaît ses amis.*
A mouse may help a lion. *On a toujours besoin d'un plus petit que soi.*
Revenge is a dish that can be eaten cold. *La vengeance est un plat qui se mange froid.*
One step at a time. *Une chose à la fois.*
There's a time and place for everything. *Chaque chose en son temps.*
Where there's a will, there's a way. *Quand on veut, on peut.*

20 **Traduisez.**

1. Mon père est menuisier (*joiner*), ma mère est comptable (*accountant*) et moi, je suis étudiant en droit.
2. Deux fois par semaine, je vais au cinéma avec un ami.
3. Avant d'être jardinier, il a été professeur pendant dix ans.
4. Elle est toujours de mauvaise humeur quand elle prend tôt son petit déjeuner.
5. Ne sors jamais sans un peu d'argent.
6. Ce gâteau est dur comme un roc.
7. Cinq livres le litre, c'est trop cher pour moi.
8. En tant que pilote, permettez-moi ce conseil : vérifiez que vous n'avez pas un pneu à plat.
9. Elle ne se baigne jamais sans bouée (*buoy*).
10. C'est dommage de voir un tas d'ordures (*refuse dump*) dans un si beau paysage.

21 **Constituez des énoncés corrects à partir des mots suivants.**

1. a / a / there / man / car / outside / waiting / in / is
2. an / an / a / a / eye / tooth / eye / tooth / for / for
3. an / a / the / doctor / apple / day / away / takes
4. a / a / of / joy / thing / beauty / forever / is
5. a / a / a / trousers / I / cardigan / pair / blouse / yesterday / and / of / bought

22 **Utilisez *such a* ou *such Ø*.**

1. He seems to be .... happy man!
2. I've never seen .... stormy weather in August.
3. .... useful machine would help me much.
4. We had .... awful summer that we remained abroad for two months in Autumn.
5. How can you manage to see with .... dirty glasses?
6. They are debating .... great issue that you can't disturb them right now.
7. .... light earth must be easy to plough.
8. The emergency required .... quick action that he couldn't think twice about it.

23 **Intégrez l'article *a* / *an* si nécessaire et justifiez.**

1. You have such (Ø / a) beautiful garden!
2. What (Ø / a) bunch of (Ø / a) liars!
3. That was such (Ø / a) nice evening!
4. You always have such (Ø / a) heavy luggage!
5. Such (Ø / a) refinement is quite uncommon.
6. What (Ø / a) bore! (*Quel raseur !*)
7. We've been having such (Ø / a) stormy weather recently that we keep indoors.
8. What (Ø / a) pity you couldn't come!
9. Such (Ø / a) intelligence I have never seen.
10. That was such (Ø / a) fun!

24 **Transformez les phrases suivantes selon le schéma :**

► This job is too difficult: I can't do it. ▷ It's too difficult a job. / I can't do so difficult a job. / I can't do such a difficult job.

1. This story is too incredible: I can't believe it
2. This explanation is too abstract: I can't understand it.
3. This trip is too expensive: I can't afford it.
4. This loaf of bread is too hard: I can't cut it.
5. This mountain is too high: I can't climb it.

25 **Expliquez la différence de sens entre les paires suivantes.**

1. I know few people who would accept to do it for you.
2. I know a few people who would accept to do it for you.

3. Few people have arrived yet.
4. A few people have arrived yet.

5. I have a few good bottles of wine left in my wine cellar.
6. I have few good bottles of wine left in my wine cellar.

7. I know little about this subject.
8. I know a little about this subject.
9. There is little water left in the tank.
10. There is a little water left in the tank.

26 **Traduisez.**

1. Je ne connais que peu de choses sur sa vie.
2. Pour moi, ce n'est pas un vrai médecin.
3. Un demi-verre de vin, c'est une trop petite quantité pour être ivre.
4. Dans une demi-heure, vous serez convaincu qu'il vous reste quelques amis.
5. Voudriez-vous me verser un peu d'eau froide dans mon café ? Il est trop chaud.
6. Elle n'est pas très bonne cuisinière.
7. J'ai juste quelques petites choses à te dire.
8. Elle m'a reconduit à la maison en un rien de temps.
9. Tu as quelques autres possibilités. Cette solution est trop risquée.
10. Un peu d'amour ne peut faire de mal.

L'article the

→ 157-160

27 **Lisez à voix haute les groupes suivants et dites si *the* se prononce /ðə/ ou /ðiː/.**

1. the honest proposal 2. the honour 3. the expensive clothes 4. the hour 5. the university 6. the hospital 7. the horrible mistake 8. the historical landmark 9. the umbrella 10. the I.C.B.M. 11. the C.D. players 12. the hair 13. the M.P. 14. the ewe (*la brebis*) 15. the hotel

28 **Justifiez l'emploi de *the* dans les phrases suivantes.**

a. Renvoie à du déjà dit. b. Renvoie à un élément de la situation.
c. Renvoie à du déjà connu culturel. d. *The* devant un nom déterminé par ce qui le suit.
e. Généralité. f. Nominalisation.

1. He'd better not sit on **the** floor (.........).
2. **The** sky (.........) is still overcast.
3. We landed at Gatwick. **The** airport (.........) is not too far from **the** city (.........).
4. I've just bought a new computer. **The** former one (.........) broke down last week.
5. **The** customer (.........) is always right.
6. Don't forget to lock **the** door (.........).
7. Listen! She is playing **the** piano (.........).
8. This is **the** school (.........) I went to when I was a kid.
9. You won't believe it, I went to **the** same one (.........)!
10. **The** best of friends (.........) must part.

29 **Utilisez soit l'article Ø, soit l'article *the*.**

1. (Ø / The) President of (Ø / the) France is meeting (Ø / the) English Prime Minister today.
2. (Ø / The) man who's playing(Ø / the) cello in (Ø / the) orchestra is my husband.
3. (Ø / The) World cup drew (Ø / the) tourists from all over (Ø / the) world to (Ø / the) France.
4. All (Ø / the) people who were able to attend (Ø / the) matches were delighted.

5. Your visit has made (Ø / the) letter I had meant to write superfluous.
6. (Ø / The) child hadn't seen (Ø / the) car coming and was run over.
7. (Ø / The) only witness said (Ø / the) car didn't even stop and one of (Ø / the) passers-by immediately phoned (Ø / the) police.
8. (Ø / The) ambulance arrived next and (Ø / the) doctors said (Ø / the) child would recover quickly from (Ø / the) trauma.
9. I like bathing in (Ø / the) Mediterranean and sleeping in (Ø / the) sun.
10. All (Ø / the) people on (Ø / the) strike had gathered in (Ø / the) hall of (Ø / the) building in (Ø / the) Regent Street and no one could get inside (Ø / the) office-block.

30 **Insérez l'article voulu : Ø , *a* / *an* ou *the*.**

.... trial had lasted for .... eighteen days, and from .... moment .... judge had entered .... courtroom .... public benches had been crowded. Suddenly there was .... buzz in .... corridors, and .... members of .... jury entered .... one after .... other. .... press and .... public alike began to come back into .... court. All .... eyes were on .... foreman of .... jury, ... fat, jolly-looking little man wearing .... suit, ... striped shirt and .... bow-tie. He seemed .... sort of .... fellow with whom, in .... normal circumstances, I would have enjoyed .... pint at .... local pub.

Adapted from .... *Trial and* .... *Error* by Jeffrey Archer.

31 **Insérez l'article voulu : Ø, *a* / *an* ou *the*.**

I was awakened earlier than usual by .... insistent call of .... nature. Accompanied by my copy of .... *Weekly Telegraph*, I was deeply absorbed by .... home news when .... loud rumbling noise alerted my senses. .... apartment began to shake, ... curtains swayed vigorously and .... crockery rattled on .... shelves, I was galvanised into .... action. Spurred on by .... dread that like some ancient Pompeian, I might be preserved in .... volcanic ash to be viewed thus by .... future generations of .... tourists, I hurried out.
Living in .... Arequipa, ... city in .... Peru prone to .... frequent seismic movements, one becomes accustomed to .... instability of .... environment. However I have taken it as .... definitive warning that I shall have to find somewhere else to read .... newspaper.

Adapted from .... *Weekly Telegraph*, ... issue n° 358.

32 **Intégrez un déterminant : Ø, *a* / *an* ou *the*.**

.... sun rose up, at first like .... yellow ball, then like .... disk of .... polished brass. .... trees, ... cornfields, ... farms, ... pastures, ... horses and .... workmen in .... fields, all appeared instantly bathed in .... soft light. .... objects .... great distance away, ... little towers, ... smoking chimneys. Slowly .... dew became visible, hanging upon .... trees like .... ladies' ear-rings. Soon everything was under .... warm stillness.

Adapted from *Alexander* by H. E. Bates.

 → 160-162

33 **Intégrez un déterminant possessif en relation avec le contexte.**

1. He hoped that .... fame and .... popularity would stop .... creditors from asking for .... money.
2. "Pleased to meet you! I read .... article in *Newsweek* on the plane," I said, and I went on telling him I was fascinated by .... style.
3. She took a seat opposite .... husband on the other side of .... desk.
4. What I like in soldiers is .... uniforms. As for .... rifles, I'd rather not see them.
5. She was very proud of .... house, ... furniture, but not much of .... husband.
6. She checked .... rear-view mirror, but he was still right behind .... car. .... petrol gauge was nearly empty.
7. She handed .... canvas over to him. "It's .... best yet! As long as we're sensible about .... prices, we should sell at least half of .... pictures before the exhibition closes!"
8. I looked at the two women but decided not to make any comment about .... make-up or .... hair.

34 **Intégrez un déterminant : Ø, *a / an, the* ou un déterminant possessif.**

1. You're .... sort of .... young man we want.
2. By .... time she came round to .... apartment .... following afternoon, he had realised .... truth.
3. He disappeared into .... bathroom. There he cleaned .... teeth, dropped .... toothbrush into .... mug and brushed .... hair.
4. Then he returned to .... bedroom and threw himself on .... bed.
5. .... final words as he closed .... door behind him were lost in .... noise of .... traffic.
6. .... car skidded across .... gravel in .... front of .... house, coming to .... halt in .... flowerbed just below .... kitchen window.
7. .... second later .... van came crashing into .... back of her car, slamming it against .... wall of .... house and shattering .... glass in .... kitchen window.
8. When she reached .... far end of .... gallery, she became aware of .... office in which .... short, balding man, wearing .... old tweed jacket and .... corduroy trousers, was examining .... picture.
9. His occupation, as described in .... passport, was .... banker.
10. He was .... branch manager of .... Barclays Bank in St Albans, ... Hertfordshire, which in .... banking circles is about .... equivalent of being .... captain in .... Royal Air Force.

35 **Intégrez un déterminant : Ø, *a* / *an*, *the* ou un déterminant possessif. Plusieurs solutions sont parfois possibles, justifiez-les.**

I knew .... Louise before she married. She was then .... frail, delicate girl with .... large and melancholy eyes. .... father and mother loved her with .... anxious adoration, because some illness, ... scarlet fever, I think, left her with .... weak heart and she had to take .... greatest care of herself. .... boyfriend gave up .... games he excelled in because by .... coincidence she had .... heart attack whenever he proposed to leave her for .... day. He could not be such .... brute as to leave her alone. She'd been to all .... best heart specialists in .... world, and they all said that .... life hung on .... thread. But she had .... unconquerable spirit.

Adapted from *Louise* by S. Maugham.

3 This / That

1 Associez *this* / *these* ou *that* / *those* avec les notions suivantes.

ce qui est proche • ce qui est terminé • ce qui vient d'être dit • ce que l'on aime • le passé • le présent immédiat • ce qui est éloigné dans le temps • ce que l'on n'aime pas du tout • ce qui va être expliqué par la suite • ce qui est éloigné dans l'espace

2 Associez *this* / *these* ou *that* / *those* avec les mots suivants.

now • then • here • there • over there • yesterday • already • admired • hated • imminent • before • near • distant • loved • I • remember • noise • they • introduce • unknown

3 Mettez au pluriel.

this man • that day • this mouse • that goose • this news • that people • this leaf • that chief

4 Mettez au singulier.

1. These coming years will be fantastic.
2. Those crossroads are dangerous.
3. These species are rare.
4. Those analyses are wrong.
5. These phenomena seldom happen.
6. Those barracks have to disappear.
7. These aircraft are too old.
8. Check those data, please.
9. These churches are magnificent.
10. Where have you put those keys?

5 Dans les phrases suivantes, soulignez *this* / *these* et dites s'ils sont déterminants ou pronoms.

1. Plenty of refugees come across the border these days.
2. A lot of people spend their vacation in one of these tents every year.
3. A man needs a drink in this climate to help keep him in shape.
4. I've already had a talk with this Tibetan who's going with you.
5. Only a small plane stands a chance in these mountains.
6. We'll fly up to Leh this afternoon.
7. "Joro, this is Mr Chavasse." His English was excellent but there was more to it than that.
8. What it comes down to is this: you don't trust her.

Adapted from *Year of the Tiger* by Jack Higgins.

Dans ces mêmes phrases, expliquez l'emploi de *this* / *these*.

6 **Dans les phrases suivantes, soulignez *that* et dites s'il est déterminant ou pronom.**

1. I'd like to see you as soon as possible, if that's alright with you.
2. I was not a suspected person, if that's what you mean.
3. He had been very ill. That was why I went to see him.
4. If that's all for the moment, we'd better be going, I've got plenty to arrange before that plane takes off.
5. That's the best idea you've had yet.
6. "Remember to keep that face covered. It's as Gallic as a packet of Gauloises." "I'll try to remember that."
7. We have our differences from time to time. Nothing more than that.
8. He was again conscious of that slight feeling of nausea.

Adapted from *Year of the Tiger* by Jack Higgins.

Dans ces mêmes phrases, expliquez l'emploi de *that*.

7 **Traduisez.**

1. Ces garçons sont insupportables !
2. Je ne peux porter tous ces livres ! Aide-moi.
3. Tu peux vraiment courir aussi vite que ça ?
4. À cette époque-là, il n'y avait pas d'électricité.
5. Voici mon meilleur ami, Tim Parsons.
6. Tu me prends pour un traître, c'est ça ?
7. Ceux de Londres arriveront plus tard.
8. Celles que nous avons achetées le mois dernier étaient parfaites.
9. Ceux du premier rang peuvent se lever.
10. Celui que tu as choisi ne me plaît pas.

8 **Traduisez.**

1. In this moonlight, I can fly through the passes with no trouble, and that was always the most dangerous part of the operation.
2. No one would dare to spend a night in the open in this area.
3. The man produced a packet of cigarettes. "Try one of these."
4. This little adventure will make most interesting reading: "The mysterious Englishman," if that's what you are, "lands by night, disguised as a Tibetan."
5. It was hard not to like a man like this.
6. I'm doing a series on Buddhism and this is one of the few monasteries still functioning in this part of Tibet.
7. I've heard of this ceremony. It's something few travellers ever see. The Downfall of the King of Hell.
8. It is as simple as that.
9. What the hell is this supposed to be? Whisky?
10. The peasants worship him and this helps our cause enormously.

Adapted from *Year of the Tiger* by Jack Higgins.

4 Les quantifieurs

1 **Soulignez les fonctions que vous pouvez associer au mot “quantifieur”.**

exprimer une quantité suffisante • déterminer • exprimer un nombre • dire que l'on connaît déjà le nom qui suit • annoncer un complément d'information à droite dans le texte • désigner une certaine quantité • exprimer la totalité • reprendre ce qui a été dit avant • signaler une quantité nulle • présenter un nouvel élément • donner une idée d'abondance • exprimer la possession • impliquer un nombre indéfini • remplacer un nom • exprimer une petite quantité

2 **Soulignez les quantifieurs dans la liste suivante. Dites ce qu'ils expriment et donnez la nature grammaticale des autres mots.**

both • the • mine • some • such • few • any • an • much • all • this • a lot • a little • a • one • that • his • enough • yours • thirty • plenty • no • either • these • whole • those • whose • each • so • every

Both, the two, either, neither

→ 170-172

3 **Choisissez la (les) forme(s) correcte(s).**

1. Both (my friend / my friends / of my friend) have married older women.
2. Both (them / of them / they) were students at Eton.
3. (The / a / Ø) both her sons live next door.
4. Jack and Jill have known each other for years. (Both / The two) got married last week.
5. You can see (both / the two) of them walking down the street right now.
6. (The two / Both) of these books are novels.
7. That's a good bargain! You can have (both / the two) for less than one pound.
8. My (both / two) parents are teachers.
9. (Both / The two) his parents are painters.
10. They are (both / the two) at my school.

4 **Traduisez.**

1. Je ne peux pas choisir, je les aime tous les deux.
2. Décide-toi ! Tu ne peux pas épouser les deux : c'est soit l'un, soit l'autre.
3. Mais ils sont tous deux si charmants !
4. Soit tu te maries, soit tu restes célibataire !
5. L'un ou l'autre me convient, en fait.
6. Tu peux ne pas te marier. Je ne le suis pas non plus.
7. Mais mon père et ma mère insistent !
8. Ils ont tort tous les deux.
9. Soit je leur obéis, soit je m'en vais de la maison.
10. Je suis sûre que tu n'aimerais pas cela non plus !

5 **Traduisez.**

1. To make it sweeter, you can add either one or two lumps of sugar.
2. You can take either street to the hospital.
3. She can write with either hand.
4. He's the kind of man you either love or hate.
5. It's your choice: either she leaves or I will.
6. There were flowers on either end of the table.
7. It's either that or nothing.
8. I've lived in London and Detroit but I don't like either city very much.
9. She was sitting in the back of the car with a man on either side.
10. There are telephone booths at either end of the street.

6 **Choisissez.**

1. I feel (both / either) excited and exhausted.
2. They're (both / either) very intelligent or very imaginative.
3. (Both / Either) these books are too expensive.
4. (Both / Either) solutions are wrong.
5. I've never met (both / either) her or her sister.
6. We (both / either) said we would come.
7. There's tea or coffee. You can have (both / either).
8. My children (both / either) have green eyes.
9. Do (both / either) of you know where he is?
10. (Both / Either) you and I like going to the pictures.
11. Now she can (both / either) speak and write Japanese.
12. You can't have it (both / either) ways.
13. You left it (both / either) on the kitchen table or in the living-room.
14. My sister and I (both / either) went to England last summer, but my brother didn't.
15. We were treated with (both / either) indifference and contempt.

All, whole, each, every

→ 172-177

7 **Intégrez *all* dans les groupes nominaux suivants. Que constatez-vous?**

these people • my friends • the papers • those nice things • day long • three men • these new methods • your life • the time • her money

8 **Traduisez.**

1. All dogs are animals but not all animals are dogs.
2. All the people you have met are friends of mine.
3. All five children are good musicians.
4. All wool tends to shrink.
5. You've had all the fun and they've had all the difficult work.
6. All these letters must be posted before five p.m.
7. They've worked hard all summer.
8. We've been waiting for you all that time.
9. They were gone all last week.
10. They arrived in all haste.

9 **Traduisez.**

1. She doesn't cook all that well.
2. I'd never have thought that you, of all people, would appreciate her.
3. All my best wine has been drunk.
4. All the spectators applauded the performance.
5. All this is now yours.
6. She was dressed all in white.
7. My old grannie lives all alone.
8. She was all upset about the bad news.
9. The score was two all.
10. You'll have to work all the harder after two weeks' absence.

10 **Traduisez.**

1. Tout vient à point à qui sait attendre.
2. Tout est pour le mieux dans le meilleur des mondes.
3. Tout ce qui brille n'est pas or.
4. Tout est bien qui finit bien.
5. C'est tout ou rien.

11 ***Whole* ou *all* ?**

1. You haven't got (whole / all) day to do it.
2. The (whole / all) school meets together twice a year.
3. On the (whole / all), I'm rather happy.
4. She was (whole / all) smiles when I told her we were going out.
5. (Whole / All) I'm asking for is a little tenderness.
6. The (whole / all) point of the quarrel was the mother-in-law.
7. This rule applies to drivers as a (whole / all).
8. (Whole / All) I could do was wait.
9. He is the best grammarian in the (whole / all) world.
10. Two halves make a (whole / all).

12 **Accordez le verbe entre parenthèses.**

1. Each bedroom (have) a shower.
2. Each extra day (cost) ten pounds.
3. Each of the children (receive) a present for Christmas last year.
4. Each day (pass) without any news.
5. Each of the buildings (have) to be repaired.
6. Each coming day (be) a new day.
7. Each of you (be) allowed to give their opinion.
8. Each man (know) what they have to do.
9. Each week (bring) its load of pain and joy.
10. Each one of us (be) concerned by this matter.

13 **Dites quelle est la nature de *each* (déterminant ou pronom) dans les groupes suivants.**

each coming day • thirty pounds each • each one • each of you • each of the dogs

14 Formez des phrases correctes à l'aide des mots entre parenthèses (parfois les deux sont possibles).

1. They (every / each) had a suitcase to carry.
2. (Every / Each) one did as they wanted.
3. I saw those two films last week. (Every / Each) of them has a definite appeal.
4. You don't have to pay for (every / each) drink.
5. (Every / Each) time you see her, you feel miserable.
6. (Every / Each) of us knows the truth.
7. They watched her (every / each) move.
8. Take one (every / each).
9. (Every / Each) gave him a coin for Boxing Day.
10. I met her twice. It was (every / each) time a pleasure.

15 Quelle différence faites-vous entre :

1. each student **et** all the students
2. each of them **et** all of them
3. They've got one book each... **et** They've all got one book...
4. Each of them had a story to tell... **et** They all had a story to tell...
5. Each one of us is different... **et** We are all different...

16 Choisissez la (les) bonne(s) solution(s).

1. She works ....
   • all day • every day • all days • each day
2. They stayed abroad .... of two months.
   • the whole • every • all • each
3. Have you given .... those present one book?
   • all • the whole • each • every
4. .... one of us did their best.
   • all • the whole • each • every
5. .... thing should never have happened.
   • all • the whole • each • every
6. Is that .... you've done today?
   • all • the whole • each • every

17 Remplacez *all* par *every* quand c'est possible (d'autres changements peuvent intervenir en conséquence).

1. He read all the book in two days.
2. He has read all the novels I have given him.
3. The wife had all the work and the husband all the fun.
4. How come you drank all the wine without giving me any?
5. I'm sorry, I think I've broken them all.
6. All of the films I have seen yet are rather disappointing.
7. The policemen wanted to know all the details of her timetable.
8. All the money that was left was spent later.
9. All her fellow-students were present at the meeting.
10. They had left all the dishes on the table.

18 **Traduisez.**

1. There is an exception to every rule.
2. You can't please everyone.
3. Everything has an end.
4. There is a time and place for everything.
5. Everything comes to he who waits.

Much, many, enough et leurs équivalents

→ 177-180

19 **Intégrez l'un des quantifieurs suivants : *much, many, enough*.**

1. I'm sorry, I'm in a hurry and I can't give you .... time.
2. I know .... people in this room.
3. People who work hard always have .... courage in life.
4. She is a workaholic and always has .... work on her hands.
5. When you are really fed up, you say .... is ....
6. It requires .... courage to jump from that height.
7. She has given away .... opportunities.
8. This town is nothing but buildings. There isn't .... worth seeing here.
9. I'm full up, I've really had ....
10. I like eating and drinking, like .... children.

20 **Choisissez le quantifieur approprié.**

1. I still have (a lot / a good deal of) to do before dinner.
2. (Many / A great deal of) people have found that movie dreadful.
3. I'm sorry but I have (much / enough) problems already.
4. CDs still cost (a good deal / a lot).
5. (Lots / A good many) people would like to be in your situation.
6. (A good deal of / Much) their work is going to be published.
7. There's (many / plenty) more gravy for those who're not on a diet.
8. Stop drinking! I think you've already had one glass too (much / many).
9. There's (many / enough) water left for a bath.
10. You shouldn't put so (plenty / much) salt in the water when you boil eggs.
11. If you haven't got (many / enough) time for me, just forget me.
12. There isn't (a lot of / much) I can do about it.

Some

→ 180-183

21 **Soulignez les fonctions que vous pouvez appliquer à l'emploi de *some*.**

exprimer une quantité nulle • exprimer une certaine quantité • montrer que l'énonciateur ne connaît pas exactement le nombre d'éléments • désigner un élément éloigné • montrer qu'une certaine quantité existe • annoncer des propriétés nouvelles • montrer que tous les éléments ne sont pas concernés • montrer précisément un élément • dire que l'on a apprécié particulièrement ce qui suit • renvoyer à ce qui vient d'être dit

22 **Dans les énoncés qui suivent, dites si *some* est déterminant (D), pronom (P) ou adverbe (A).**

1. Some people had arrived earlier.
2. They were born some twenty years ago.
3. Could I borrow some money?
4. Would you like some more tea?
5. Some like it hot.
6. Some Mr Johnson came this afternoon.
7. Would you care for some coffee? Oh yes please, I'd like some.
8. The house was some twenty miles from the sea.
9. Some would say this is unacceptable.
10. Some of them knew the truth but refused to speak.

23 **Dans les énoncés suivants, choisissez entre Ø et *some*.**

1. Yes, I'd like (Ø / some) tea, I'd like Orange Pekoe please.
2. I never have (Ø / some) vegetables with meat.
3. Since you're asking me, alright, I'll have (Ø / some) more wine, but not much.
4. He spoke about (Ø / some) Mr Smith I had never heard of.
5. (Ø / Some) children like playing hide and seek.
6. (Ø / Some) people like spending their holidays by the seaside, others in the mountains.
7. (Ø / Some) children have never seen the sea.
8. I'd like(Ø / some) flowers, (Ø / some) roses I guess.
9. Stop complaining! (Ø / Some) money is better than no money.
10. That was (Ø / some) meal!

24 **Dans les énoncés suivants, indiquez la prononciation de *some* : /sʌm/ ou /səm/.**

1. I had some nice books for Christmas.
2. Some people would appreciate that.
3. Would you like some more coffee?
4. I'll try to visit you some time next month.
5. Some day there will be peace on earth.
6. This really is some champagne!
7. Some friends of yours have phoned today.
8. There's something wrong going on.
9. It's some forty miles from here.
10. She isn't someone reliable.

25 **Traduisez en utilisant *some* et indiquez sa prononciation : /sʌm/ ou /səm/.**

1. Si tu en as besoin, il reste de la glace dans le réfrigérateur.
2. Tu sais que tu as laissé de l'argent sur la table du salon ?
3. Quelques enfants jouaient au tennis pendant que d'autres se baignaient dans la rivière.
4. Elle lisait une espèce de journal.
5. Ça, c'est un joueur d'échecs.

 → 183-186

26 **Dans les énoncés qui suivent, dites si *any* est déterminant (D), pronom (P) ou adverbe (A).**

1. Is there any living soul here?
2. Can't that car go any faster?
3. You want sweets but I'm afraid I haven't got any.
4. Any car will do so long as I can get there on time.
5. Could any of you boys give me a hand?
6. Is there any politician worth listening to?
7. There isn't any hope left.
8. I don't appreciate any of your silly jokes.
9. Do you feel any better now?
10. Not any teacher could teach those pupils.
11. Come any time!
12. I refuse to stay here any longer.

27 **Intégrez *some* ou *any* dans les phrases suivantes.**

1. I didn't eat .... meat for lunch.
2. I'm sure I need .... cherries for this recipe.
3. They own .... land near a camping site.
4. We crossed the Channel without .... difficulty.
5. All that is required for the job is .... experience.
6. To avoid .... further delay, passengers are required to board immediately.
7. Are there .... cartridges in that box?
8. They say you just have to swallow .... pills and you lose .... weight.

28 **Intégrez *some* ou *any* dans les phrases suivantes.**

1. Think hard! There must be .... solution to this problem.
2. He was .... good old friend of my father's.
3. I can't see .... good armchair in this room.
4. I wonder whether .... athlete could have run so fast.
5. .... book you have written here!
6. .... fool would know that.
7. "I need .... help." " I'm sorry, I can't give you ...."
8. You can't give a child .... sweets and take them away the next minute.

29 **Intégrez *some* ou *any* dans les phrases suivantes, puis traduisez.**

1. You want apricots but I don't think there are .... left.
2. Tell me how many you have, if ....
3. I've made apple pie. Would you like ....?
4. I'm sorry but I can't walk .... faster.
5. .... of the houses were destroyed by the flood.
6. She gained .... two thousand pounds betting on horses.
7. I don't think she will ever feel .... better.
8. How about having .... more cake?
9. .... of his friends are real drop-outs.
10. I refuse to go .... farther.

Few, a few, little, a little → 187-188

30 **Associez *a few* ou *a little* avec les mots suivants.**

people • water • houses • wine • sheep • time • times • fish • faster • criteria • chicken • series • mice • love • help

31 **Traduisez.**

1. J'ai peu d'amis fiables.
2. J'ai un peu peur de lui.
3. J'ai quelques bonnes raisons de ne pas l'aimer.
4. Tu ne pourrais pas conduire un peu plus vite ?
5. Cela te demandera un peu de patience.
6. Il m'a donné trop peu de temps pour saisir ces quelques pages.
7. Il reste quelques problèmes à résoudre.
8. Peux-tu me laisser seule une peu ?
9. Donne-moi quelques explications.
10. Je vois trop peu de gens en ce moment.
11. J'ai trop peu de temps libre pour passer quelques jours avec toi.
12. Quelques rares journalistes ont rapporté l'événement.
13. Peu d'écologistes approuvent le nucléaire.
14. Je sais peu de choses à son sujet.
15. On dit que le ministre aurait eu quelques histoires d'amour avec quelques jeunes femmes.

No, none, nothing → 188-191

32 **Complétez à l'aide de *no*, *none*, *nothing*.**

1. She speaks very good English and she's .... fool.
2. I got .... sleep last night.
3. Two is company but three is ....
4. It occurs to me that .... ordinary man would be able to speak Chinese so perfectly.
5. You don't get something for ....
6. This is .... of your business.
7. It's got .... to do with politics.
8. He shivered for .... accountable reason.
9. This girl had a strange effect, like .... woman he'd known before.
10. Something is better than ....

33 **Complétez à l'aide de *no*, *none*, *nothing*.**

1. Ask .... questions and hear .... lies.
2. A blind man's wife needs .... paint.
3. Believe .... of what you hear and half of what you see.
4. A bad excuse is better than ....
5. There's .... so blind as will not see.
6. .... for ....
7. There's .... so deaf as those who will not hear.

8. My father used to say that .... man was God.
9. There is .... new under the sun.
10. .... venture, ... gain.

Les nombres

→ 191-194

34 **Écrivez en toutes lettres.**

137,000 people • 0.9143 • 40,000,000 inhabitants • 3.7853 • 0.394 • 2.205 • 378 • 499 • 219.98 • 29,028

35 **Associez les mesures dans les deux systèmes et lisez-les à haute voix.**

an inch • a foot • a yard • a mile • an acre • a pint • an ounce • a pound • a stone • a gallon

1.609 km • 40.4672 a • 28.35 g • 30.48 cm • 453.59 g • 0.56791 l • 0.9143 m • 3.7853 l • 6.350 kg • 2.54 cm

36 **Associez les mesures dans les deux systèmes et lisez-les à haute voix.**

1 cm • 1 m • 1 km • 1 l • 1 kg • 1 cm^2 • 1 ha • 1 km^2 • 1cm^3 • 1 m^3

0.386 sq.mile • 1.1760 pint • 219.98 gallons • 0.155 sq.inch • 0.621 mile • 0.394 inch • 0.061 cubic inch • 3.280 ft • 2.205 lb • 2.471 acres

37 **Lisez et écrivez en toutes lettres les numéros de téléphone suivants.**

00 44 18187498523 • 00 44 16034556588 • 00 33 02356065079 • 00 33 02326007057

38 **Écrivez en toutes lettres les dates suivantes.**

le 3 novembre 1953 • le 17 octobre 1985 • le 21 mai 1979 • le 27 mars 1988 • le 2 août 1940

5 La mise en relation des noms

L'utilisation des prépositions

→ 195-196

1 **Intégrez la préposition manquante : *from, by, for, in, to, on*.**

1. It's only two weeks .... my birthday.
2. They asked me to write a cheque .... a hundred pounds.
3. Let me introduce my daughter .... my previous husband.
4. I've just read an article .... the *Times*.
5. All philosophers are embarked .... a quest .... knowledge.
6. I've lost the key .... the garage.
7. She has developed an interest .... African art.
8. Day .... day his health got better.
9. The workers .... strike were asking for a rise .... wages.
10. The Russian economy doesn't seem to be .... the road .... recovery.
11. The guests were teachers .... all over the world.
12. There's a solution .... every problem.
13. We had to take the road .... London.
14. They are twins and it's difficult to tell the one .... the other.
15. I love the Fifth .... Beethoven.
16. I missed the late train .... Norwich.
17. Have you ever been .... a tour of London .... night?
18. He is a good specialist .... biology.
19. Don't forget your appointment .... tomorrow.
20. She's secretary .... the manager.

Le génitif

→ 196-200

2 **Formez des génitifs à l'aide des deux séries de mots suivantes.**

France • the children • my parents • the President • Jenny and Peter • Dickens • Ulysses • St Paul • today • anyone

travels • cathedral • foreign policy • men • wedding party • novels • toys • weather report • friends • guess

3 **À partir des exemples fabriqués dans l'exercice 2, remplissez le tableau suivant.**

- ▶ groupe nominal 's (adjectif) nom : *the man's (blue) cap,* ....
- ▶ groupe nominal ' (adjectif) nom : *the pupils' (heavy) satchels,* ....
- ▶ groupe nominal 's : *Marks and Spencer's,* ....

4 **Dites si le déterminant souligné détermine le premier nom ou le second.**

▶ He was riding a lady's bike. [*a* détermine *bike* / *lady* se comporte comme un adjectif
▷ le génitif est classifiant : un vélo de femme]

▶ She was carrying my mother's bag. [*my* détermine *mother* (= *her bag*) / *my mother* est le déterminant de *bag* ▷ génitif déterminatif : le sac de ma mère]

1. She was wearing a man's clothes.
2. The man's trousers were dirty.
3. He wanted to buy a woman's hat.
4. All that was needed was a year's experience.
5. She was holding a policeman's six-shooter.
6. He didn't attend Ø last week's meeting.
7. I could hear a woman's footsteps on the pavement.
8. His novels' success was not surprising.
9. She was a rich man's wife.
10. Ø Britain's hooligans are unfortunately very famous.

5 **Dans les phrases ci-dessus, classez les génitifs en deux catégories :**

– génitifs déterminatifs (ils prennent la place du déterminant) ;
– génitifs classifiants (ils prennent la place d'un adjectif).

Attention : certains peuvent appartenir aux deux.

6 **Transformez les phrases ci-dessous en génitifs.**

▶ My daughter is ill. ▷ my daughter's illness

1. My brother has yellow eyes.
2. I've got the newspaper published today.
3. I visited the cathedral dedicated to Saint Peter.
4. Merlin worked magic.
5. Dublin has a fair city center.
6. I've got the same eyes as my father.
7. John has received a letter.
8. Mary wrote a book.
9. Kennedy was murdered.
10. Manson murdered Sharon.
11. Spielberg has made many films.
12. He was imprisoned for ten years.
13. I have bought a knife looking like those of butchers.
14. The train has departed.

7 **Dites où l'on peut trouver les marchandises suivantes en associant les mots des deux séries (il est bien sûr interdit de répondre : *at the supermarket*!).**

▶ You can find fish at a fishmonger's.

jewels • flowers • chicken • tomatoes • shoes • material • cigarettes • meat • hats • medicine • cream • thread and needles • pans • tins • oysters

haberdasher • jeweller • butcher • ironmonger • chemist • dairyman • shoemaker • draper • oyster seller • grocer • hatter • greengrocer • florist • poulterer • tobacconist

8 **Dites pourquoi la seconde partie du génitif a été omise dans les phrases suivantes après l'avoir éventuellement rétablie.**

1. Tim's parents and Lucy's had never met.
2. My brother's in-laws are far nicer than my sister's.
3. He went to the MacFarlanes' last week.
4. She is a cousin of her mother's.
5. I've never been to the dentist's.
6. St John's is famous for heart surgery.
7. I didn't find anything interesting at the jeweller's.
8. Ulysses' were incredible adventures.
9. Elliot's voice was the same as E.T.'s.
10. Is this bike the lady's?

9 **Traduisez.**

1. He is out of harm's way now.
2. The poor woman's two young children were slightly wounded in the crash.
3. Better be an old man's darling than a young man's slave!
4. That monster had goat's legs and raven's wings.
5. They were wearing widdows' garments.
6. It took us a whole day's work.
7. My father's mother's favourite activity was going to the bookseller's.
8. That friend of Jenny's had got a demon's eyes and an angel's face.
9. For God's sake, can't you behave!
10. Have you ever been at Sotheby's?

10 **Pourrait-on transformer les expressions soulignées en génitifs? Si non, pourquoi ?**

1. Let me introduce the two young children of the chieftain.
2. I'd been hoping that the workers of that contractor could help me build my house.
3. The nurse had finished bandaging the head of the wounded man.
4. There was an expression of tremendous joy on the man's face.
5. This is the way of the world.
6. The hospital room had that particular smell of disinfectant.
7. She had examined every article of clothing carefully.
8. No one could have got her knowledge of the situation.
9. The victory of the French was a surprise.
10. They had now reached the end of the corridor.

11 **Traduisez les expressions soulignées.**

1. Le problème de ce garçon, c'est la timidité.
2. Tous attendaient avec impatience la fin du siècle.
3. Le vin de l'an dernier était meilleur.
4. Attention ! Tu vas abîmer le pied de la table.
5. C'est le devoir d'une mère que de protéger ses enfants.

La formation des noms composés

→ 200-201

12 **Associez les mots de la colonne A à ceux de la colonne B.**

A	B
1. milk chocolate	• a bag made of leather
2. chocolate milk	• vegetables that grow in a garden
3. malt whisky	• whisky made with malt
4. whisky malt	• leather used to make bags
5. a race horse	• a garden where you grow vegetables
6. a horse race	• milk flavoured with chocolate
7. a vegetable garden	• a race for horses
8. garden vegetables	• malt used to make whisky
9. bag leather	• chocolate made with milk
10. a leather bag	• a horse that runs in races

13 **Retrouvez la relation qui unit les mots composés suivants.**

teacup • address-book • bank account • daydream • fingertip • handshake • landowner • money box • vegetable garden • leather coat

14 **Mettez les mots composés suivants au pluriel.**

a mouse-trap • an on-looker • a corkscrew • a grown-up • a race-horse • a sit-in • a blood transfusion • an after-thought • a landscape gardener • an oak forest • an in-patient • a story-teller • a pin-up • a dining-room • an all-day session

6 Les adjectifs

1 Vrai ou faux ? Entourez la réponse choisie.

1. Les adjectifs apportent une information concernant un nom. V / F
2. Un adjectif dit dans quelle situation se trouve un nom. V / F
3. Un adjectif peut être greffé à un pronom. V / F
4. Les adjectifs se placent toujours avant les noms. V / F
5. Tous les adjectifs peuvent être modifiés par tous les adverbes. V / F
6. Tous les adjectifs peuvent être soit épithètes, soit attributs. V / F
7. L'adjectif se place à la droite des composés de *some, any* et *no*. V / F
8. Les adjectifs peuvent être suivis d'une préposition. V / F
9. On place les adjectifs dans l'ordre que l'on veut. V / F
10. On ne trouve jamais *and* entre deux adjectifs épithètes. V / F

2 Intégrez les adjectifs entre parenthèses dans les groupes nominaux soulignés.

1. This was another of <u>her ideas</u>. (crazy)
2. Do you know <u>her daughter's name</u>? (last)
3. His discovery aroused <u>interest</u> in <u>circles</u>. (considerable) (various)
4. Your invention has <u>no application</u>. (practical / conceivable)
5. He soon returned to <u>his love</u>, mathematics. (greatest)
6. The car was parked in the driveway of <u>a house.</u> (white-painted / pleasant)
7. He looked at <u>the peaks</u> of the mountains. (white / great)
8. <u>A calm</u> took possession of him. (strange / fatalistic)
9. <u>Her dress</u> was down to her ankles. (woollen / long)
10. They sat down on <u>the bank</u>. (high / grassy)

3 Traduisez.

1. Tout ceci n'est que pure coïncidence.
2. Pourriez-vous dire quelque chose de gentil pour changer ?
3. Cette première édition du roman est tout à fait unique.
4. C'est tout à fait impossible, désolée.
5. Son visage était un peu trop blanc.
6. C'était un projet bien trop ambitieux !
7. Fais attention, j'ai une aussi bonne mémoire que toi.
8. Ces abricots ne sont pas assez mûrs (*ripe*) pour être mangés maintenant.
9. Ne t'en fais pas, c'est arrivé par le plus pur des hasards.
10. C'est une question trop compliquée pour moi.

4 Chassez l'intrus.

1. chief • main • essential
2. available • sheer • possible
3. satisfied • content • happy
4. enormous • huge • much

5 **Traduisez les paires suivantes.**

1. a full wine glass / a glass full of wine
2. the only room available / the only available room
3. the people concerned / the concerned people
4. the involved explanation / the explanation involved
5. You met the proper person. / You met the person proper.

Adjectifs et prépositions

→ 204-205

6 **Intégrez la préposition requise par l'adjectif.**

1. I was very angry .... myself .... being such a fool.
2. She was so afraid .... spiders she had nightmares when she saw one.
3. Being jobless he felt anxious .... his future.
4. The teacher was cross .... the pupils.
5. She was really cross .... his permanent lies.
6. He had lost all that was dear .... him in life.
7. The jobless are often desperate (*vouloir à tout prix*) .... work.
8. He had suffered so much that he had sworn to get even .... her one day.
9. The old woman was grateful .... him .... helping her cross the street.
10. The trees were heavy .... fruit this year.
11. Parents sometimes prove more impatient .... their children than teachers.
12. Younger people shouldn't be impertinent .... older people.
13. He refused to get involved .... such a detestable person.
14. She is as mad .... him as he is mad .... football!
15. Stop being so mean .... me, you might need me one day.

7 **Choisissez l'adjectif qui convient à la structure de la phrase.**

1. Don't be so (angry / nasty) to your little sister!
2. Everything she saw around her seemed (new / sheer) to her.
3. He was so (unconscious / oblivious) to danger that he did incredible things.
4. This palace has never been (designed / open) to the public.
5. She was absolutely (full / petrified) with horror during that Stephen King film.
6. I can't lend you any money, I'm (short / pressed) for cash at the moment.
7. I was very (proud / happy) of my daughter when she managed to walk again after her accident.
8. My son is very (fair / quick) at figures and mental arithmetic.
9. The witness said he was (reliable / sure) of what he had seen.
10. He was (anxious / scared) of not waking up after the operation.

L'ordre des adjectifs

→ 205-206

8 **Remettez dans l'ordre les mots entre parenthèses.**

1. The (tall / French / white / seventeen-year-old / handsome) boy was shaking hands with a girl.
2. A (tiny / wooden / cane / rather common) chair stood in front of a magnificent huge stone fireplace.

3. Why don't you buy this blouse instead of that (grey / flannel / old-fashioned) shirt?
4. He drove a (brand new / black / sports / flashy) car along the Boulevard.
5. I'd rather have a (ice-cold / Bloody / small) Mary than a malt.
6. She has lost her ring in the (hot / night / noisy / crowded / *and*) club.
7. World-wide medical research is trying to overcome the (African-born / twenty-year-old / deadly) virus of Aids.
8. For my birthday my friend gave me a (very / rather / leather / expensive / black / large) bag which I could never have afforded to buy.

Les adjectifs en -ed ou -ing ➜ 207

9 **Exprimez la conséquence produite par les énoncés suivants en complétant les amorces à l'aide d'un verbe copule et d'un adjectif.**

► It's amazing that you should be here, I .... (be) ▷ I am amazed!

1. The circus artists were really amusing, all the people present .... (be)
2. All the spectators found the acts astonishing, even someone so blasé as my brother .... (look)
3. The situation was confusing and the two protagonists were speechless, so .... (be)
4. The news is always so depressing that the most optimistic of the viewers can't help .... (feel)
5. The defendant's attitude to his wife was so disgusting that even the council for the defence confessed to .... (be)
6. The howling of the wind was so frightening that hours later I still couldn't sleep, so .... (be)
7. The subject of his conference was so interesting that I went to see him at the end and told him how .... (be)
8. I found the results of the test worrying and I saw on the doctor's face that he too .... (feel)
9. This story-teller is so fascinating that anybody listening to him .... (grow)
10. The lesson was so boring that even the most attentive pupils .... (get)

Les adjectifs composés ➜ 208

10 **Complétez les phrases suivantes en utilisant des adjectifs composés.**

► A subject that you know well is well-known / is a well-known subject.

1. A baby that his mother feeds well is ....
2. Cakes that are made at home are ....
3. A girl who has long legs is ....
4. Someone who has good manners is ....
5. If something breaks you heart, you feel .... because it is ....
6. A country which produces corn is a ....
7. A car that looks expensive is an ....
8. If a story seems never to end, it's a ....
9. If a woman uses her left hand only, you say she is ....

11 **Terminez ces phrases en utilisant des adjectifs composés de mesure.**

▶ A session that lasts four days is a four-day session.

1. A rest that lasts ten minutes is a ....
2. A holiday that lasts two months is a ....
3. A man who is fifty years old is a ....
4. A magazine that has forty pages is a ....
5. A tank that holds sixty litres is a ....
6. A book that costs five pounds is a ....
7. An answer that is worth two thousand dollars is a ....
8. A walk that covers ten miles is a ....

Les adjectifs substantivés

→ 208-209

12 **Transformez les éléments soulignés en adjectifs substantivés.**

▶ Poor people, homeless people, destitute people are all needy people. ▷ The poor, the homeless, the destitute are all needy people.

1. People who can't see, can't hear, can't speak are said to be disabled people.
2. A century ago, black people were discriminated against by white people.
3. There's always more than a generation gap between young people and old people.
4. Some films are forbidden to young people under fourteen.
5. What is sublime and what is beautiful are what I appreciate most in works of art.
6. People living in Wales are as British as people living in England.
7. I love reading books dealing with things uncanny (*mystérieuses*) or supernatural.
8. You can't imagine what disabled people's difficulties can be.

13 **Traduisez.**

1. Certaines places de parking sont réservées aux gens handicapés.
2. Les sans-abris sont de plus en plus nombreux aujourd'hui.
3. As-tu lu *Les Nus et les Morts* de Norman Mailer?
4. Trois jeunes sur quatre aiment aller au cinéma.
5. Ce qui est difficile est fait immédiatement, l'impossible prend plus de temps.
6. L'homme riche a de la glace en été, le pauvre en hiver.
7. Les muets ne peuvent communiquer avec les aveugles par le langage des signes.
8. Darwin a exposé sa théorie de la survie des mieux adaptés (*fit*) dans *De l'origine de l'espèce*.

7 Les comparatifs / Les superlatifs

Comparatif d'égalité
→ 213-215

1 **Introduisez un comparatif d'égalité entre les énoncés suivants en tenant compte des éléments entre parenthèses.**

1. His hair was black. / A raven's wing is black. (négation)
2. My sister works in a hospital. / My father works in a hospital. (même)
3. Her necklace is long. / My necklace is long. (deux fois plus)
4. The English teacher is funny. / The music teacher is funny. (négation)
5. I make mistakes. / My neighbour makes mistakes. (autant)
6. I've had sweets. / My little sister has had sweets. (quatre fois moins)
7. American wine is good. / Any other wine is good.
8. She likes going to the theatre. / He likes going to the theatre.

2 **Traduisez.**

1. N'achète pas ce livre, il est quatre fois plus cher ici que dans l'autre librairie.
2. J'ai autant d'amis que toi.
3. Elle n'est malheureusement pas aussi intelligente qu'elle en a l'air.
4. Elle parle un aussi bon anglais qu'un présentateur (*announcer*) de la BBC.
5. Pourrais-tu parler deux fois moins vite pour que je comprenne deux fois plus rapidement ?
6. Par ce temps, nous sommes aussi bien ici que dehors.
7. Je ne pense pas qu'elle soit si fâchée que cela.
8. Arrête de faire toujours la même chose que moi !

Expression de la différence
→ 215-221

3 **Insérez la forme correcte du comparatif de supériorité.**

1. I'd be (happy) if I had less work.
2. A death is always (sad) than a birth.
3. Could you give me something (spicy) and (tasty)?
4. She is far (intelligent) than you think.
5. I couldn't get any (near) because of the traffic getting (heavy) all the time.
6. She must be his (old) sister since there were only two of them.
7. He looked (angry) than hurt.
8. I have never seen (smashing) a car.
9. If the door was (narrow) you would get more space here.
10. They were married for (good) and for (bad).

4 **Écrivez les comparatifs de supériorité des adjectifs suivants.**

big • fat • wide • deep • high • narrow • feeble • heavy • handsome • right • true • good • wrong • bad • real • thin • meagre • acid • fair • old

5 **En vous aidant de l'exercice précédent, associez les éléments des colonnes A et B.**

A	B
1. mots d'une syllabe	• comparatif avec *more*
2. mots d'une syllabe terminés par consonne + voyelle + consonne	• comparatif en *-er* en redoublant la consonne finale
3. mots de plus de deux syllabes	• comparatif en *-ier*
4. *pleased, real, right, wrong*	• comparatif avec *more*
5. mots de deux syllabes en *-er*	• comparatif avec *more*
6. mots de deux syllabes en *-y*	• comparatif en *-ier*
7. mots de deux syllabes en *-ly*	• comparatif en *-er*
8. mots de deux syllabes en *-ful*	• comparatif en *-r*
9. mots de deux syllabes en *-re*	• comparatif avec *more*
10. mots de deux syllabes en *-ing*	• comparatif avec *more*
11. mots de deux syllabes en *-ed*	• comparatif en *-er*
12. mots de deux syllabes en *-less*	• comparatif avec *more*
13. mots de deux syllabes en *-e*	• comparatif en *-r*
14. mots de deux syllabes en *-le*	• comparatif avec *more*

6 **Traduisez.**

1. Si tu n'es pas plus soigneux (*careful*) à l'avenir, je ne t'achèterai plus rien.
2. C'est bien plus facile que vous ne le pensez !
3. Si tu veux mon avis, elle est plus bête (*stupid*) que méchante (*nasty*).
4. Je n'ai jamais connu quelqu'un de plus riche que lui.
5. Tout ceci me semble plus réel désormais, j'avais peine à y croire.
6. Ton intuition (*insight*) est plus juste que tu ne le crois.
7. Je n'irai pas plus loin, j'ai les jambes plus fatiguées que le reste.
8. Il n'a pas voulu que j'en lise plus.
9. Les handicapés sont arrivés plus tard que les autres mais n'ont pas été les derniers.
10. J'ai vu Tim et Tom la semaine dernière : le premier a grossi, le second a maigri (*grow* + adjectif au comparatif).

7 **Réécrivez les mots entre parenthèses sous forme d'accroissements ou de diminutions progressifs.**

► Professional cycling is getting (criticized). ▷ Professional cycling is getting more and more criticized.

1. It's getting (hard) to find someone you can really trust.
2. His speech was so long that the audience felt (interested).
3. Means of communication are becoming (quick).
4. It was pouring outside and I was (in a hurry) to leave.
5. Going on holiday costs (money).
6. Village schools have (pupils). Some will have to close.
7. She was (pleased) as she heard the nice speech of the manager.
8. (People) use the Internet.
9. The imaginary world was getting (real).
10. There are (hitchickers) on the roads these days.

8 Complétez à l'aide des adjectifs ou adverbes entre parenthèses.

1. .... I know you, ... I appreciate your company. (more / less)
2. .... he earns, ... he spends. (more / more)
3. .... she gets, ... beautiful she is. (old / beautiful)
4. .... her clothes, ... they suit her. (dear / less)
5. .... you try, ... it is. (hard / good)
6. .... friends he has, ... he feels. (more / happy)
7. .... you come, ... we leave. (early / soon)
8. .... he loves her, ... she loathes him. (more / more)
9. .... drinks you have, ... you become. (more / dangerous)
10. .... he goes, ... chances he has of coming back. (far / few)

9 Traduisez.

1. Actions speak louder than words.
2. Attack is the best form of defence.
3. Better be envied than pitied.
4. Better late than never.
5. The grass is always greener on the other side of the fence.
6. The more, the merrier.
7. The pen is mightier than the sword.
8. Prevention is better than cure.
9. The sharper the storm, the sooner it's over.
10. The sooner begun, the sooner done.

10 Mettez en rapport les éléments des colonnes A et B.

A	B
1. This is the nicest piece of news	• (of / in / ø) I know.
2. He is the most famous senator	• (of / in / ø) in the French team.
3. That's the worst place	• (of / in / ø) the day.
4. China is the most populated area	• (of / in / ø) in France.
5. The day I got my divorce was the happiest day	• (of / in / ø) the world?
6. It's the strangest remark	• (of / in / ø) the world.
7. This is the best ever book	• (of / in / ø) Congress.
8. Chartres' is the most interesting cathedral	• (of / in / ø) my life.
9. Alain Proviste is the most talented player	• (of / in / ø) I have ever heard.
10. What is the highest building	• (of / in / ø) the history of literature.

8 Les pronoms personnels et possessifs

Les pronoms personnels

→ 222-228

1 Transformez le complément d'attribution en pronom.

1. He used to bring flowers to his wife every other day.
2. The milkman brought milk to the Jonsons every morning.
3. Could you give my share to my children?
4. All her friends gave presents to Mary for her child's birth.
5. She had promised a few things to her husband so that he would not go.
6. I send my best regards to your parents.
7. They never showed their holiday photographs to John.
8. I had to teach linguistics to crowds of students.
9. He was supposed to tell the truth to the jury.
10. She gave it to her best friend.

2 Transformez les phrases suivantes en utilisant le style indirect.

1. She said: "All I know is that they don't like me."
2. She wondered: "I don't know whether I should go or stay with you."
3. She asked: "Can you give me a hand, the two of you?"
4. They said to me: "You should be more careful! You have hurt your leg again!"
5. He said to them: "Mind your own business from now on."
6. She started by saying : "In this novel, I have tried to show what my life was in those days."
7. She shouted to him: "You'd better hurry or we'll be late!"
8. How could you say "I'm pleased to meet you!" to such a detestable man!

3 Traduisez.

1. Personne d'autre que toi ne sait où elle se trouve, alors c'est toi qui vas aller la chercher.
2. "Qui a acheté tout ceci ? – C'est moi. – Toi ? – Oui, c'est moi qui suis allée faire les courses."
3. "Je ne les ai pas encore rencontrés. Et toi ? – Moi, je les ai vus hier."
4. J'en ai assez ! Il me tape sur les nerfs !
5. Il est trois fois plus gros qu'elle et pourtant, elle mange deux fois plus que lui.
6. On sonne. Cela doit être elle. Elle est toujours en retard quand elle vient chez nous.
7. "Comment s'appelle ton chat ? – Kitty. Elle est très indépendante."
8. C'est son père qui veut lui parler au téléphone mais elle n'est pas là et il ne va pas me croire quand je vais le lui dire !
9. "Qui a dit : 'On ne sait jamais.' ? – Ce que je sais, c'est que ce n'est pas moi."
10. "Nous arrivons de New York. – Enchantés. Nous, nous arrivons de Cuba."

4 **Traduisez.**

1. It's important that you should know it.
2. I won't be able to come to your wedding and I apologize for it.
3. It was very difficult for me to believe you didn't know it either.
4. It's very kind of you to do it for me.
5. I thought it best to tell you about it first.
6. It doesn't matter, besides, I really don't care (about it).
7. It was obvious that nobody found it essential to sell it.
8. If it is really so easy to do, why don't *you* do it?
9. It's always he who speaks last that is right.
10. It's he who broke it ! (*He* broke it!)

Les pronoms possessifs

→ 228-229

5 **Complétez à l'aide des pronoms possessifs en utilisant les indices fournis.**

1. I don't think this is .... (my car) although .... (my car) is the same colour and the same make.
2. That friend of .... (you have friends) is no match to .... (my friend).
3. She had taken one of .... (their books) in order not to write on .... (her book).
4. You have never met that doctor of .... (we have a doctor) I told you about.
5. .... (your hair), ... (their hair) and .... (his hair) have nothing in common.

6 **Traduisez en faisant appel à des pronoms possessifs en français.**

1. That self-styled doctor of yours strangely looks like ours, don't you think?
2. She was looking at me with those smiling eyes of hers.
3. Take theirs if you haven't got yours, but no way will I lend you mine.
4. You can bring your children along, mine will be delighted to play with yours.
5. Theirs is a very beautiful house, nothing in common with his!
6. Nothing serious! He's just a friend of mine...
7. Have you told that husband of yours to hurry up? Because of that laziness of his, we'll be late!
8. That diamond of mine, as you say, is far more authentic than hers.
9. His hair is naturally curly, not mine.
10. Between yours, theirs and mine, I'll always prefer my own children.

One

→ 229-231

7 **Traduisez.**

1. One day you will understand that it is better to have one reliable friend than ten good pals.
2. I'd like one gorgeous red rose please. It's for the one woman in my life.
3. You said one million, not one million two hundred? How could you make such a mistake?

4. My one and only leisure activity is playing a game of squash from time to time.
5. She had twins. One is a boy, the other a girl. They both have a beauty spot on their right cheeks.
6. I have bought a few good bottles. What about opening one tonight?
7. Which peaches do you want? Green ones and unripe ones as usual?
8. My car is too small, I'll have to buy a bigger one.
9. One and one and one is three.
10. Have you heard this one? One day, a German meets a Belgian and says...

8 **Mettez au pluriel les mots soulignés (attention à l'accord des verbes).**

1. I don't know all of them. I only know this one.
2. This blue one and that green one will do.
3. I'd rather have the one that is in the shop-window.
4. This one looks very much like the one I borrowed from you.
5. The one I like has nothing in common with that ugly one.

"On"

→ 232

9 **Traduisez.**

1. On aurait dû te prévenir de mon retard !
2. On y va ? Êtes-vous prêts ? Dépêchez-vous ou on va rater le début du film !
3. Alors on est content de son voyage, mon gars ?
4. On a eu un temps épouvantable au mois de juillet !
5. Il y a quelqu'un qui demande à te parler, elle est dehors, devant la barrière.
6. À la direction, on dit qu'on va licencier les deux secrétaires.
7. On m'a demandé de faire ce rapport pour demain.
8. On ne devrait jamais faire confiance à un vendeur de voitures d'occasion, tu sais ! (*You should...*)
9. On s'est bien amusés hier. Et toi, qu'as-tu fait ?
10. On dit dans la presse que trois personnes ont été grièvement blessées.

10 **Traduisez.**

1. I'll try to prove that two and two is not always four.
2. You'd never think it rained so much last summer.
3. He is said to have been made to confess to crimes whose authors had never been found.
4. It was stolen while you were sleeping! Have you never been told to lock your door?
5. One should never say such things to someone who is depressed!
6. You know, we never know what the future has in store for us.
7. We'll be waiting for you outside the station at eight sharp.
8. So there are things you want to tell me? What shall we start with?
9. I had been told I would get a crew-cut but they didn't touch my hair.
10. People always say that a friend in need is a friend indeed and that is absolutely true.

9 Les pronoms réfléchis et réciproques

1 **Intégrez un pronom personnel ou réfléchi selon le contexte.**

1. Look at ....! John! You've been jumping in water-puddles again!
2. She spends considerable time looking at .... in the mirror.
3. They really enjoyed .... at the party last night.
4. You should think about .... first.
5. What's happened to ....? You look terrible!
6. Take care of .... I'll come and see the three of you next week.
7. While he was getting .... ready, his son told him what he would do that day.
8. Whenever they thought about ...., they regretted their absence.
9. If they hadn't joined that sect, I think they wouldn't have killed ....
10. Their daughter .... was present at their wedding.
11. I think you can easily do it .... without any help.
12. Instead of perpetually looking at ...., you should look about ....
13. You'd see some are far more miserable than .... if you paid more attention to others.
14. He didn't have any money on .... so he couldn't even pay for ....
15. What do you reproach .... for? You didn't do it!

2 **Transformez les phrases suivantes en utilisant un pronom réciproque.**

1. John kept looking at Mary and Mary kept looking at John.
2. Brothers love their sisters and sisters love their brothers.
3. She congratulated him for his degree and he congratulated her for hers.
4. We have never met them and they have never met us.
5. I send him letters and he sends me letters.

3 **Traduisez.**

1. Plus je pense à nous et plus je me dis que nous devrions nous voir moins souvent.
2. Ils ont perdu le dernier match et s'en veulent énormément (*be annoyed with oneself*).
3. Elle a honte d'elle-même depuis que tout le monde sait qu'elle a triché.
4. Il n'y a rien de mieux que d'essayer de s'entraider.
5. Les gens parlaient entre eux et je ne pouvais pas me faire entendre.
6. Votre livre se vend bien, vous pouvez être fiers de vous.
7. Détends-toi, dors dix minutes et quand tu te réveilleras, tu te sentiras très bien.
8. Je vais me féliciter moi-même si personne d'autre ne le fait !
9. J'ai rencontré le président en personne et il s'est intéressé à ce que je faisais.
10. Elle a appris toute seule à jouer du piano.

3 La phrase

1 L'ordre des mots dans la phrase simple

Les phrases affirmatives et négatives ➜ 238-240

1 **Reformulez la phrase en la commençant par l'adverbe souligné.**

► I shall never forget what he did for us. ▷ Never shall I forget what he did for us.

1. It had hardly been raining when the hurricane hit the house.
2. I understood only then what he was saying.
3. We shall never forgive them for what they did.
4. I have often complained about it, but to no use.
5. I have seldom seen so much happiness.

2 **Reformulez la phrase en commençant par l'amorce proposée.**

► It only occurred to me then that he was in love with me. *Only then...* ▷ *Only then* did it occur to me that he was in love with me.

1. As soon as she left her home the sun started shining. *No sooner* ....
2. There has never been such a disaster before. *Never before* ....
3. I was so angry that I decided to write a letter to the director. *So angry* ....
4. My anger was such that I became speechless. *Such* ....
5. The boss was to be seen nowhere. *Nowhere* ....
6. He arrived late and he didn't even apologize. *Not only* .... *but* ....
7. His conduct was so absurd that they all laughed. *So* ....
8. I have never had such an idea before in my life. *Never before in my life* ....
9. I remember your grandmother well. *Well* ....
10. You are to talk about it on no account. *On no account* ....

3 **Traduisez en anglais les réponses en utilisant *so* ou *neither*.**

► I knew him well. *Moi aussi.* ▷ So did I.

► I've never liked that writer. *Elle non plus.* ▷ Neither (ou : nor) has she.

1. "I've passed my exams!" "*Moi aussi.*"
2. "You've got wonderful eyes!" "*Toi aussi.*"
3. "I can't stand that guy." "*Eux non plus.*"
4. "You've put on weight." "*Toi aussi.*"
5. "He looked ill." "*Son amie aussi.*"
6. "We'll manage." "*Nous aussi.*"
7. "She often thinks about it." "*Sa mère aussi.*"
8. "He can't remember." "*Pierre non plus.*"
9. "I worked very hard." "*Les autres aussi.*"
10. "That's something we had never considered." "*Nous non plus.*"

4 **Reformulez la phrase en *if* à l'aide de *had* ou de *should* (style très soutenu).**

► If I had known, I would have called you. ▷ Had I known, I would have called you.

► If ever you left earlier, it would not be a problem. ▷ Should you leave earlier it would not be a problem.

1. If he had arrived earlier the problem would have been solved immediately.
2. If ever she arrived now we would still have time.
3. If he had had a better idea, things would have been different.
4. If ever you changed your plan, please let us know in advance.
5. If it started raining now we would have to cancel our project.
6. They would not be here, if they had passed their exams.

5 **Traduisez.**

"Peut-être est-il trop tard pour commencer notre réunion.
– Il est en effet trop tard. Aussi pouvons-nous décider de partir.
– Mais voilà notre chef.
– Désolé, il y avait tellement de camions sur la route ! Parmi eux se trouvait même un tracteur ! Jamais je n'oublierai ce cauchemar. À peine avais-je quitté la maison que les ennuis commencèrent. Si j'avais su, je ne serais pas sorti de chez moi.
– Nous non plus."

6 **Mettez en relief l'élément souligné à l'aide de *it is... / it was...***

1. Annabel wrote a love story when she was ten.
2. Annabel wrote a love story when she was ten.
3. Annabel wrote a love story when she was ten.
4. He married his own cousin last year.
5. He married his own cousin last year.
6. He married his own cousin last year.
7. You, Mr President, are telling us a lie.
8. You, Mr President, are telling us a lie.
9. You, Mr President, are telling us a lie.
10. We understood what he did at that moment.
11. We understood what he did at that moment.
12. We understood what he did at that moment.

7 **Reformulez la phrase en commençant par *What* et en ajoutant *is / was*.**

► Ben bought a car. ▷ What Ben bought was a car.

1. Sophie's looking for a new apartment.
2. Steve wanted a cheeseburger.
3. She broke a vase.
4. They will like Brooklyn Bridge.
5. She has visited New York.
6. I might see the parade in London.
7. They want to buy three copies of that book.
8. He says that he's never felt that way before.
9. Errol is sticking to the idea that life is for living.
10. I've never understood what they liked about him.
11. She'll always feel sorry about not understanding her daughter.
12. You just can't understand how much I loved her.

Les phrases interrogatives

➜ 241-246

8 **Transformez les phrases suivantes en interrogatives.**

► Tracey is at home. ▷ Is Tracey at home?

1. She can speak German.
2. He will go to New Zealand next year.
3. You're going out tonight.
4. The unemployment rate has come down in Britain.
5. They prefer tea to coffee.
6. Your parents never leave their country.
7. They have a nice house.
8. They would rather stay inside.
9. Steve has many brothers and sisters.
10. Brenda said she'd be late.

9 **À partir des phrases interrogatives obtenues, répondez aux questions l'affirmative puis par la négative. Utilisez l'auxiliaire qui convient.**

► Tracey is at home. ▷ Is Tracey at home? ▷ Yes, she is. / No, she is not.

10 **Soulignez le sujet dans la phrase interrogative.**

► Who remembers the story? ▷ <u>Who</u> remembers the story?

► Who do you love? ▷ Who do <u>you</u> love?

1. Where did you go?
2. Who called?
3. Who did you see?
4. Who wrote that stupid letter?
5. Which one said that?
6. Which letter did you write?
7. What did they do?
8. What happened?

Dites si le mot interrogatif est sujet du verbe. Que se passe-t-il lorsque le sujet n'est pas le mot interrogatif ?

11 **Transformez les phrases suivantes en interrogatives, en commençant par le mot interrogatif proposé.**

1. Something happened. *What ....?*
2. You were doing something last night. *What ....?*
3. Somebody rang. *Who ....?*
4. Somebody wants some more tea. *Who ....?*
5. She went somewhere. *Where ....?*
6. They looked at something. *What ....?*
7. You did it in a certain way. *How ....?*
8. They arrived at a certain time. *When ....?*
9. Somebody left a note on my desk. *Who ....?*
10. Omar lived in California then. *When ....?*

12 **Posez des questions à partir des phrases proposées, en remplaçant *something*, *someone* et *some time* par un mot en *wh-*.**

► You are looking at someone. ▷ Who are you looking at?

1. You sent the flowers to someone.
2. He relied on someone.
3. They cared for someone.
4. Carey was listening to something.
5. She was thinking about something.
6. He thought of someone.
7. We both laughed at something.
8. You sent for someone's doctor.
9. The hooligans broke into someone's house.
10. You said he would be back some time.

13 **Transformez les questions suivantes en interrogatives indirectes en utilisant l'amorce proposée.**

► When will he come back? *I wonder...* ▷ *I wonder* when he will come back.

1. "Where are they going?" *Their friends wonder* ....
2. "Who called?" *Laurie wants to know* ....
3. "When will you see her again?" *I'd like to know* ....
4. "Who was on the phone?" *Let's ask them* ....
5. "How old are her grandparents?" *Peter wants to know* ....
6. "What did they buy?" *I'd be pleased to know* ....
7. "Why are you crying?" *I'm asking you* ....
8. "What were you listening to?" *I'd be interested to know* ....
9. "How did you manage it?" *I'm just asking* ....
10. "Why did she run away?" *Could you tell me* ....

14 **Transformez les questions suivantes en interrogatives indirectes en utilisant l'amorce proposée. Attention à l'emploi des temps après un verbe au prétérit.**

1. "What were you doing at this time yesterday?" *The policeman asked* ....
2. "Which of these books did you like best?" *The librarian wanted to know* ....
3. "Why did Louise lie to me?" *She enquired* ....
4. "Where will you spend your Easter holiday?" *She forced him to tell her* ....
5. "Who have you been seeing?" *He was furious and asked her* ....

15 **Ajoutez un adjectif ou un adverbe après *how*, en vous aidant de la notion donnée entre parenthèses.**

1. How .... is the lake? (profondeur / depth)
2. How .... is your sister? (âge / age)
3. How .... is the Tower of London? (hauteur / height)
4. How .... do you go to New York? (fréquence / frequency)
5. How .... brothers and sisters do you have? (quantité / quantity)
6. How .... money can you lend me? (quantité / quantity)
7. How .... are you planning to stay here? (durée / duration)
8. How .... is it from London to Manchester? (distance)
9. How .... is the swimming pool? (longueur / length)
10. How .... is the road? (largeur / width)

16 Dites si l'expression *how long* exprime une longueur dans le temps (une durée) ou dans l'espace (une dimension).

1. How long is the lake?
2. How long are you planning to stay here?
3. How long did you live with her?
4. How long is the new car he's just bought?
5. How long have you been learning Spanish?
6. Did they tell you how long they stayed in South Africa?
7. How long ago did their family arrive in Britain?
8. How long have they been married?
9. I wonder how long he is going to talk.
10. How long did it take you to drive to Manchester?

Dans quelles phrases pourrait-on remplacer *how long* par *since when* ?

17 Traduisez les phrases 1, 2, 3, 6 et 7 de l'exercice 16.

18 Les équivalents de "comment". Traduisez.

1. Alors, comment allez-vous aujourd'hui ?
2. Sais-tu comment est sa mère ?
3. Comment sais-tu qu'il ne viendra pas ?
4. Comment se fait-il qu'il ne t'ait rien dit ?
5. Comment l'as-tu su ?
6. Comment pourrais-je lui faire comprendre ?
7. Comment veux-tu que je le sache ?
8. Comment l'a-t-elle fait ?
9. Tu peux me dire comment il est, ce type ?
10. Comment faire ?

19 Complétez à l'aide de *what* ou de *which*.

1. .... did he say?
2. Hello! .... would you like?
3. You don't want to see him? .... do you mean by that?
4. .... time did they leave?
5. .... of these meals do you recommend?
6. .... is the matter with him?
7. .... will you tell her when you see her?
8. .... sentence should I rewrite in my essay?
9. I have too many sweaters. .... one should I wear?
10. .... will you be wearing tonight?

20 Complétez à l'aide de *what*, *which* ou de *who*.

"Hi, Phil! It's me, Linda."
".........'s that?"
"Linda."
"Oh, ... do you want?"
"I just wanted to say 'Hi'!"

"......... do you mean 'Hi'! Do you know .... time it is?"
"......... does it matter? I have so much to tell you, Phil."
"Look, why don't you call another one of your friends?"
"......... one?"
"I don't care .... one. Just call .... you want."
"OK, of John, Peter and Steve, ... should I call?"
"That's your business, not mine. Talking of ...., could you lend me your car?"
"......... one? The Rover or the Mercedes? But .... happened to your own car?"
"It broke down and I desperately need one, Linda."
"That's *your* business, honey, not mine. Bye."

21 Traduisez.

1. Quel temps fait-il ?
2. Comment sont ses parents ?
3. Comment vont tes parents ?
4. Depuis combien de temps sont-ils en Allemagne ?
5. À qui est ce livre ?
6. Ils sont en Écosse pour combien de temps ?
7. Il y a combien de temps qu'il n'a pas plu ?
8. Mais enfin, tu n'as pas vu cette voiture ?
9. Pourriez-vous me dire à qui appartient cette voiture ?
10. Je me demande parfois pourquoi il a bien pu faire ça.
11. Je me demande dans quelle mesure il est vraiment déterminé à réussir.
12. Quelles chances a-t-elle de réussir son permis de conduire ?

Les phrases exclamatives

→ 246-249

22 **Modifiez la phrase à l'aide du mot donné entre parenthèses.**

▶ It was difficult. (how) ▷ How difficult it was!

1. It was nice to see you. (how)
2. She has changed over the years. (how)
3. You are a sweetheart. (what)
4. Your cousin is nice. (how)
5. He was a fool not to listen to her advice. (what)
6. This tea is hot. (how)
7. It was a relief to see them. (what)
8. This programme is stupid. (how)
9. It feels strange not to be with my daughter. (how)
10. He made a fuss (*faire des histoires*) about nothing. (what)

23 **Modifiez la phrase à l'aide du mot donné entre parenthèses.**

▶ I was stupid. (so) ▷ I was so stupid.

1. It was great to see you. (so)
2. I behaved in a stupid way. (such)
3. I have to study. (so much)
4. It hurts to listen to you. (so much)
5. She was mad at him. (so)
6. I was a fool to believe you. (such)

7. He really cares for you. (so much)
8. I'm sorry but I am in a hurry. (such)

24 **Reliez les deux phrases à l'aide du mot entre parenthèses.**

► It rained. We left a week earlier. (so much) ▷ It rained so much that we left a week earlier.

1. There were mistakes. I couldn't read his paper. (so many)
2. We had terrible weather. We decided to leave after an hour. (such)
3. I was in a hurry. I didn't notice the accident. (such)
4. The book was funny. I couldn't stop reading. (so)
5. I was late. It was useless to try to make it. (so)
6. They were given wine to drink. They got drunk in less than an hour. (so much)
7. It rained. We decided to cut short our holiday. (so much)
8. It was a lousy film. We didn't watch it to the end. (such)

25 **Complétez les phrases à l'aide de *what (a), how, so, so much, so many* ou *such (a)*.**

1. .... fool I was not to listen to her advice.
2. There's .... I have to learn.
3. I have .... to tell you.
4. .... nice to see you!
5. It was .... nice to meet you.
6. Chris was in .... hurry that she forgot to call you.
7. I have to work .... hard to please them.
8. .... lovely this is!
9. There were .... people in the streets you could hardly move.
10. You are .... artist that I would like to buy a painting from you.
11. He has .... hair on his chest that he looks like a bear.
12. His admiration for your art is .... great that he'd pay any price for it.
13. They have .... to offer us.
14. There was .... wind we had to stay indoors.
15. I cannot stand .... bad manners.

26 **Reformulez la phrase en faisant une interro-négative exclamative. Puis traduisez.**

► He is sweet. ▷ Isn't he sweet! *Comme il est charmant !*

1. They speak well.
2. They behaved badly.
3. I'm smart.
4. I know.
5. It's clever.
6. He is old now.
7. She looks sweet.
8. It tastes nice.
9. Time flies. (*Le temps passe vite.*)

2 Les constructions verbe + verbe

Verbe + to + verbe ou verbe + V-ing ou verbe + verbe → 250-255

1 **Mettez le verbe entre parenthèses à la forme qui convient : *to* + verbe ou V-*ing*.**

► She wants (leave) tomorrow. ▷ She wants to leave tomorrow.

1. If you choose (leave), please let us know.
2. I swear (tell) the truth.
3. We all enjoyed (travel) together.
4. He promised not (talk) to Joan's neighbours again.
5. I can't stand (drive) on motorways.
6. We spent all our time (wait) for him!
7. I advise you (listen) very carefully.
8. I just love not (have) to go to work!
9. I expect him (give up).
10. I told my parents not (worry).

2 **Mettez le verbe entre parenthèses à la forme qui convient.**

When it was too late he decided (tell) his Mum about his secret love affair. He knew how (not / shock) her and wanted (be cautious) with her so as (not / cause) any problem. He is very sweet and hates (hurt) people's feelings but at the same time he couldn't bear (not / let her know). So he asked her (promise) (not / talk) while he was speaking. He had to wait for (she / sit up) in her bed and then started (explain) that he disliked (she / pry) into his affairs and that he enjoyed (lead) his own life. He kept (talk) never daring (look) at her. When he stopped (speak) he realized that she was sound asleep.

3 **Construisez une phrase à partir des éléments proposés, en employant *to*, V-*ing* ou la base verbale.**

► I want x (x = they must leave immediately). ▷ I want them to leave immediately.

1. I advise x (x = you shouldn't write that letter).
2. They swear x (x = they never stole that bike).
3. They swear x (x = they will never steal again).
4. My parents have always let x (x = I can do anything I want).
5. I was listening very carefully. I heard x (x = she whispered to her husband).
6. I distinctly remember x (x = he took your keys).
7. I would prefer x (x = I won't see her right now).
8. I like x (x = I listen to opera).
9. I would like x (x = I listen to an opera).
10. The government proposed x (x = it gives money to fund the programme).
11. I promise x (x = I will not do it again).
12. This time I won't forget x (x = I'll tell them).

Récapitulatif

→ 250-259

4 Traduisez.

1. Peux-tu m'aider à remplir ce formulaire ?
2. Si tu choisis de rester, il faudra coopérer.
3. J'aime qu'on m'admire. J'aimerais tant qu'on m'admire.
4. Je veux que tu me dises la vérité.
5. Tu refuses de me dire où il est ?
6. Vous étiez tous d'accord pour voir ce film, non ?
7. Finalement, on l'a persuadée de nous accompagner.
8. J'attends que ses amis arrivent.
9. Ils ne supportent pas qu'on les touche.
10. Ses parents ne le laisseront pas partir.

5 Traduisez.

1. Ils font semblant de ne pas me voir.
2. Inutile de me dire comment ça marche.
3. Ça ne me dérange pas de ne pas y aller.
4. Il n'a pas arrêté de pleuvoir.
5. Je l'ai entendue chanter.
6. Je ne sais pas comment le lui dire.
7. Les clients avaient l'intention de boycotter ce produit.
8. Essaie de te concentrer, pour changer.
9. Prendre ce train, cela veut dire voyager pendant quinze heures.
10. Je regrette de ne pas en avoir parlé.
11. Soyez patient, je viendrai vous aider un jour.
12. Le toit a besoin d'être réparé.

3 Les propositions causatives-résultatives

Les équivalents de "faire"

→ 260-264

1 **Complétez la phrase à l'aide de *make*, *have* ou *get*.**

1. It'll take time but I'll .... Mustapha to give you a hand.
2. He .... us work extremely hard and we don't regret it now.
3. I'll .... him call you.
4. I .... this cake made especially for you.
5. She .... him park his car on a double yellow line.
6. I'll .... him do the dishes tonight.
7. Don't worry, I'll .... my brother to write your essay for you.
8. This actor always .... me laugh.
9. You'll .... me blush if you go on like that!
10. As a child I .... my brother write my essays for me.

2 **Traduisez.**

1. J'ai fait peindre ma chambre par mon frère.
2. Faites frire le poisson dans un peu d'huile.
3. On m'a fait ouvrir ma valise. (emploi du passif)
4. Ne vous en faites pas, je vous ferai aider par un policier.
5. Me suis-je fait comprendre?
6. J'ai essayé en vain de me faire obéir.
7. Il s'est fait voler sa montre.
8. Il y avait énormément de circulation et cela fait que je suis arrivé en retard.
9. L'idée l'a fait sourire.
10. Ils m'ont fait boire de la vodka.

3 **Traduisez.**

1. J'ai réussi à lui faire ranger son fouillis (*clear up his /her mess*).
2. Maman a fait venir le médecin.
3. Je vous le ferai savoir dès que possible.
4. Ça y est, j'ai fait réparer la voiture.
5. Ils se sont fait couper les cheveux.
6. Les pauvres, ils se sont fait avoir par leur avocat.
7. Toutes ces belles histoires font rêver.
8. Le prince fit reconstruire le château.
9. Quand j'étais petit, mon père me faisait faire mon lit tous les matins.
10. N'essayez pas de me faire croire qu'il est ici.

4 **Combinez les deux phrases en une seule puis traduisez.**

► I have painted my bathroom. Now it is red. ▷ I have painted my bathroom red.
J'ai repeint ma salle de bains en rouge.

1. She has washed her car. Now it is clean.
2. Jo shouted last night. Now, her voice is hoarse.
3. Steve read a lot. Now he is almost blind.
4. She ran quickly and then she was out of the shop.
5. They starved and then they died.
6. They starved themselves and then they died.

5 **Combinez les deux phrases en une seule, à l'aide de *into*, *out of* ou *to*.**

► Dad talked to me. So I made an appointment with my dentist. ▷ Dad talked me into making an appointment with my dentist.

1. They blackmailed her. So she had to resign.
2. They threatened her. So she had to sign the document.
3. My mother tricked me. So I picked up my aunt at the airport.
4. Erwin talked to Sue. So she didn't accept the offer.
5. The President clearly fooled the State Secretary. So the State Secretary supported the resolution.
6. Sheila argued. So Betsy didn't become a nurse.
7. His parents begged him: he should not marry the girl.
8. My dad persuaded me. So I did a degree in maths.

4 La coordination et la subordination

1 **Dans ce texte, soulignez les coordonnants et dites quels sont les segments coordonnés entre eux.**

The Duke recognized the strategic importance of the castle, which was mentioned for the first time in the twelfth century. It lay at the junction of major trading routes: the wheat and wine route (from north to south) and the salt and silver route (from west to east). When it came into the possession of the Duke, it was given to his son, who had it rebuilt. During a battle, the Duke's son held out against attacks for more than a month, but the castle was finally pillaged and burnt. Five centuries later, the castle was given to the town of Rigmarole, which offered it to the Prince of Mornmouth and his young and beautiful wife. The Prince asked an architect if he could either restore it or build a new one. He replied that he would restore it but that he would do it slowly and meticulously, so that it would take ten or fifteen years. In the end, both he and the Prince had to wait twenty years before the dream came true.

2 **Soulignez les propositions subordonnées dans le texte suivant.**

Dear John,
I suppose that you'll be using my bedroom while you're in London. I'm afraid I've lost the key to the large cabinet that is next to the bed. So if you have anything confidential you should keep it under the carpet, as no one will think of looking there. You can use my books, which are all in my bedroom, though I'd appreciate if you wouldn't lend them to anyone, as books are rarely returned. I have been told by Carey, who came round last night, that you intend to give a party during your stay in London. It's all right with me but make sure that nothing gets broken and that everything stays clean. You know I hate coming back to a dirty house.

5 Les subordonnées relatives

Les pronoms relatifs

→ 270-274

1 Dans ce texte, entourez les pronoms relatifs et soulignez l'antécédent.

The Duke, who was getting old, recognized the strategic importance of the castle, which was mentioned for the first time in the twelfth century. It lay at the junction of major trading routes: the wheat and wine route (which ran from north to south) and the salt and silver route (which ran from west to east). When it came into the possession of the Duke, it was given to his son, who had it rebuilt. During a battle, the Duke's son held out against attacks, which were led by the Duke's arch enemy, for more than a month. But the castle, whose walls were not thick enough, was finally pillaged and burnt. Five centuries later, the castle was given to the town of Rigmarole, which offered it to the Prince of Mornmouth and his young and beautiful wife. The Prince asked an architect, whom he had known for years, if he could either restore it or build a new one. He replied that he would restore it but that he would do it slowly and meticulously, so that it would take ten or fifteen years. The roof, whose tiles were imported from Italy, took longer than he thought. In the end, both he and the Prince had to wait twenty years before the dream came true.

2 Dans le texte précédent, donnez la nature de l'antécédent (humain ou non humain) et la fonction du pronom relatif (sujet, complément, génitif).

3 Réunissez les deux phrases à l'aide d'un pronom relatif.

► The solid table was consumed in a few minutes. It had stood thirty years in the same place. ▷ The solid table that had stood thirty years in the same place was consumed in a few minutes.

1. My mother pushed her neighbour roughly forward. My mother was a relatively aggressive person.
2. We lived in a street. It contained a garage called Ever-Ready.
3. We lived in a street. Its name was Langdon Park Road.
4. It was a narrow room. It had two windows between two wings of the building.
5. Once in a while she appeared with something. That thing took you by surprise.
6. My uncle was always generous. He had never married.
7. The house is old. We live in it.
8. This man was on television last night. His photograph is in my wallet.
9. Brian asked me a lot of questions. He's a police inspector.
10. The shop belongs to my husband. I'm walking towards it.

4 **Ajoutez le pronom relatif qui convient. Si plusieurs possibilités existent, précisez-le.**

1. The friends with .... we play tennis live in our neighbourhood.
2. The friends .... we play tennis with live in our neighbourhood.
3. Marsha, ... had always refused to marry, suddenly decided to embark on a new life.
4. My girlfriend is the girl .... is sitting on the bench over there.
5. My husband, with .... I often argue, agrees with me on that point.
6. This is the book .... I told you about and .... you must read at once.
7. He's given me four bottles of perfume, none of .... I like.
8. Sandy, ... uncle I am, never forgets my birthday.
9. This is the best show .... I have ever seen.
10. This is the only car .... will do 60 miles per hour in 10 seconds.
11. The Japanese, ... language is not well known outside Japan, tend to learn English, ... is now a universal language.
12. They travelled with lots of clothes, some of .... were unnecessary in this warm weather.
13. The Prime Minister is aware of the problem .... played such an important role in the downfall of his predecessor.
14. The leaders know about the loss of sovereignty .... the euro implies.
15. The government had not cut the interest rate since 1998, after .... investors chose other investments.

5 **Dans les phrases suivantes, repérez les pronoms relatifs, les propositions relatives et les antécédents.**

► As I said before, there were several beggars in the street. The one who walked like a prince asked for a cigarette.

▷ *pronom relatif* = who / *relative* = who walked like a prince / *antécédent* = the one

1. The medicine is Amilile, the same that women use regularly.
2. The darkness was thin, like some old dress that has been worn and worn for many winters.
3. The artist left after shooting the woman who no longer wanted to live with him.
4. On the desk were two novels which she had received as Christmas presents.
5. The other book was one that she actually lived with.
6. The music came from records that dated from the 1920s.
7. I was a poet who had a job in a coffee shop.
8. These records were souvenirs of our father, a man whom we barely remembered, a man whose name was never mentioned.

6 **Dans les phrases 3, 4, 5 et 6 de l'exercice 5, dites si la relative est nécessaire pour identifier l'antécédent.**

► As I said before, there were several beggars in the street. The one who walked like a prince asked for a cigarette.

▷ who walked like a prince : *relative nécessaire pour identifier l'antécédent. Si on la supprime, on ne sait plus de quel mendiant il s'agit.*

Traduction des pronoms relatifs ➜ 274-280

7 **Les équivalents de "dont". Traduisez.**

1. Voici la personne dont je pense qu'elle serait un bon candidat.
2. Je n'aime pas du tout la façon dont il conduit.
3. Que faire de ces livres dont personne ne veut ?
4. Ce musée possède de nombreuses peintures, dont une seule est du XXe siècle.
5. L'histoire, dont je me souviens bien, est moins intéressante que le style.
6. Voici une machine dont l'utilité est évidente.
7. C'est une pièce de théâtre dont la modernité avait surpris tout le monde.
8. Elle possède plusieurs voitures dont une seule est utilisable.
9. Ce dont je me rends compte, c'est qu'il n'est jamais trop tard.
10. Ce dont je suis fier, c'est de mon accent.
11. Il a acheté une maison ancienne mais dont le toit est tout neuf.
12. Les amis dont je te parle n'habitent pas ici.

8 **Dans les phrases suivantes, que pouvez-vous dire de l'antécédent ? Traduisez le pronom relatif *which*.**

1. He became a drug addict, which is not surprising.
2. That was the end of my third section, which means that I can now move on to my conclusion.
3. You've always loved him, which not many have done.
4. My boyfriend has been offered a new job, which implies that we cannot stay in this town.

9 **Les équivalents de "ce qui...", "ce que...". Traduisez.**

1. Ce que je regrette, c'est qu'il ne m'en ait pas parlé.
2. Ruth a toujours refusé de m'en parler, ce que je regrette.
3. Ce qu'elle m'a dit ne te regarde pas.
4. Ce qu'ils veulent, c'est qu'on les laisse tranquilles.
5. Tu vois ce qu'il y a là-bas ?
6. Ce qui est regrettable, c'est qu'il ne s'en rende pas compte.
7. Aller les voir ? C'est précisément ce que je refuse.
8. Ils sont tous partis avant la fin du match, ce qui est vraiment incroyable.
9. Ce qu'il te faut, c'est une nouvelle montre.
10. Il est arrivé avec ce qui ressemblait à une voiture.

10 **Traduisez en faisant appel à un relatif + *ever*.**

1. Qui m'aime me suive.
2. J'irai où tu iras.
3. Nous pouvons partir quand tu veux.
4. Quiconque sait faire cet exercice a tout compris.
5. Quel que que soit l'endroit où nous mangeons, il n'est jamais content.
6. De toutes ces voitures, vous pouvez choisir celle que vous préférez.
7. Nous ferons tout ce que tu voudras.
8. Le premier d'entre vous qui trouve la bonne solution aura droit à mon estime.

6 Les subordonnées nominales en V-ing

1 **Remplacez *it* par une proposition sujet en V-*ing*.**

► They complain all the time / it is unbearable. ▷ Their complaining all the time is unbearable.

1. Melvin was late / it annoyed Michael.
2. Henry passed his exam / it rejoiced his parents.
3. I failed my exam / it did not sadden my boyfriend.
4. They hesitated / it could have been dangerous.
5. She rang five minutes after the accident / it puzzled the policeman.
6. He left a note / it didn't make things easier.

Dans quelle phrase aurait-on pu utiliser *to* + verbe ?

2 **Réunissez les deux phrases en une seule, à l'aide de V-*ing*.**

1. I hate something / I am late.
2. Do you mind something / I leave right now.
3. Jane remembers something / she wrote a letter of complaint to her boss.
4. We dislike something / we are not invited.
5. He left without something / he did not say goodbye.
6. On something she immediately rang her best friends / she learnt the news.
7. After something the minister decided to resign / she failed to convince the prime minister.
8. Don't forget that before something you have to fasten your seatbelts / you take off.
9. Thank you for something / you listened with so much interest.
10. I don't object to something / you smoke in here.
11. My students are used to something / they travel a lot.
12. I prefer his new habit to something / he woke up very late.
13. We all look forward to something / Errol visits us soon.
14. They were caught / they were dreaming of the Mediterranean.
15. They were busy / they were repairing their old car.

3 **Traduisez les phrases obtenues dans l'exercice 1.**

7 Les subordonnées conjonctives

Ø ou that ? ➜ 287-288

1 **Utilisez la conjonction Ø ou *that* pour introduire la proposition subordonnée. Préférez la conjonction Ø à *that* à chaque fois que cela est possible.**

1. I knew .... it would be too difficult.
2. He always said .... you were the best.
3. Phil told me .... he would be late and .... we needn't wait for him.
4. Did she know .... you were married?
5. I think, if I am to judge by his performance, ... he is our best hope for a medal.
6. Don't worry, I will tell him .... you called.
7. They supposed, after hearing all the witnesses, ... the suspect was not among them.
8. I believe .... he is out, but I can check if you insist.
9. Joan thought .... you were American.
10. Vivien said ...., as it had not snowed for quite a few days, they would not go skiing.

Équivalents des subordonnées françaises ➜ 287-289 et 293

2 **"Trouver" + adjectif. Traduisez.**

1. Elle trouve bizarre qu'il n'ait pas téléphoné.
2. Je trouve inquiétant qu'elle ne réponde pas.
3. Vous trouvez normal qu'ils soient partis aussi rapidement ?

3 **Traduisez ces phrases qui comportent des propositions infinitives.**

1. Elles se sont plaintes de ne pas être écoutées.
2. Je doute de pouvoir vous répondre.
3. Ils disent vouloir vous aider.
4. Je pense aller à Edimbourg demain.
5. Vous imaginez vous en tirer (*get away with it*) comme ça ?
6. J'admets ne pas savoir comment faire.

4 **Traduisez ces phrases qui comportent des propositions conjonctives sujets.**

1. Qu'il n'arrive que demain est surprenant.
2. Qu'il ne pleuve qu'une fois par an ici me paraît bizarre.
3. Qu'il m'en veuille est normal.
4. Qu'elle n'arrive pas à se décider est compréhensible.
5. Qu'il n'ait pas téléphoné m'inquiète.
6. Qu'ils aient aimé Wagner n'est pas si facile à comprendre.

5 "D'autant plus que..." Traduisez.

1. Il le regrettera d'autant plus qu'un jour je serai riche.
2. Je ne sais pas comment elle va. D'autant plus qu'elle ne m'écrit plus.
3. C'est d'autant plus dangereux que tu ne sais pas conduire.
4. Ce test est d'autant plus facile pour Sean qu'il est en anglais.

Emploi des temps dans les subordonnées conjonctives → 288-298

6 **Mettez le verbe entre parenthèses à la forme qui convient.**

1. They insisted that she (start) her job immediately.
2. It's incredible that she (be) so arrogant.
3. It's vital that they (be) here as soon as possible.
4. Mum suggested that we (go) swimming this afternoon.
5. I strongly recommend that you (remain) quiet for a moment.
6. So, what does the doctor suggest we (do)?

7 **Traduisez.**

1. Il est incroyable qu'elle ait dit ça.
2. Il est surprenant qu'une telle chose se soit produite.
3. Il n'est pas normal qu'ils se soient comportés ainsi.
4. Il est regrettable que vous vous soyez disputés.

8 **Mettez le verbe entre parenthèses à la forme qui convient. Puis traduisez les phrases ainsi obtenues.**

1. I'll phone you as soon as I (get) home.
2. He said he would come as soon as he (drive) Karen home.
3. We'll buy a new TV set when our old one (break down).
4. My parents said we'd buy a new TV set when our old one (break down).
5. We'll leave when you (finish) your work.
6. We're moving to Miami next month. Come and visit us whenever you (want).
7. The judge said she would invite the press once her investigation (be) over.
8. I know he'll arrive when it (be) too late.

9 **Reliez les deux phrases à l'aide de *no sooner... than...* et de *hardly... when...***

► She had left him. He started crying. ▷ No sooner had she left him than he started crying.
▷ Hardly had she left him when he started crying.

1. I saw her. I stopped my car.
2. It started raining. We left the beach.
3. She rang. They started laughing.
4. We got off the plane. We were gripped by the cold.
5. I began accelerating. My husband screamed at me.

10 **Mettez le verbe de la principale à la forme voulue.**

1. If I had known, I (not come).
2. He (not go) if it starts raining.
3. The examiners (cancel) the exam if they had been told about the cheating.
4. Brenda (not talk) to Kevin if she had known the truth.

5. If he comes with his grandparents we (not be able to) go climbing.
6. If you arrived two days earlier you (can) meet my new girlfriend.
7. If you pass your exam I (take) you to the restaurant.
8. If you ever passed your exam I (take) you to the restaurant.

11 **Mettez le verbe de la subordonnée en *if* à la forme voulue.**

1. Imagine all the things we could do if you (be) here with me.
2. If you (make) an effort I'm sure you would succeed.
3. I might have married her if things (be) different.
4. If the president (not be) so rash she would have been reelected.
5. They can come to my party if they (behave oneself).
6. She could make it if ever she (apply) her energy to it.

Récapitulatif

→ 287-298

12 **Reliez une phrase de gauche avec une phrase de droite.**

1. He insisted on trying again	• as soon as it stops raining.
2. They looked at each other	• all the more as it is easy to read.
3. They'll do it	• provided you bring it back with a full tank.
4. We'll leave	• until you are over 30.
5. The government will negotiate	• where it turns out of sight.
6. Take my advice: don't get married	• than he offered to marry her.
7. The path runs around a corner	• as long as you take good care of them.
8. No sooner had he met her	• in case he had to describe it.
9. She is so famous	• even though he knew it was useless.
10. They immediately stood up	• when they can.
11. How can he know London	• since he said he'd never been to England?
12. He took a picture of the monument	• to greet the new mayor.
13. You may borrow my car	• if they stop striking.
14. The students enjoy this novel	• as though they had never met.
15. You may have any of my books	• that she would never think anyone could be disrespectful to her.

Dans lesquelles des phrases ainsi obtenues peut-on inverser l'ordre des deux propositions ?

13 **Dans les phrases suivantes, soulignez la subordonnée conjonctive et entourez la conjonction.**

1. I got your letter right after you phoned.
2. It won't be long until he apologizes.
3. Strike while the iron is hot.
4. I'll take my shoes off so as not to wake you up.
5. Oliver wrote that letter for you to know the truth.
6. They complained to the management so that they wouldn't have to do it again.
7. They complained to the management, so that they won't have to do it again.
8. Since you really want to know, I'll tell you the plain truth.

9. Pete hasn't seen her since she returned from her holiday in Leeds.
10. I still love her, even though I'll never admit it to her.
11. However intelligent he may be, he still has to work very hard.
12. She would like to be a shop assistant, whereas her parents would like her to be an actress.

14 **Dans les phrases suivantes, soulignez la subordonnée conjonctive et entourez la conjonction.**

1. He drowned while he was trying to rescue his dog.
2. Strange though it may seem, I've never been on the London underground.
3. As it was dark they didn't see the bicycle.
4. The telephone rang as I was cooking for Dominique.
5. Don't disturb me, unless it's a matter of life and death.
6. In case you didn't know, I am also the owner of that car.
7. I'd be happy to go with you, as long as your parents don't mind.
8. I like going out with a group of people, provided nobody tells me what to do.
9. The government backed down for fear that there might be riots.
10. What if he decided to emigrate to South Africa?
11. I hate him for telling me lies.
12. I want to hate him to forget that I love him.

8 Discours direct et discours indirect

Tell ou say ? ➜ 300

1 **Remplacez *say* par *tell* et *tell* par *say* dans les phrases suivantes. Apportez les modifications nécessaires.**
Attention ! C'est impossible dans deux phrases. Lesquelles ?

1. She told me nothing.
2. Unfortunately, they did not say anything to their parents.
3. He told you lies.
4. The headmaster said to the assembly that discipline should be encouraged.
5. Stop telling everyone that you're my boyfriend!
6. They told their best friends that they did not want to get married.
7. You keep telling the same jokes over and over again!
8. Say it to the teacher before it's too late.

2 **Employez *say* ou *tell* à la forme qui convient.**

1. He .... : "Good morning."
2. Has he .... you where he would spend his holiday?
3. He didn't .... where he was going.
4. I'm only .... aloud what everybody is thinking.
5. He .... me something that made me laugh.
6. You should .... the truth and nothing but the truth.
7. There's something I want to .... you.
8. This is a free country, I can .... what I want.
9. She .... me how happy she was.
10. Did they .... you not to wait for them?
11. Would you mind .... me your name and address?
12. Could you .... that again, please?

Questions, conseil, ordre, suggestion au discours indirect ➜ 301-302

3 **Transformez les questions en subordonnées à l'aide de l'amorce proposée.**
▶ Do you have a driving licence? *The policeman asked me...* ▷ The policeman asked me if I had a driving licence.

1. "So, do you want to marry him or not?" *My mother enquired* ....
2. "Did you have a nice meal?" *She asked me* ....
3. "Have you lost anything?" *He wondered* ....
4. "Are you going out tonight?" *She wanted to know* ....
5. "Will the children be home for dinner?" *My husband asked* ....
6. "Has the minister resigned yet?" *The neighbour wondered* ....

4 **Transformez les questions en *wh-* en subordonnées à l'aide de l'amorce proposée.**

1. "Where did you meet him?" *She asked* ....
2. "When will you be back?" *She enquired* ....
3. "What did he say to you?" *They wanted to know* ....
4. "Why was Chris late?" *John wondered* ....
5. "Who has gone?" *They asked* ....
6. "How did it happen?" *She wondered* ....
7. "Where are they?" *The judge wanted to know* ....
8. "When are they coming back?" *Their mother asked* ....

5 **Réécrivez les phrases en utilisant l'amorce suggérée. Quand plusieurs possibilités existent, signalez-les.**

1. "Shut up" he said. *He ordered* ....
2. "Open your books on page 43." *She asked* ....
3. "Never say you're sorry." *He advised* ....
4. "You should go to the cinema." *He suggested* ....
5. "I'm sorry I didn't warn you." *The guest apologized* ....
6. "Don't lie to me." *She told* .... / *She forbad(e)* ....
7. "Don't park your car here." *The policeman warned* ....
8. "Why don't you come round for tea?" *She invited* ....

L'emploi des temps au discours indirect

→ 303-305

6 **Passez du discours direct au discours indirect en utilisant l'amorce.**

▶ "The train leaves at 5:32." *She said...* ▷ She said the train left at 5:32.

Au présent

1. "We want to go to Disneyland." *The children cried* ....
2. "John and William never write to us." *Mr and Mrs Litten complained* ....
3. "It's too late to catch the train." *He said apologetically* ....

Au prétérit et au pluperfect

4. "I met the man of my dreams yesterday." *She announced* ....
5. "Anyway, Liz had never trusted Al." *Her mother explained* ....
6. "I had a dream about my children." *The Reverend claimed* ....
7. "I remembered looking at her." *The policewoman testified* ....
8. "If John came two days earlier it would make things simpler." *They insisted* ....

Au present perfect

9. "I've come to say goodbye." *The boy said* ....
10. "I've decided to get a divorce." *The President's wife cried* ....
11. "Sorry, Miss, you've just missed your train." *The station master told Kirstie* ....

Renvoi à l'avenir

12. "Mr Byrd will be here in a moment." *The secretary explained* ....
13. "I shall not speak to her." *Her former husband exclaimed* ....
14. "Things will get better." *The clairvoyant predicted* ....

Modaux

15. "Thomas, you must come in at once." *Mother told Thomas ....*
16. "I can swim that length in 30 seconds." *Michele bragged ....*
17. "You may sit down." *The priest then said ....*
18. "You could stand up when I come in." *The headmaster shrieked ....*

7 **Passez du style direct au style indirect en utilisant l'amorce.**

1. "He is going to New York." *He asserted ....*
2. "I've made a mistake." *She acknowledged ....*
3. "It's too late to react." *He admitted ....*
4. "We've never been invited." *They confirmed ....*
5. "I'll probably move to London in September." *He answered ....*
6. "I've got no time to lose." *She objected ....*
7. "Nick, you're too stupid for the job." *The boss shouted ....*
8. "I didn't have the courage to talk to her." *Alex accepted ....*

8 **Transformez ces phrases de dialogue en discours indirect. Attention aux pronoms personnels.**

"Henry, have you found anyone who can help me?" asked Nathalie.
"I've found a priest who will be able to help you. His name is Father McCrory. Go to him. He may be able to tell you something," Henry replied.
"Thank you. I suppose that will help."
"Do you have any relatives around here?"
"Only an aunt."
"Oh! That helps a bit, doesn't it?"
"She had the house in Langdon Park Road."
"Anyway, I feel sure Father McCrory could help you. He knew everybody in this neighbourhood. Try not to be too sad. One never knows."
"I know. Life goes on."

Discours indirect libre

→ 306-307

9 **Soulignez les exemples de discours indirect libre dans le texte suivant.**

Mrs Litten was feeding the fire. Tears rose to her eyes. Why had it happened to her? Did she deserve such a harsh treatment? She had always been kind to everybody and could not understand what was going on in her life. The other women did not say a word but Mrs Litten felt their sympathy. She crept closer to her son and asked him, "Melvin, can you pray?" "No, mother." Mrs Litten could understand her son's feelings. Perhaps he could not pray today because of the pain he felt. In a few days, perhaps next week, he would probably feel differently. He might even break down. That would be terrible. If he broke down, it would take weeks for him to recover. Outside the wind abated as if it feared to disturb the mother and her son.

10 **Transposez le texte de l'exercice 9 au style direct.**

4 Annexes

1 Les prépositions

Adjectif + préposition

→ 310-311 et 205

1 **Ajoutez la préposition qui convient après l'adjectif (vous pouvez utiliser un dictionnaire).**

1. They were afraid .... the dog.
2. I am angry .... you.
3. They were annoyed .... their children.
4. He is not ashamed .... his parents.
5. I am aware .... the problem.
6. He is very bad .... maths but good .... French.
7. Look, I am bored .... this film.
8. I feel quite close .... my parents.
9. I am crazy .... you.
10. The students were all disappointed .... the new course.
11. My town is very famous .... its porcelain.
12. I am very fond .... music.
13. This house is full .... mystery.
14. I am furious .... you. Yes, I am furious .... the way you treated your sister.
15. The whole family was glad .... his success.
16. Are you interested .... what I'm saying?
17. He was jealous .... his brother's success.
18. You should be kind .... your sister.
19. I have always been nice .... her.
20. I am pleased .... / satisfied .... what you have done.
21. We are all proud .... you.
22. I am sorry .... what I said.
23. We were surprised .... the way he behaved himself.
24. The judge was tired .... hearing the same excuse over and over again.
25. I am worried .... the future.

2 **Ajoutez la préposition qui convient après l'adjectif.**

1. I am amazed .... his skills.
2. He felt annoyed .... the policeman for being so uncooperative.
3. We are very worried .... our daughter's health.
4. She is busy .... her new job.
5. He is clever .... building miniature boats.
6. We were delighted .... the news.
7. Even though he is 30 he is still dependent .... his parents.
8. This problem is different .... the other one.
9. I am disgusted .... the way he treated his friends.
10. Everybody was excited .... the news of the victory.

11. I am not yet very familiar .... this new computer.
12. Bess is already fed up .... her new job.
13. I am now frightened .... meeting him in the street.
14. I am grateful .... you, ... telling me the truth.
15. Laurie said she was impressed .... your new book.
16. I don't think Thomas is very keen .... visiting her again.
17. She is mad .... him (*en colère contre lui*) for not telling her that he was married.
18. She still loves him. In fact she is still mad .... him (*folle de lui*).
19. Why should I be responsible .... my brothers and sisters, when they are so rude .... me? In fact, I am even scared .... them and I am sick .... having to live with them.
20. I am terrible .... driving.
21. That's typical .... him, always on the road.
22. They felt upset .... the news.

Verbe + préposition ➜ 311-313

3 **Employez la préposition qui convient (servez-vous d'un bon dictionnaire).**

1. I often think .... you.
2. We always go .... Spain in the summer.
3. He suffers .... loss of memory.
4. There is no need to hide the truth .... us.
5. The hero managed to escape .... the battle.
6. I would like to apologize .... being late.
7. I didn't steal that car .... anyone. I borrowed it .... Miss Page.
8. Do you know what sea separates England .... France?
9. That country would like to take part .... / to participate .... our games.
10. He will never succeed .... his examination.
11. Could you translate this text .... German for me?
12. You should divide this cake .... six portions.
13. They turned that clever child .... a good-for-nothing.
14. Is this table made .... solid wood?
15. Children depend .... their parents.
16. I could live .... bread and butter.
17. Don't spend all your money .... sweets.
18. We would like to congratulate you .... your victory.
19. Fill it .... petrol to make it work.
20. You should cover your car .... something to protect it.
21. I'm looking .... my keys. I need them to lock the house.
22. Stop laughing .... those poor children.
23. I don't approve .... their behaviour.
24. How much did you pay .... it?
25. Could you comment .... this text?

Place de la préposition

→ 311-313

4 **Posez des questions à l'aide de l'amorce proposée.**

▶ I sent it to John. *Who...* ▷ Who did you send it to?

1. I replied with a polite letter. *What* ....?
2. We went to Scotland last summer. *Where* ....?
3. She killed him with a knife. *What* ....?
4. I am in love with Tracy. *Who* ....?
5. We are dependent on our grandparents. *Who* ....?
6. We slept in George's house. *Whose* ....?
7. He is married to my cousin. *Who* ....?
8. I felt more interested in this story. *Which* ....?

5 **Reliez ces phrases à l'aide d'un pronom relatif.**

▶ I know a guy. You've just been talking to him. ▷ I know the guy (who) you've just been talking to.

1. This is a book. John is keen on it.
2. I wrote a story. No one is interested in it.
3. She is my cousin. I have often told you about her.
4. They are friends. We depend on them for food.
5. They are former schoolchildren. We are so proud of them.
6. Here is a house. The three men broke into it (*l'ont cambriolée*).
7. These are rare books. I've been looking for them everywhere.
8. The Smiths are our neighbours. Passers-by keep looking at them.

6 **Complétez ces phrases à l'aide des doubles compléments donnés entre parenthèses. Pour certaines, deux constructions sont possibles.**

▶ Sandy gave (a book / Fred). ▷ Sandy gave Fred a book *ou* Sandy gave a book to Fred.

1. The dog brought .... (Peter / two bones)
2. The magician showed .... (the hat / his partner)
3. My parents sent .... (me / a letter) and I left .... (a message / Anny)
4. She wants to book .... (a plane ticket / Bob)
5. I'll teach .... (maths / her) and she'll pay .... (it / me)
6. The manager explained .... (the problem / his employees)
7. We'll provide .... (them / enough food)
8. The murderer described .... (his act / the jury)
9. I'd like to remind .... (my friends / the presents I gave them)
10. There is no need to ask .... (him / his help)

Les principales prépositions de lieu

→ 313-316

7 **Retrouvez l'équivalent anglais des prépositions suivantes.**

à travers • au-dessus de • le long de • derrière • parmi • au-dessous de • près de • en bas de • à l'intérieur de • à côté de • au large de / séparé de • en face de • devant • autour de • vers

near • inside • opposite • down • above • next to • by • along • past • towards • close to • across • through • among • off • behind • round • below • in front of • over

8 ***Across* ou *through* ? Choisissez la préposition qui convient.**

1. Let's walk (across / through) that street.
2. They managed to row (across / through) the lake in 15 minutes.
3. This road will take you (across / through) the forest.
4. The teacher drew a line (across / through) the blackboard.
5. Which river flows (across / through) New york?
6. It took five years to build a bridge (across / through) the river.
7. They entered the house (across / through) the large window.
8. He shouted at me from (across / through) the hall.
9. Jason passed his fingers (across / through) Mary's hair.
10. That car drove (across / through) a red light (*a brûlé un feu*)!

9 ***At* ou *in* ? Choisissez la préposition qui convient.**

1. We met (at / in) a party, not (at / in) the street!
2. I'll pick you up (at / in) the bus stop.
3. They arrived (at / in) the factory half an hour late.
4. Time seems to fly faster when I'm (at / in) work than when I'm (at / in) home.
5. We were (at / in) school together when we were 12.
6. The Kaufmans arrived (at / in) Canada, more precisely (at / in) Montreal, in 1998.
7. We started with an argument but (at / in) the end we became good friends.
8. Would you rather live (at / in) the country (*à la campagne*) or (at / in) town?
9. You either left your bag (at / in) the garden or (at / in) the swimming pool.
10. I have to see my boss (at / in) the end of the week.

10 **Complétez par l'une de ces prépositions : *in*, *to*, *into*, *on* ou *onto*.**

1. Let's all go .... the pub to celebrate!
2. He walked .... the room majestically.
3. She felt weak and fell .... the floor.
4. You'll find your friends .... the living room.
5. He threw the book .... the fire.
6. Come on! Step .... the platform (*quai*).
7. The car crashed .... the wall.
8. She threw the keys .... the table.

11 ***Among* ou *between* ? Choisissez la préposition qui convient.**

1. This ferry sails (among / between) Dover and Calais.
2. There were (among / between) five to seven people.
3. (Among / Between) those present were ten orphans.
4. They had less than 12 dollars (among / between) them.
5. The property was divided (among / between) his wife and himself.
6. The property was divided (among / between) all his grandchildren.
7. (Among / Between) you and me, I must admit that I've never liked her.
8. He is now half way (among / between) youth and middle age.

Les principales prépositions de temps ➜ 316-319

12 **Utilisez l'une des trois prépositions : *on*, *at*, *in* ou Ø.**

1. I'll meet you at the station .... 3:15.
2. He arrived here .... Christmas day.
3. When shall I see you? .... tonight or .... tomorrow?
4. She rang .... Wednesday morning to say she'd start working .... the next day.
5. I last saw her .... Easter, that is, ... the 14th of April.
6. I'm usually away .... weekends, but you can contact me .... the evening.
7. .... her arrival, everybody became silent.
8. Tell her I'll be back .... a few days, ... Monday week (*lundi en huit*) to be precise.
9. This town was founded .... the sixteenth century, ... the year 1503.
10. They'll come back .... three months, that is .... August.
11. Nobody was here .... time : they were supposed to arrive .... the morning.
12. Most of them got here .... the afternoon and some even .... night!

13 **Traduisez le segment souligné en employant *by*, *from... to*, *since*, *for* ou *during*.**

1. Je vous attendrai de trois à quatre.
2. Pouvez-vous terminer ce travail d'ici demain ?
3. Que faisiez-vous durant l'été ?
4. Je n'ai pas travaillé de juin à septembre.
5. Téléphonez-moi ce soir au plus tard à 6 heures.
6. Je suis à l'université depuis l'année dernière.
7. Pendant cinq ans il ne nous a pas écrit.
8. Je la vois régulièrement depuis trois ans.

Autres prépositions ➜ 319-320

14 **Reliez un énoncé de gauche à un énoncé de droite pour exprimer la cause ou le contraste.**

1. Stop dawdling, because of you	• the express to London will leave at 10:05.
2. Due to a late arrival of the train,	• the sports event was cancelled.
3. Unlike Ruth	• we'd better not count on her.
4. Given their children's reluctance	• I've always liked going to the pub.
5. Considering what Brenda said	• we may never be in time for our appointment.
6. Owing to the heatwave	• they decided not to go to New Zealand.

15 **Reliez un énoncé de gauche à un énoncé de droite pour exprimer la cause ou le contraste.**

1. Why don't you go out for a walk	• despite her parents' encouragement.
2. They decided to go on foot	• thanks to Patty's generosity.
3. We managed to go to New York	• in spite of the weather conditions.
4. What you have done is	• on account of their being late.
5. The meeting was postponed	• contrary to the headmaster's orders.
6. She failed	• instead of wasting your time watching TV?

16 **As ou *like* ? Choisissez.**

1. I felt .... an idiot after what I said.
2. .... a teenager he was always very shy.
3. .... a professional adviser I strongly support your choice.
4. My father behaved .... a child when he saw her.
5. It was exactly .... a dream!
6. It fits her .... a glove.
7. He now works .... an accountant in a famous bank.
8. He drinks .... a fish.
9. Don't talk to me .... that!
10. It looks .... rain. (*On dirait que le temps est à la pluie.*)

17 **Traduisez le segment souligné.**

1. Ils sont arrivés à pied de la gare.
2. Je l'ai vu à la télévision.
3. À mon avis ce film est sans intérêt.
4. J'ai parlé à Sophie au téléphone.
5. Les ouvriers sont en grève depuis lundi.
6. Les choses sont différentes de ce côté-ci de la Manche.
7. Barbara a été au chômage pendant six mois.
8. Elle vit au troisième étage.
9. J'ai dû conduire sous la neige.
10. La maison était en feu.
11. Je suis arrivé en train.
12. Je n'ai pu dormir dans l'avion.

Récapitulatif

➜ 310-320

18 **Complétez avec la préposition qui convient.**

1. She came home .... work every night .... eight.
2. .... Sunday evenings she sometimes went .... a lecture .... philosophy.
3. She had been a bookkeeper .... twenty-one years.
4. Mrs Briggs was proud .... her record .... a bookkeeper.
5. .... a young girl she had studied very hard .... business school.
6. She had been served .... Joe or Perry, ... three or four years.

19 **Traduisez.**

1. À qui désirez-vous parler ?
2. Donne-le-lui.
3. Je vous ai déjà expliqué comment ça fonctionne.
4. Louise a demandé de l'argent à Karim.
5. J'ai demandé le prix au vendeur.
6. Cela me rappelle ma première leçon de conduite.
7. Cet acteur célèbre habite à deux pas d'ici.
8. Elle n'aime plus la danse. Elle est maintenant branchée informatique.
9. Quand il est retourné chez ses parents, il ne s'est plus senti chez lui.
10. C'est selon moi la seule façon de s'y prendre (*go about it*).

20 **Traduisez chacun des segments soulignés en utilisant une préposition.**

À mon avis, chanter sous la pluie est une mauvaise habitude.
Si vous chantez seul dans la rue ou à votre travail, on vous prendra pour quelqu'un de bizarre. Par exemple, l'autre jour j'ai voulu rentrer chez moi à pied plutôt qu'en bus. J'habite en banlieue, à cinq kilomètres du centre-ville. Je n'étais pas pressé. Il fallait simplement que je sois rentré pour huit heures. Je me sentais en vacances. En passant par le parc qui se trouve en face de la mairie, je me suis à chanter un air d'opéra. Tout le monde me regardait de haut en bas, voire se retournait sur moi. Finalement, j'ai dû m'arrêter tellement j'avais peur de ces gens.
C'est selon moi une limite à la liberté. D'autant plus que j'ai une belle voix. Je prends des cours de chant depuis seize ans, en fait depuis mon enfance. Quand j'étais enfant, je voulais chanter comme ténor, comme Pavarotti. Certes, j'en suis loin, malgré tous mes efforts. Mais, entre vous et moi, est-ce si important ?
Quand nous sommes entre amis, ça n'a pas d'importance. D'ailleurs je suis prêt à vous chanter, ma chère collègue, le grand air de ténor de *Turandot*, juste pour vous. Comment ça, "hors de question" ? Vous ne voulez pas m'écouter ? C'est à cause de gens comme vous que la liberté est bafouée. Je serais mieux dans une île déserte qu'au mileu d'ignorants. À Pâques, c'est-à-dire dans deux mois, je donnerai ma démission. Je préfère être au chômage qu'avec vous tous. À votre arrivée en septembre, j'ai pensé que vous étiez mieux que les autres. Comme je me suis trompé !

2 Les adverbes

Portée et place de l'adverbe

→ 323-332

1 **Dans les phrases suivantes, soulignez les adverbes et dites ce qu'ils modifient.**

1. Quite frankly, I have other things to worry about.
2. You're too good to be true.
3. Honestly I didn't say anything against you.
4. I'll always love you.
5. This film is incredibly long – and dull.
6. He's still looking for his keys.
7. I read it quite recently.
8. He expressed his opinion convincingly.

2 **Mettez l'adverbe à la place qui convient.**

1. He is away. (often)
2. She does not answer her mail. (always)
3. I'll write to them. (never)
4. It rains here. (hardly ever)
5. He's complaining about the service. (always)
6. We've enjoyed the show. (really)
7. It can't be true. (possibly)
8. "Won't you call her?" "I will. / I will not." (certainly)

3 **Commencez la phrase par l'adverbe entre parenthèses.**

► He left the house and it started raining. *Hardly...* ▷ Hardly had he left the house when it started raining.

1. She opened her mouth and I recognized her voice. *No sooner* ....
2. They had never seen such a beautiful show. *Never before* ....
3. He had said a few words and he began crying. *Hardly* ....
4. The children closed their eyes and fell asleep. *No sooner* ....

Place de all, both et each

→ 324

4 **Mettez *all*, *both* et *each* à la place qui convient.**

1. We've decided to move to Chicago. (all)
2. They are lodging a complaint against their boss. (all)
3. We are properly married. (both)
4. They have returned to their parents' home. (each of them)
5. We will write soon. (all)
6. They can be quite tiresome. (both)
7. We had cucumber sandwiches for lunch. (each)
8. "I'm fed up with this show." "We are." (all)

5 **Traduisez.**

1. Il a expliqué son rôle de manière inattendue.
2. Elle a bien chanté son air.
3. Ils ont répondu avec colère.
4. Si tu l'as déjà vu, on peut voir un autre film.
5. C'est joliment dit.
6. Il se mit à pleuvoir soudainement.
7. J'irai bientôt la voir à Glasgow.
8. Il s'est finalement éteint à l'âge de 92 ans.
9. Si tu vas en haut, n'oublie pas d'éteindre la lumière.
10. Quand avez-vous parlé à la victime pour la dernière fois ?

6 **Utilisez *still* ou *yet*.**

1. Do you .... love me?
2. Have you talked to the boss ....?
3. I .... believe that he lied to us.
4. He hasn't said anything ....
5. They .... won't admit it.
6. I haven't written that letter ....

7 **Traduisez en faisant appel à *yet* ou *still*.**

1. Il n'a pas encore acheté sa nouvelle voiture.
2. Le bébé ne parle toujours pas.
3. Je crois qu'ils sont encore au lit.
4. Jonathan n'a pas encore terminé son travail.
5. L'accusé (*defendant*) n'a pas encore parlé.
6. L'accusé ne parle toujours pas.

8 **Mettez l'adverbe de fréquence à la place qui convient.**

1. The warmth of friendship mellowed her contacts. (seldom)
2. One or two of the club women had called on her. (only)
3. Mrs Briggs believed in keeping her distance, too. (always)
4. Has she been to Denmark ? (ever)
5. They are not ready on time. (often)
6. On Sunday evenings she went to a lecture on philosophy. (sometimes)
7. You can just tell (*savoir*, ici) when he is happy. (never)
8. He had seen Mrs Briggs so generous before. (never)
9. She wanted to see him again. (never)
10. It's the worst concert I've heard. (ever)
11. It doesn't rain here. (often)
12. "Have you met any of my cousins?" "No, I have..."(never)

Adverbes de degré

➜ 327-330

9 **Traduisez.**

1. C'est un peu mieux.
2. J'ai vraiment cru qu'elle était partie.
3. Je crois qu'Ives est un peu soûl.
4. Ça leur a beaucoup plu.
5. Cet endroit est tellement mieux maintenant.
6. Tiens, il a neigé un petit peu.
7. Je leur ai à peine parlé.
8. Presque 80 000 personnes ont assisté à ce concert.
9. Les amis de Peter sont complètement nuls (*hopeless*).
10. Je ne suis pas assez riche pour pouvoir me payer cet hôtel.
11. Je n'ai pas vraiment faim. Je n'ai vraiment pas faim.
12. Elle avait presque envie de démissionner.

10 **Traduisez.**

1. Malheureusement, j'ai loin d'avoir fini.
2. J'ai compté à peine vingt personnes.
3. Mon petit frère sait à peine parler, encore moins (*let alone*) écrire.
4. Il a fait encore plus chaud que l'année dernière.
5. C'est plutôt un pays riche.
6. Ils sont assez paresseux.
7. Je ne veux même pas lui parler au téléphone.
8. Même Kevin ne serait pas d'accord avec toi.

11 ***So* et *too*. Traduisez.**

1. Ne marche pas si vite.
2. Ce livre est beaucoup trop difficile à lire.
3. Il mange tellement. Il mange trop.
4. C'est un voisin beaucoup trop dangereux.
5. Il a tellement mangé qu'il en a été malade.
6. J'ai trop à faire ; je suis débordée (*overworked*).
7. C'est trop. Je ne pourrai pas tout manger.
8. C'est si propre qu'on ne veut plus s'en servir.

Adverbes d'ajout, de liaison, de modalité

➜ 330-332

12 **Adverbes d'ajout. Traduisez.**

1. Ils parlent aussi l'allemand et l'italien.
2. Que pouvions-nous faire d'autre ?
3. Moi aussi, je veux être musicien.
4. Nous avons aussi des ordinateurs portables, si vous voulez.
5. Autre chose pour vous, Madame ?
6. De plus, il ne nous est pas permis de les vendre.
7. Non seulement elle joue bien, mais elle compose aussi de la musique.
8. Mon réveil n'a pas sonné. De plus, j'ai eu du mal à faire démarrer la voiture.

13 Adverbes de liaison. Traduisez.

1. Tom felt ill, but went to work all the same. However, he didn't manage to concentrate.
2. I've never liked Harry and yet I've decided to help him.
3. It is true nevertheless that I was a bit harsh on him.
4. I know you don't like having guests around. Still, you could make an effort.
5. Stop cheating, otherwise I'll report you.
6. Actually, I can't talk to you right now. I'll call you back.
7. Incidentally, can I suggest you rewrite the first paragraph?
8. "Don't worry, we'll manage somehow." "I somehow doubt it."
9. These figures don't prove anything. And besides, who worked them out?
10. We have more and more customers and therefore we need more workers.
11. She is the eldest daughter and thus heir to the title.
12. It's not very useful. It's beautiful, though, don't you think?

14 Adverbes de modalité. Retrouvez l'équivalent anglais des mots ou expressions suivants.

1. probablement 2. franchement 3. on pourrait dire que... 4. assurément
5. peut-être 6. heureusement 7. sans aucun doute 8. à mon avis 9. on espère que...
10. sûrement 11. bien sûr 12. il faut le reconnaître 13. manifestement
14. il est surprenant que... 15. certainement 16. de toute évidence
17. vraisemblablement 18. naturellement

3 La formation des mots

Les mots dérivés

→ 334-336

1 Soulignez les préfixes dans les mots suivants. Puis traduisez chaque mot.

counter-clockwise • asymmetry • incoherence • re-evaluate • forearm • disconnected • undo • irreproachable • mistrust • amoral • foreground • illegal • forecast • rebuild • misspell • undoubtedly • immature • non-smoker • ex-husband

2 Décomposez les mots suivants en précisant la nature de chaque élément. Puis traduisez.

▶ stewardess = nom formé d'un nom (*steward*) et du suffixe du féminin (*-ess*) : <u>hôtesse de l'air</u>

▶ happiness = nom formé d'un adjectif (*happy*) et d'un suffixe exprimant une condition (*-ness*) : <u>bonheur</u>

waitress • boyhood • stardom • useful • sadden • driver • hairy • refusal • friendliness • catastrophic • childless • foolish • laughable • strangely • violonist • catholicism • backwards • childlike • popularize • symbolical

La composition

→ 337

3 Décomposez les mots suivants, en précisant la nature de chaque élément. Puis traduisez.

underpaid • undercooked • outrun • overeat • overdressed • upgrade • outgrow • uplifting • overreact • overlap • underrate • overrate • outdistance • upstage

4 Commentez l'expression *out-Herod Herod* qui signifie "être très violent", "en rajouter".

Corrigés

1 Le groupe verbal

1 Les verbes à particules et les verbes prépositionnels

1

1. go away 2. took off 3. take (your passport) along 4. get (my money) back
5. put on 6. eat out 7. move along 8. do (the kitchen) over 9. given up 10. come about

2

1. blew up (*exploser, se mettre très en colère*)
2. call in (*s'arrêter à*) 3. called off (*annuler*)
4. call (you) up (*appeler au téléphone*) 5. carry on (*continuer*) 6. cut down (*réduire*) 7. cutting in (*interrompre*) 8. ended up (*finir par*)
9. getting along (ou : on) (*s'entendre avec*)
10. get across (*faire passer*) 11. hang around (*traîner*) 12.put (us) up (*héberger*) 13. put off (*remettre à plus tard*) 14. running out (*manquer*) 15. turn (me) on (*"brancher", plaire à*)

3

1. broken out 2. carried out 3. got about
4. got through 5. turned down 6. keep up / give up 7. burst in 8. worn off 9. turned out 10. hang on

4

1. He has not answered my letter yet.
2. He is looking for his keys. 3. He lacks courage. 4. Yesterday, we waited for a taxi for 20 minutes. 5. Have you phoned Judith? 6. I will ask them for further information. 7. What do you think of that? 8. I've thought about what you said. 9. She remembers him. 10. Do you trust him (her)? 11. She plays the violin beautifully. 12. What are you staring at? 13. He entered the room without knocking. 14. You have not dealt with the subject. 15. Do you need a dictionary? 16. I have enough money to pay for the meal. 17. We will discuss this matter later on. 18. I hope for better days.
19. Will you attend the meeting? 20. I can't explain this word to you.

2 Be - Have - Do

1

1. that is / he has 2. he has had / at Paul's / it is 3. she is 4. it has 5. she is 6. what is / she is 7. he has 8. it is / let's (ou : let us) 9. he is
10. We have got / He has agreed / It is wonderful / He is the right age / he has got / he has worked

2

1. Did you have 2. she has not got (ou : hasn't got / does not have / doesn't have) 3. I have never had 4. they had 5. Have you really got (ou : Do you really have) / I have to 6. I do not usually have 7. we did not have to 8. I have had 9. we did not have (ou : hadn't got) 10. we have (ou : have got) / we do not have

3

1. He will be fourteen in December. 2. You ought to be ashamed. 3. He has (got) blue eyes. 4. Are you hungry or thirsty? 5. We had a lot of visitors last summer. 6. Will you have some more? 7. Did you have a good time?
8. They are the same age.
9. I've got (ou : have) everything I need.
10. How tall (ou : high) is it?

4

• **pose l'existence de...**
2. <u>There is</u> / <u>there are</u> 6. <u>There were</u> / <u>There were</u>
• **établit un repère dans le révolu**
4. <u>It has been a long time since</u> 5. <u>Twenty years ago tonight</u> 7. <u>52 years ago</u>
• **exprime la durée**
1. <u>I've done it for years</u> 3. <u>they had not seen each other for years</u> 8. <u>a hundred years</u>

5

1. *Je ne suis pas une débutante; il y a des années que je le fais.* 2. *Gagner est un mot important. Il y a un individu qui arrive à faire ce qu'il voulait et il y en a des centaines de milliers qui échouent.* 3. *Ils avaient vingt ans, il y avait des années qu'ils ne s'étaient pas vus.* 4. *Il y a longtemps que tu n'es pas venu en ville.* 5. *Il y a vingt ans ce soir, je dînais ici avec mon ami.* 6. *L'immeuble grouillait de chats. Il y avait même quelques chiens... Il y avait beaucoup de plaintes.* 7. *Il y a 52 ans, j'ai trouvé un sac plein d'argent. J'ai pris ce sac et je m'en suis servi pour gagner plus d'argent.* 8. *Il n'y a que cent ans que cette école existe.*

6

1. There is an Indian restaurant in my street. I had dinner there three days ago.
2. "When did you last see your mother?" "Almost two years ago."
3. He has been an M.P. for 28 years.
4. "How long is it since you last visited

London?" (ou : "When did you last visit London?") "Five or six years."
5. It is 9,000 km from Paris to San Francisco.
6. I have known him for eight years.
7. How far is it to the next bus stop?
8. Twenty years ago it was different.

7

1. I guess I did 2. do you / I do 3. we did 4. you did, did you 5. didn't you 6. please do 7. do you 8. didn't you 9. did you 10. I really don't

8

1. I told you, didn't I? (ou : I did tell you, didn't I?) 2. You don't know the man, I do. 3."I could get a better job." "I doubt that." "You do? Why?" 4. "He lives here now." "He does, does he? I didn't know that." 5. "He told me something about you." "He did? What was that?" 6. I do not understand why he came so early. Do you? 7. "I told you to use the computer." "That's what I did." 8. We know where it is. Do you?

3 Le présent

1

runs • works • pays • lies • cries • catches • laughs • goes • hurries • passes • relaxes

2

1. What time does she get up? 2. Is it raining? 3. What are you reading? 4. Does she agree (with me)? 5. Do you like sweets? 6. When is he coming back? 7. When does she leave home everyday? 8. What do they do? 9. Does she know him? 10. What are you waiting for?

3

1. am I dreaming 2. dream / love 3. is having 4. look / are you thinking 5. are you writing / I always write 6. is coming / do you want 7. is coming up / thinks 8. say / frightens / are not being 9. don't have / we do / do they / are you talking about / have / you're coming / are not trekking 10. look / are you looking for / I'm not actually looking for / I'm passing through 11. leaves / is anyone coming 12. gives up / starts / seems / is looking for

4

Présent simple utilisé pour :
- **énoncer une caractéristique du sujet**

1. is 4. don't like / do you ask 6. sits / reckon 8. don't want 9. am sorry / doesn't matter 11. don't care / doesn't bother / don't know
- **relater un film d'actions successives**

3. begin 7. ties / rises / yawns / begins / stops / looks down / shakes
- **décrire une habitude**

2. do you shop 12. say / say

Présent en be + V-ing utilisé pour :
- **décrire une action en cours de déroulement**

3. is falling / is dropping 6. he's thinking / I'm thinking 11. you're all being
- **insister sur un fait ou une action**

5. We're expecting 8. I'm saying
- **exprimer un point de vue dépréciatif**

9. I'm always doing 12. You're always saying
- **annoncer la réalisation d'une action déjà envisagée**

1. I am just going 10. is speaking

5

1. I'm not cooking today. 2. I'm thinking about moving to London. 3. What I'm trying to say is that you can't come back here. 4. If I don't do it now, it won't be ready tonight. 5. You both need a break. Why don't you go away? 6. I thought I'd better tell you: I'm going away. I feel like a change. 7. "Does your mother agree?" "She does." 8. "It's Patrick. How are you?" "Patrick!" "I hope I'm not disturbing you." 9. "He'll be looked after, don't worry." "Are you telling me he's not well?" 10. Every night he tells the kids a story and then goes to bed.

4 Le prétérit

1

1. I saw 2. they carried 3. did you fly 4. she taught 5. she did not think 6. I thought 7. did he forgive 8. he lost 9. I sent 10. did you send 11. he did not sleep 12. they did not catch 13. he laid 14. did you lie 15. he lay 16. he fell 17. she felt 18. did they win 19. he struck 20. he brought 21. did they buy 22. it meant 23. did you meet 24. he paid 25. she led

2

1. was (R.R.) / decided (R.R.)
Lorsque j'avais 18 ans, j'ai décidé d'étudier la médecine.
2. was asked (N.R.) / saw (D.I.)
Que devrais-je dire si l'on me demandait quand je l'ai vu pour la dernière fois ?
3. shook (R.R.) / was (R.R.) / thought (R.R.) / he looked (D.I.)
Assis à côté d'elle, Adam secoua (secouait) la tête. Il était grand, brun. Elle pensa qu'il ressemblait à l'un de ces hommes parfaits des publicités de magazine.
4. talked (R.R.) / were (N.R.)
Il lui parla (parlait) comme si elle était un bébé.

5. went (N.R.)
Que se passerait-il si j'y allais ?
6. felt (R.R.) / didn't... stay (D.I. libre)
Elle se sentait irritée. Pourquoi de telles pensées ne restaient-elles pas enfouies dans son cerveau ?
7. did it seem (D.I. libre) / wondered (R.R.)
"Vous pensez vraiment que c'est une bonne idée ? Il apparaît que..." Comment cela apparaissait-il ? se demanda-t-il.
8. knocked off (R.R.) / said (R.R.) / had (D.I.) / packed up (R.R.) / hit (R.R.)
Elle arrêta de travailler de bonne heure, dit qu'elle avait mal à la tête, fit sa valise et prit la route.
9. discussed (N.R.)
Le mieux serait que tu en discutes avec elle.
10. slowed down (R.R.) / were sleepwalking (N.R.) / seemed (N.R.)
Dans les jours qui suivirent l'enterrement, ses mouvements ralentirent, comme si elle marchait pendant son sommeil (elle était somnambule) et que tout mouvement demandait beaucoup d'effort.
11. didn't tell (N.R.)
J'aimerais beaucoup mieux que tu ne lui racontes pas.
12. was (N.R.) / knew (N.R.)
Si seulement j'avais leur âge tout en sachant ce que je sais maintenant.

3

1. I was thinking 2. were enjoying / was 3. Beck did not know / she was talking about / she persisted / he ran off / was annoying 4. I was asking 5. happened / was going / had / was following / turned around / never saw 6. were you doing / came in

4

1. *Mr James S.* ***killed*** *his wife in a dream yesterday night. He* ***dreamed*** *that his daughter who* ***was sleeping*** *in the same room* ***was being attacked*** *by assassins and he* ***fired*** *on them, with the result that he* ***killed*** *his wife.*
Yesterday Mr S., his wife and their two daughters **went** to bed as usual about 10. Towards midnight Mr S. **thought** he **heard** the window open. Turning over, he **saw** two masked men enter the room with knives. One **went** and **stood** over the daughter. In frantic terror Mr S. **fired** the pistol which he **was clutching** in his hand beneath the pillow. Switching on the light he **saw** that blood **was trickling** from his wife's head. He then **realized** he had been dreaming but his wife **was** dead.
2. "I **saw** the vet ride to the pub..." "What on?" "On his bike." "I **thought** he **had** a scooter." "That's right. He **was riding** his scooter when he **met** the rep." "Was he a man with a mac?" "Yes, with a mac and specs." "I **saw** him then." "As I **was saying** (ou : I **said**), the vet **met** the rep and they **went** into the pub with the ref..." "So there was the ref and the vet and the rep, so what?" "They **were talking** (ou : **talked**) of rugger." "Rubbish, there's nothing like soccer!" "Right as I **was saying** they **were talking**; suddenly I **saw** a woman with a pram... " "Where **was she coming** she from?" "She **was coming** out of the hairdresser with a new perm. "So what?" "So she **cried** 'Look! The vet's scooter's gone!' and gone it **was**! At full revs! A young man had gone off with it!"

5

1. She was 28 and she was going to conquer the world. 2. She didn't know what they were looking for. 3. He asked if she knew who the keys belonged to. 4. He didn't only want to please her. 5. The children were not listening. They were too busy watching the match. 6. This puzzled her (ou : him). They reached the beach: everyone was enjoying the lovely weather, a lot of people were swimming.
7. Every evening after work he would go (ou : he used to go) and see her (ou : he went to see her); he would tell her about his day at work; she would pretend that she was listening. 8. It was a lovely morning. She looked around: the dew was shining on the grass, the birds were singing. 9. When the waves were breaking, Jimmy was always at the beach. He liked to surf. 10. And now the woman bent down and released the dog. As if he was obeying some command, he slipped into the bushes.

Prétérit ou present perfect ?

1

Verbes au prétérit
She once said : *once* implique que la déclaration est classée dans le passé.
She was born in Illinois in 1935 : *1935* = fait révolu.
she attended the University of Ottawa : fait révolu, elle n'est plus étudiante
settled in Canada in 1957 : *1957* = fait révolu
I always wanted : état passé, elle est écrivain
it seemed impossible : impression passée, coupée du présent
She was awarded : fait classé dans le passé
was published in 1993 : *1993* = fait révolu
I wanted : fait révolu
Before they were : *before* = fait révolu, coupé du présent

Verbes au present perfect
has become : bilan dans le présent
She has lived there since that date : action commencée dans le passé continue dans le présent (rôle de *since that date*). Traduction en français : "elle y habite".
I have written : bilan dans le présent
has written : c'est le résultat présent qui importe
has always meant : action commencée dans le passé qui continue dans le présent (rôle de *always* = toujours, y compris au moment présent)
This change has had : bilan dans le présent
they have had : bilan dans le présent

2

1. Have you tasted 2. invented / mixed / taught / has become 3. has been electrocuted / was found / touched / was electrocuted
4. happened / met / swapped / I have not heard / she has not heard 5. gave / has stepped 6. has been 7. said / 've made 8. have never had / saw

3

1. changed / lost / slid 2. has created / became / told 3. have completed / have come / belonged / abandoned / was enveloped

---

5 Le present perfect

1

1. Have you been 2. She has caught 3. I haven't heard 4. He has forgotten 5. They have just gone 6. She has spent 7. Have you spoken
8. Have you thought 9. She has wept 10. We haven't paid 11. I have never ridden 12. He has taught 13. Have you won 14. They haven't met
15. Have you read

2

1. I have been reading 2. Have you been smoking 3. They have been fishing 4. We have been waiting 5. have they been looking 6. have you been doing 7. He has been sleeping
8. have you been wearing 9. I have been shopping 10. I have been asking

3

1. (**for**) Je le connais depuis huit ans. 2. (**for**) Il a voyagé pendant six mois en Australie.
3. (**since**) Cela fait longtemps qu'il a joué cette sonate. 4. (**since**) Sont-ils vraiment ici depuis lundi ? 5. (**since**) Je ne les ai pas vus depuis la naissance de leur fils. 6. (**for**) Est-ce que je peux laisser ça ici pendant deux heures ?
7. (**since**) Depuis quand regardes-tu la télévision ? 8. (**for**) Elle est mariée depuis deux ans. 9. (**since**) Ça fait vingt ans qu'elle est morte. 10. (**for**) Je l'aimerai toujours.

4

1. I have been stuck... for seven years 2. He has been known... since a teenager 3. to have been seen since the founding 4. it had been raining for ten days 5. Since 1990... has won 6. has tripled since 1971 7. had been wandering... for nearly an hour 8. has happened... since he turned 9. Since July 1st... have been having (ou : have had) / are prohibited for a year

5

1. He has been awake for three hours.
2. He has been awake since three (in the afternoon).
3. He has been at sea for more than six weeks.
4. She has been professor of political economy at Oxford since 1991.
5. We haven't been paid for five weeks.
6. "How long have you been doing this?" "Since I left university, nine years ago."
7. A whole year has passed since he (ou: she) came back.
8. I've been trying to open this door for 45 minutes.
9. Her novel has been a best seller for nearly a year.
10. The garden had been neglected for years when we bought it.

6

1. You've been phoning for ages. Haven't you nearly finished? 2. "You look exhausted." "Yes, I've been jogging and I've not run for years." 3. What have you been doing? I've been waiting for you for hours. 4. Have you already done your homework? I've been working for hours and I've not finished yet.

7

1. he has been sleeping 2. he has slept 3. I have ever slept 4. I have taught / have never met 5. I have been teaching 6. have you smoked 7. have you been smoking 8. he has painted 9. she has been painting 10. he has drunk

8

1. have you been doing 2. I have not laughed
3. I have been trying / I have hardly said 4. I have never seen / It has been happening
5. have been found / have been making / have been making / has been growing

Présent ou present perfect ?

1

1. "I **am going** out. **Do you want** anything?" 2. "Pleased to meet you, Sandy. Where **do you come from** you from?" "I **come** from Maryville. "How long **have you been** here?" "I've just only arrived." 3. **Does he know** what we **are talking about**? 4. What **are you four plotting**? 5. The bus **leaves** at half past ten. 6. "Your report is a disgrace." "It's not fair. **I'm trying hard (I've been trying hard)**, really." 7. He **has run** restaurant for more than twenty years. 8. It's the first time she **has kissed** him. 9. "Wake up! It's the day **I've been waiting for**. Come on, get up!" "What is it? **I'm sleeping!**" 10. The jeans market **is shrinking**. Jeans sales **have slumped** by more than 3 million pairs in the year to May. Yet, denim **remains** fashionable – as long as it's used for anything but jeans. Whether **it is** hip or nostalgic its appeal is universal.

2

1. What happens when the doors are shut? 2. What's all this noise? What's happening? 3. "Did you hear the phone?" "Yes, I'm coming." 4. I have used this pen for years. 5. He bought his ticket this morning: he's flying to London this afternoon. 6. It's the first time I have been away from her. 7. You're always sleeping! 8. How long has he been sitting here? 9. This is a problem that has been creeping up on us for years. 10. Have you been working all that time?

3

1. What about last night, did you sleep at all? 2. You didn't listen to what he said. 3. We went there three years ago. 4. "How many comedies has Shakespeare written?" "I don't know, but he wrote them when he was young." 5. I've been walking too fast, that's why I'm tired. 6. How many tablets have you had? 7. You never came back home once in five years. 8. "Why did you accept?" "I couldn't say no." 9. What have you been doing to this knife? The blade is twisted. 10. "We were just about to start without you." "Sorry, I got lost."

4

1. works 2. worked 3. has been working 4. has worked 5. is working 6. does not work 7. did not work 8. has never worked 9. has written 10. wrote 11. has been writing 12. writes

6 Le past perfect

1

1. he had never seen 2. she moved / she had planned 3. she had gone 4. they talked / they had visited / never seemed 5. she had cried / she began 6. she behaved / had changed 7. he had forgotten 8. she was / had he forgotten 9. she took / she had expected

2

1. A Chicago judge today **granted** divorce to Mr R. on the grounds of his wife's silence. The plaintiff **informed** the Court that, although his wife **had lived** in his house, she **had not spoken** to him for eighteen years. He **declared** that it **was** like living with a ghost. He **had consulted** physicians in the effort to get her to talk but it **was** impossible to surprise her into uttering a word.
2. Through the arrest of three former prisoners of the San Quentin prison in California who **had been released** on parole at various times last year, it **became** known today that counterfeit $ 10 bank notes, with which they **had been supplied were manufactured** on the prison's own printing presses. In examining the men's prison records, the Secret Service **found** that all three **had had** access to the printing shop while they were serving their terms.
3. I **went** back to Oxford recently. I **had not been** back since we all **left** , almost twenty years ago. I **was surprised** to see how little the city **had changed.** Although there **were** new buildings everywhere and the main crossroads **had been widened**, the main landmarks **remained** in place.

3

1. I had gone / there was / I passed / she was smiling / there was / I stood / came
2. stopped / stared / needed / had needed
3. she was standing / he began / she hadn't had time
4. she looked / sniffed / it was / she had been missing (ou : had missed) / she had thought of / had been (ou : was)
5. cheated / crash-landed / had been filming (ou : had filmed) / had

4

1. She **pushed** open the door. Women **were sitting** at the table. She **saw** her mother among them. In five years her hair **had gone** grey and she **looked** very old. Everyone **stopped** what they **were doing.**
2. "What **happened**?" "A massive heart attack. He'**d had** two or three warnings before but... "

"Where **was** he?" "He **said** he **wasn't feeling** (ou : **hadn't been feeling)** great. Yesterday morning. **Was** it yesterday or the day before? Anyway, he **felt** (ou : **was feeling)** sickish and **had** a bit of pain across here." She **touched** her chest. "And he**'d been having** these pains in the upper arm. I **told** him to take his tablets. And off he **went** to open the bar. The next time I **saw** him he **was** dead."

Maîtriser les formes verbales

1

1. taught / met / fell 2. read 3. have known 4. thought / had forgotten 5. laid / left 6. have... ridden 7. lay down 8. fell / broke 9. have... run 10. has caught

2

1. lose 2. understood 3. choose 4. rung 5. brought 6. didn't think 7. set 8. does the sun rise 9. found 10. wrote this letter

3

1. someone tells / the world is going / I simply don't believe 2. have you had / do you have / I have never done / I have kept / I have done 3. you did not live / I brought / I came 4. everything was not becoming 5. we are having / don't you come

4

1. do you know / I have been saying / do you understand 2. I have told you / you were not paying 3. she died 4. I saw / he had been fighting 5. I had known 6. have been saying / it has certainly been true 7. they picked up / he was carrying / they had never seen 8. you turned / (you) went / I haven't finished / you haven't been working / you have been reading / you have been doing 9. I had been staying 10. he was going

7 Le passif

1

1. start / do not finish 2. are offered 3. is taken 4. are being neglected / is pressing / are being overlooked / are opting 5. was built / was remodelled / was partially destroyed / was acquired / operated / it was sold 6. occurred / were killed / were carried / were buried 7. have spent 8. has been recorded 9. has largely replaced 10. it has often been said / have been written 11. has not changed 12. will be found 13. will come 14. be easier said than done 15. may well not close 16. we will send / will be sent / must be placed 17. will give / can be included 18. can the suburbs be blamed 19. can we make 20. be taught

2

1. The concert was sponsored... / was being transmitted... *Le concert était parrainé... /était retransmis en direct...*
2. according to how much attention is paid to them... *selon l'attention qu'on leur prête...*
3. children are cared for... / I was asked... *on s'occupe des enfants... /on m'a demandé...*
4. are spread all over the island... *partout sur l'île se trouvent (ou : il y a)...*
5. The washing must be done... *Il faut que la lessive soit faite...*
6. is seldom used... *s'emploie rarement...*
7. are collected... / are to be sold... *sont récoltés... /se vendront (ou : sont destinés à la vente)...*
8. lots of things to be done... *beaucoup à faire...*
9. was born... *est née...*
10. need to be played with and talked to... *ont besoin qu'on joue avec eux et qu'on leur parle...*

3

1. Our programme will be watched by millions of viewers. 2. They must be made acceptable. 3. The Admiral's Cup was instituted in 1957 by the Royal Ocean Racing Club. 4. ... he was obeyed by everyone. 5. ... most of the tea was being brought back by steamers. 6. He had been told about them by his father. 7. Those who arrive first will be greeted by the president. 8. Several experiments in that field have been carried out by scientists... 9. In the modern world, magic has been replaced by technology. 10. Who was it written by?

4

1. I am told... 2. *Transposition peu souhaitable.* 3. The park gates will be opened / they are usually locked... 4. *Transposition peu souhaitable.* 5. Goods were regularly being stolen... *Pour* he set a trap, *transposition peu souhaitable.* 6. *Transposition peu souhaitable.* 7. The news of the strike had been announced... 8. *Transposition peu souhaitable.* 9. If every house was painted / the balance of nature would seriously be disturbed...

5

1. People under 16 are not admitted.
2. Yes, it was built in 1880.
3. The plane was delayed.
4. He ought to be locked up.
5. He is sure he can solve the problem.
6. Yes, evening dress will be worn.

7. I do not agree.
8. She was not offered the job. (ou : She hasn't been offered the job.)
9. His colleagues gave him a TV set when he retired.
10. Yes, he was an English painter, he was recognized as a revolutionary genius, he made his name with painting seascapes, he has left some 300 paintings.

6

1. Education is acknowledged to be... 2. Frank Lloyd Wright is considered to have been... 3. Chicago is known to be... 4. The man... is understood to have been... 5. He was reported to be dismayed... 6. She is believed to have paid... 7. The couple are (ou : is) believed to have suffered... 8. This gold nugget is expected to fetch...

7

1. ethnic minorities are still discriminated against. 2. They are not properly looked after. 3. A visa has to be applied for... 4. he was shouted down... 5. the conflict has been put an end to... 6. It is being looked into... 7. She was lost sight of... 8. are disapproved of... 9. can only be guessed at. 10. are often referred to...

8 Le renvoi à l'avenir

1

1. will occur 2. is going to come / will find out 3. Is he coming? 4. is staying 5. 'll keep 6. 'll probably see 7. 'll sell / will buy 8. are going to be

2

1. We will know tonight. [*simple prédiction*] 2. He's leaving in a few days. [*projet personnel /décision*] 3. It's easy, I'll show you. [*décision prise par le sujet au moment de l'énonciation*] 4. "What would you like to drink." "I'll have tea." [*décision prise au moment de l'énonciation*] 5. I'll believe it when I see it. [*simple prédiction*] 6. "Can you come on Sunday?" "I'm afraid I can't. I'm going to the theatre." [*projet*] 7. He's not going to retire now, he's got too much to do. ["*futur d'intention*"] 8. Well, I'll tell you what we are going to do (ou : what we'll do). [*décision prise au moment de l'énonciation*] 9. The show is about to start. [*événement imminent*] 10. I'm not going to watch the match, I've got work. [*intention*]

3

1. will have seen 2. it will reach 3. we'll be going home 4. they'll be discussing 5. they will have survived 6. will you be moving out 7. you'll be wanting 8. you will have left 9. you will be spending (ou : you will spend) 10. will look 11. will have lost 12. you won't find (ou : will not find) / it will have melted away

9 Les modaux

1-2

quasi certain
(**must**) 2. Il devait y avoir quelqu'un d'autre (qu'eux) pour conduire la voiture.
(**must**) 8. Il doit y avoir de meilleures chansons (à chanter) que celle-ci.
(**should**) 10. Elle devrait être de retour dans quelques minutes.
probable
(**'ll**) 6. Le téléphone sonna. "C'est sans doute our moi !" dit-il.
possible
(**may**) 4. Il se peut qu'elle ait été responsable de l'accident.
incertain
(**might**) 1. Ça pourrait être une bonne idée.
(**might**) 3. J'ai pensé que vous aimeriez peut-être voir les enfants avant qu'ils n'aillent se coucher.
(**might**) 7. Il se pourrait qu'il devienne célèbre un jour.
imaginable
(**could**) 5. Il se pourrait bien qu'il gagne un millier de dollars.
difficilement imaginable
(**couldn't**) 11. Ça ne pourrait pas arriver de nouveau.
impossible
(**can't**) 9. Ce n'est pas possible qu'il soit mort !

3

1. You must be joking. / He must have been lying.
2. You may be surprised. / He may have given her a diamond ring.
3. We might never see each other again. / She might be waiting for us at the airport.
4. She can't be as old as... / She can't be sleeping. / I can't have lost his address.
5. He should speak English fluently... / They should have arrived now.

4

1. She might become a vet. 2. There must be some other solution. 3. "You think he could be gone a month?" "He might." 4. She may not

like this idea. 5. He must be three or four years younger than her. 6. That must have been just before the war. 7. It could be very embarrassing if people saw us together. 8. One might have thought he was drunk. 9. Why have you thrown (ou : did you throw) these clothes away? Somebody might have wanted them.

5

1. (**could**) J'aimerais pouvoir rester ici pour toujours. 2. (**would**) Je peux t'expliquer si seulement tu voulais bien écouter. 3. (**can**) Interflora a lancé un site Internet qui vous donne la possibilité d'envoyer des fleurs de votre travail sans même décrocher le téléphone. 4. (**will**) Cette chemise blanche classique est indémodable. 5. (**can**) Ici, vous pouvez tout acheter, des huîtres aux cigares ! 6. (**will / can**) Les ours sont essentiellement végétariens mais ils mangent toute viande qu'ils peuvent attraper ou trouver. 7. (**can't**) Ce que je ne peux pas supporter, c'est l'idée qu'il n'a cessé de mentir pendant toutes ces années. 8. (**will**) Tu veux bien me rendre un service ? 9. (**would**) James Dean était son héros à ce moment-là. Elle gardait toutes les photos des magazines et les épinglait sur les murs de sa chambre. 10. (**will**) Viens avec moi, tu veux bien ?

6

1. (**can't / can't**) "Je ne me souviens pas de l'adresse. – Tu ne te souviens même pas du nom de la rue ?" 2. (**would**) "Il dit que tu es stupide de prendre un tel risque. – C'est bien de lui ! Il a toujours quelque chose à me reprocher." 3. (**couldn't / can't**) Lorsque j'étais enfant, je ne pouvais pas comprendre les adultes et maintenant que je suis adulte, je ne peux pas comprendre les enfants. 4. (**would**) Ils voudraient nous faire croire que la situation s'améliore mais le fait est qu'elle empire. 5. (**would**) Ce serait gentil si tu voulais bien me prêter ton ordinateur portable. 6. (**could**) Il a dit que c'était parfaitement évident à ses yeux (ou : comme il voyait les choses). 7. (**could**) Si seulement il avait pu passer la nuit ici ! 8. (**will**) Lorsque la voiture démarra, il dit : "Ça tient du miracle !" (ou : "On n'a pas fini d'être étonné.") 9. (**would**) J'avais un réveil qui était réglé pour sonner à neuf heures mais invariablement je me réveillais avant. 10. (**could**) Je n'avais pas eu de leurs nouvelles du plus loin que je me souvienne, mais je savais qu'ils étaient encore vivants.

7

1. I couldn't leave him. Where would I go? 2. I couldn't have left him. Where would I have gone? 3. You should talk to her (ou : him) because you can answer her (ou : his) questions. 4. You should have talked to her (ou : him) because you could have answered her (ou : his) questions. 5. She would prefer you wrote in English. 6. She would have preferred you wrote in English (ou : you to write in English). 7. Surely things could improve, life could be better. 8. Surely things could have improved, life could have been better. 9. You would have nothing to lose and you might have a great deal to gain. 10. You would have had nothing to lose and you might have had a great deal to gain.

8

1. You must take time 2. She must be reading 3. he should be riding 4. we should celebrate 5. you can always tell 6. they can't be having 7. She could be playing 8. I couldn't hear 9. she might be working 10. Might I suggest

9

1. must be 2. must have been 3. must be leaving 4. may go 5. may have done 6. might have loved 7. might have

10

1. Couldn't it have waited 2. He could have done 3. he wouldn't speak up / it wouldn't have changed / it might have helped 4. they can't... be doing 5. I can't explain 6. I couldn't find / Could I have dropped 7. I couldn't believe / You must be thinking 8. You should have called 9. You should come 10. I shouldn't have come

11

contraindre, donner un ordre
(**must**) 1. La file de gauche doit tourner à gauche. [*fréquent*]
(**shall**) 14. Il refuse de partir ? Moi, je t'assure qu'il va partir. [*moins fréquent*]

interdire
(**must not**) 8. Tu ne dois pas mentir. [*fréquent*]
(**shalt not**) 11. Tu ne voleras point. [*moins fréquent*]

offrir / suggérer de ...
(**shall**) 7. Désirez-vous que je vous débarrasse de cette assiette ? [*fréquent*]
(**might**) 16. Tu pourrais lui en parler. [*moins fréquent*]

donner un conseil
(**should**) 4. Je pense que tu devrais voir un médecin. [*fréquent*]
(**shouldn't**) 5. Il n'aurait pas dû t'en parler. [*fréquent*]

accorder une permission
(**can**) 10. Vous pouvez partir tous les deux.

Je n'ai pas besoin de vous. [*fréquent*]
(**may**) 13. Chaque votant n'a le droit de voter que pour un seul candidat. [*moins fréquent*]
demander une permission
(**can**) 2. Est-ce que je peux laisser mes affaires ici ? [*fréquent*]
(**could**) 3. Pourrais-je vous parler, Monsieur ? [*fréquent*]
(**may**) 6. Puis-je te rappeler que tout ceci est fait en ta faveur ? [*fréquent*]
(**might**) 12. Pourrais-je vous parler un instant ? [*moins fréquent*]
refuser une permission
(**can't**) 9. Si vous avez moins de 17 ans, vous ne pouvez pas conduire une voiture en Grande-Bretagne. [*fréquent*]
(**may not**) 15. Deux lignes blanches parallèles signifient que vous n'avez pas le droit de doubler. [*moins fréquent*]

12

1. I'm hungry. Can I have a snack? 2. You must obey the law. 3. You can borrow my paper if you like. 4. May I see your passport, please? 5. Shall I help you (ou : give you a hand)? 6. You shouldn't have drunk so much. 7. They should be in bed, not watching television. 8. Visitors must not feed the animals. 9. Might I give you some advice? 10. Could I use your telephone? 11. You should have told me! 12. You must not touch (it).

13

1. would you do 2. I wouldn't worry 3. would he have told 4. They would be glad 5. that wouldn't be 6. she might have succeeded 7. I could do 8. I would not accept 9. I should imagine (ou : have imagined) 10. she couldn't live

14

1. (It is) strange that he shouldn't be here. 2. In case he should ask, tell him I'll be back on Wednesday. 3. What do you suggest I should take (ou : I take)? 4. It is funny that you should say that. 5. It is important that you should listen carefully. 6. They insisted that we should have dinner with them. 7. If you should change your mind, please let me know. (ou : Should you change...) 8. It is absurd that she should be paid less than him. 9. I gave her a map lest she should get lost. 10. He suggested that she should sell her car.

15

1. should I say 2. would never come 3. would say 4. should make 5. should have 6. would talk 7. would always go 8. should be 9. would you 10. would

16

1. would have thought 2. should I get 3. would you like 4. should change / would you change 5. should be 6. should have happened 7. would stop 8. should be 9. would be 10. wouldn't start 11. would be

---

10 Autres façons d'exprimer la modalité

1

1. can imagine 2. we could buy 3. I could (not) have answered 4. you'll be able to 5. she could keep 6. you can see 7. you were unable to 8. he could pick on / he couldn't 9. I was able to 10. she was never able to

2

1. she would have to / I would see 2. He used to be 3. she was now used to 4. He would throw 5. I used to feel 6. I used to play 7. he would order 8. he is used to spending 9. There used to be

3

1. He'd better not drive. 2. You shouldn't take notice of what he tells you. 3. I think I'd better go. I need to be on my own. 4. "He should sleep now." "Will he be alright, do you think?" "He's just in a shock. A few hours' rest ought to take care of it." 5. I decided I had better be present when she met him. 6. I've still got the flu. I ought to be (at) home in bed. 7. You'd better think carefully about what you're going to do. 8. It's a disgrace. There ought to be a notice. 9. She was just a child. She oughtn't to have known about that kind of thing. 10. I should have taken a taxi instead of walking back home.

4

1. must be prepared 2. have to say 3. mustn't cry 4. must convince 5. don't have to do 6. mustn't let 7. have to do / has to do 8. must admit 9. have to wait 10. must tell me 11. have to go 12. must absolutely go 13. don't have to lie 14. have to go 15. must admit 16. don't have to go on 17. must (ou : have to) concentrate / mustn't get 18. doesn't have to worry 19. have to be 20. must take the decision

5

1. You need not 2. does she need 3. They need not 4. You need not 5. I do not need to go

6

1. You need not have driven (ou : You did not need to drive) so fast: we had plenty of time. 2. She was well: she did not need to take (ou :

she needn't have taken) more pills. 3. They need not have worried: they would succeed. 4. You need not have written to her (ou : him). 5. There was plenty of food in the fridge: I did not need to go (ou : needn't have gone) shopping.

7

1. I must say I was rather surprised. 2. He doesn't see very well: he has to wear glasses. 3. You'll have to get used to it. 4. Why do they have to obey him? 5. He was to die four years later. 6. He must have missed his train. 7. You are to do (ou : You must do) as you are told. 8. They are to marry in two months. 9. You must be looking forward to seeing him again. 10. He must have been in England when the accident happened.

11 Le subjonctif et l'impératif

1

1. you should say that 2. I (should) stay 3. we stopped 4. this be the case 5. Come what may 6. I were you 7. (God) bless you! 8. he should be prepared for this 9. need be 10. as it were

2

1. Come back! 2. Let's ask him (ou : her)! 3. Don't run! 4. Be quiet! 5. Do be careful! 6. Don't let's complain! (ou : Let's not complain!) 7. Do as you're told. 8. Don't let them go! 9. Leave him alone. 10. Listen, will you? [*intonation descendante*]

12 Les reprises elliptiques

1

1.Oh, yes, he has. 2. No. I didn't. 3. Yes, she does. 4. Yes, I will. 5. Simon did. 6. Oh, have they? 7. No, I am not. 8. Does he? 9. I don't think so. 10. I'd love to. 11. You're not allowed to. 12. I'm afraid he has. 13. Yes, I expect so. 14. Of course she can. 15. Oh, did they? 16. I'm afraid not. 17. Oh, did she? 18. Because they told us to. (ou : Because we were told to.) 19. I don't know how to. 20. Am I?

2

1. So does he. 2. They (accentué) did not. 3. I don't. 4. So it does. 5. Neither have I. 6. No, he is not. 7. So shall I (ou : will I).
8. Neither (ou : Nor) have I. 9. Neither (ou : Nor) did I. 10. So would he.

3

1. isn't she? 2. are they? 3. didn't you?
4. will they? 5. didn't they? 6. do you? 7. could they? 8. shall we? 9. wasn't there? 10. won't you?

2 Le groupe nominal

1 Le genre et le nombre du nom

1

woman • mother • aunt • niece • wife • lioness • cow • vixen • bitch • girl-friend • female • she-bear • actress • waitress • cat • goddess • barmaid • mare • daughter-in law • sow

2

1. **nurse** : peut désigner homme ou femme 2. **she-bear** : féminin formé autrement que par dérivation -ess 3. **ship** : traditionnellement associé au féminin 4. **dog** : seul masculin des quatre 5. **spokesman** : seul nom marqué par le masculin 6. **teacher** : seul nom indifférent au genre

3

/z/ selves • ideas • kids • members • tomatoes • ears • corporations • bachelors • systems
/s/ groups • books • necks • chiefs • units
/iz/ wishes • peaches • offices • churches

4

/z/ snails • shells • gardens • numbers • borders • lawns • paths • gardeners • flowers • carnations • dahlias • vegetables • tomatoes • salads • strawberries • slugs
/s/ pellets • plants • carrots • pests
/iz/ courses • roses

5

brushes • chiefs • crossroads • photos • paths • species • ghettos • criteria • thieves • crises • loaves • brothers/brethren • potatoes • media • leaves • analyses • wolves • phenomena • aircraft • teeth

6

AC/DC : Alternating Current / Direct Current • C.D. : compact disc; CDs • C.I.A. : Central Intelligence Agency • C.V. : Curriculum Vitae; CVs • G.P. : General Practitioner; GPs (*généralistes*) • D.J. : Disk Jockey; DJs • I.C.B.M. : Intercontinental Ballistic Missile; ICBMs • K.K.K. : Ku Klux Klan

• L.A. : Los Angeles • M.C.P. : Male Chauvinist Pig; MCPs (*machistes*) • M.P. : Member of Parliament; MPs • N.A.T.O. : North Atlantic Treaty Organisation • T.U. : Trade Union; TUs (*syndicats*) • U.F.O. : Unidentified Flying Object; UFOs • V.C.R. : Video Cassette Recorder; VCRs

7

men • children • lice • feet • oxen • mice • teeth • geese • axes • theses • stimuli • cherubim • campuses • tableaux • innuendos

8

grass : pas de pluriel, indénombrable. (≠ a grass / grasses : *les herbes, les indicateurs*) • **leaf** ▷ **leaves** : dénombrable • **staff** : pas de pluriel, collectif (≠ staff / staves : *bâton*) • **illness** ▷ **illnesses** : dénombrable • **youth** : pas de pluriel, indénombrable (≠ a youth / youths : *un jeune, des jeunes*) • **dish** ▷ **dishes** : dénombrable • **box** ▷ **boxes** : dénombrable • **porch** ▷ **porches** : dénombrable • **robbery** ▷ **robberies** : dénombrable • **business** : pas de pluriel, indénombrable (≠ a business / businesses : *une entreprise*) • **kingdom** ▷ **kingdoms** : dénombrable • **silence** : pas de pluriel hors contexte spécifique (indénombrable)

9

sons-in-law • goods-trains • men-servants • tooth-brushes • men-eaters (≠ man-eaters: *anthropophages*) • woman-haters • passers-by • grown-ups • woman doctors (≠ women doctors : *femmes médecins*) • sit-ins • university-degrees • step-fathers

10

1. **photo** : nom abrégé ; pluriel en -s et non pas -es 2. **boy** : voyelle + y ; pluriel en -s et non pas -ies 3. **cliff** : pluriel en -s et non pas -ves 4. **book** : seul pluriel régulier des quatre 5. **fish** : peut prendre un -s au pluriel contrairement aux trois autres 6. **mouse** : pluriel irrégulier, les autres sont identiques au singulier et au pluriel 7. **people** : le verbe qui suit est toujours au pluriel alors que les trois autres admettent singulier ou pluriel suivant le contexte 8. **rubbish** : construction verbale au singulier, les trois autres au pluriel 9. **news** : le verbe qui suit est toujours au singulier, les trois autres admettent singulier et pluriel 10. **physics** : seul des trois à toujours se construire avec un verbe au singulier

11

<u>knife</u> • <u>family</u> • <u>drink</u> • <u>fish</u> • <u>try</u>

12

a blade of grass • a compass (*une boussole*) /a pair of compasses (*un compas*) • a stroke of luck • a head of cattle • a slice of toast • a flash of lightning • a crash of thunder • a pair of jeans • a lump of sugar • a flake of snow

13

1. mes frères de sang / mes frères d'esprit 2. deux pièces d'un penny / un coût de deux pence 3. des espèces de fruits différentes / des fruits 4. des flèches, des fléchettes / le jeu de fléchettes 5. des courants d'air / le jeu de dames 6. les coutumes / la douane 7. deux boussoles / deux compas

14

Verbe au singulier : measles, athletics, politics, billiards, news
Verbe au pluriel : glasses, shorts, spectacles, funds, clothes, outskirts, remains, savings
Admettent les deux accords : barracks, headquarters

15

1. have 2. is 3. were 4. lives (ou : live) / is (ou : are) 5. do 6. has 7. was 8. think / is 9. have 10. is / have
Rappel : les expressions *a number of, the majority of, a couple of, a group of* et *a lot of, the rest of* suivies d'un nom pluriel ou d'un pronom sont généralement suivies d'un verbe au pluriel.

16

1. has 2. swim 3. are 4. gather 5. is (ou : are) 6. was (ou : were) 7. live 8. is (ou : are) 9. were 10. is

17

Verbe au singulier : Barbados • Cyprus • Honduras • Laos • the Netherlands • Wales • the United States of America
Verbe au pluriel : the Bahamas • the Philippines • the Seychelles • the West Indies
Ceux qui admettent un verbe pluriel désignent des groupements d'îles comportant plusieurs entités séparées et individualisables.

18

Perhaps it was **the old women's long illnesses** that had got **them** in the habit of staying at home every night when **they were** young.
By ten o'clock, **they were** always back with **their dogs** in **their flats.**
Almost **all the women they** knew had **husbands, sisters or friends** of long standing with whom **they** could stay.
They had never been able to afford **maids.**

They liked fishing trout, which is a rather difficult thing to do.

19

1. Try not to forget your luggage at the airport! 2. You should follow my advice. 3. I can't find my trousers. 4. I have bought new furniture for my flat. 5. Kicking John was the best goal-keeper in the world-cup.

20

1. The headquarters of the political parties are protected by the police. 2. The public have not been told the latest news yet. 3. The barracks were destroyed by the army. 4. The audience were so satisfied that they applauded the actors in the middle of the play. 5. Ten police were wounded during the riots. 6. All luggage is examined at the customs. 7. All my family have fair hair and blue eyes. 8. The American government has decided to increase its fight against terrorism. 9. I haven't found a better means to do it. 10. Two aircraft have crashed after take-off.

2 Les déterminants du nom

1

1. Men and women are supposed to be equal. 2. Courage, love and generosity are rare values. 3. Speed can kill, drugs too. 4. If you pour too much oil in the pan, it may catch fire (ou : burn). 5. I'll have to go there by car or by plane since traindrivers are on strike. 6. The hospital is between the school and the church: I remember going to school and to church here, but not to hospital. 7. I like books, even if I don't read them. 8. What did you have for breakfast? 9. Blue and orange are my favorite colours. 10. Everybody should speak English nowadays.

2

1. Diseases like cancer, AIDS, hepatitis may one day be bad memories. 2. Days are much shorter in winter than in spring. 3. Squash is very tiring but quite relaxing at the same time. 4. Would you care for a drink? Whisky, gin, or orange juice; no champagne I'm afraid. 5. I had to stay fourteen days (ou : two weeks / a fortnight) in bed owing to a bad cold. 6. I am fed up with television. 7. I don't know anyone living in North America or Australia. 8. Mount Everest has always fascinated me. 9. You go across Regent Street, find your way to Buckingham Palace and there you may see one of the Royals. 10. President McKingates has decided to eradicate international terrorism.

3-4

Valeur générique
l'apéritif : ø (evening) drinks • *l'amour* : ø love • *les miroirs* : ø mirrors • *des glaces* : ø panes / ice-creams • *l'art* : ø art • *la science* : ø science • *la vérité* : ø truth • *les hommes* : ø men • *le style* : ø style • *des choses compliquées* : ø complicated things • *le génie* : ø genius • *du sens pratique* : ø being practical • *des statues* : ø statues • *la frivolité* : ø frivolousness • *la légèreté* : ø casualness • *l'enfance* : ø childhood
Valeur spécifique
la prière du soir des Français : the evening prayer of French people • *une affection de la peau* : a skin disease • *une façon très simple* : a very easy way • *l'extrême pointe* : the apex • *la lune* : the moon • *le soleil* : the sun • *un crime* : a crime

5

1. La parole est d'argent, le silence est d'or. 2. Il ne faut pas se fier aux apparences. 3. L'appétit vient en mangeant. 4. L'attaque est la meilleure forme de défense. 5. Charité bien ordonnée commence par soi-même. 6. Froid aux mains, chaud au cœur. 7. Les extrêmes se rencontrent. 8. Tant qu'il y a de la vie, il y a de l'espoir. 9. Si tu veux la paix, prépare la guerre. 10. Le temps fait des miracles.

6

Dans les proverbes, l'article Ø désigne une généralité, accompagné de noms dénombrables pluriels ou indénombrables singuliers.

7

1. red and yellow 2. blue and yellow and black 3. blue and white 4. red and blue and green 5. black and white 6. red and blue 7. black and blue 8. white and red 9. yellow and white 10. brown and white

8

warm weather : généralité, nom indénombrable assimilé aux noms de saison
Lex : nom propre, autodéterminé
dogs : nom dénombrable pluriel associé de façon distributive à *people*
night : nom dénombrable employé au singulier pour référer au concept de nuit
things : généralité, nom dénombrable au pluriel
people : collectif pluriel, généralité
strange people : collectif pluriel, l'adjectif crée une classe de *people*
parks : absence de localisation précise, généralité, nom dénombrable au pluriel

dog : emploi qualitatif, c'est l'idée de chien qui est envisagée, déterminant Ø associé à un nom dénombrable au singulier.
Dans la dernière phrase, la question posée est une généralité et toutes les formes nominales ont donc une détermination de type générique.

9

1. American 2. Irish English 3. Norwegian 4. Portuguese 5. Welsh

10

The Spaniards come from **Spain** and speak **Spanish**. The Greeks come from **Greece** and speak **Greek**. The Dutch come from **the Netherlands** and speak **Dutch**. The Poles come from **Poland** and speak **Polish**. The Swedes come from **Sweden** and speak **Swedish**. The Persians come from **Iran** and speak **Iranian**. The Medes come from **Media** and speak **Mede**. The Letts come from **Latvia** and speak **Latvian**. The Laps come from **Lapland** and speak **Lappish**. The Lithuanians come from **Lithuania** and speak **Lithuanian**. Russians come from **Russia** and speak **Russian**. Roumanians come from **Roumania** and speak **Roumanian**. The French come from **France** and speak **French**. The Finns come from **Finland** and speak **Finnish**. The Japanese come from **Japan** and speak **Japanese**. The Tartars come from **Tartary** and speak **Tartar**. The Turks come from **Turkey** and speak **Turkish**.

11

Transvaal (exception) • Atlantic (nom d'océan) • Bahamas (îles) • Congo (pays et rivière ; on trouve aussi : *Ø Congo*) • Netherlands (nom commun : *lands*) • Irish Republic (nom commun : *republic*) • Ivory Coast (nom commun : *coast*) • Mediterranean (nom de mer) • Seychelles (îles) • United Kingdom (nom commun : *kingdom*) • United Arab Emirates (nom commun : *emirates*)

12

New Jersey (NJ), Pennsylvania (PA), Ohio (OH), Indiana (IN), Illinois(IL), then Missouri (MO), Kansas (KS), Colorado (CO), New Mexico (NM), Arizona (AZ) and last of all, California (CA).
L'article Ø est utilisé devant les noms d'états, assimilés à des noms propres.

13

Greater London, then, Buckinghamshire, then, Northamptonshire, Warwickshire,Staffordshire, Cheschire,Greater Manchester.
L'article Ø est utilisé devant les noms de comtés, assimilés à des noms propres.

14

The Rocky mountains are in the USA. • Lake Winnipeg is in Manitoba, Canada. • St George's Channel is between Ireland and England. • Belfast is in Northern Ireland.• New Zealand is between the Pacific Ocean and the Tasman Sea. • Melbourne is in Australia. • Soweto is in South Africa. • The Kalahari desert is in the south of Africa. • Mount Etna is in Sicily. • The Isle of Wight is near the south coast of England, in the Channel.

15

1. an 2. a 3. an 4. a *ou* an (*h peu prononcé car accent sur la deuxième syllabe*) 5. an 6. a 7. an 8. a *ou* an (*h peu prononcé car accent sur la deuxième syllabe*) 9. a 10. an

16

an IOU • a useful piece of advice • an expensive item of clothing • a CD player • an honest piece of information

17

a loaf / a slice / a piece of bread • a slice / a slab / a sliver of cake • a piece of chalk • a bar / a slab / a square / a piece of chocolate • a piece of evidence • a block of ice • a sheet / a piece / a scrap of paper • a grain of rice • a flake of snow • a cake / a bar of soap

18

a shred of cloth (*un lambeau*) • a speck of dust • a clod of earth • a sliver / a pane of glass • a peal of laughter (*un éclat de rire*) • a drop of rain • a chunk of rock • a puff / a wisp of smoke • a means of transport • a spell of weather

19

Il n'y a pas d'équivalent strict entre français et anglais dans la traduction des proverbes. Ils témoignent de deux cultures différentes et l'on peut noter ici que l'anglais utilise des données concrètes là où le français préfère l'abstraction.

20

1. My father's a joiner, my mother an accountant and I am a law student. 2. I go to the pictures with a friend twice a week.
3. Before being a gardener, he was a teacher for ten years. 4. She is always in a bad mood when she has an early breakfast. 5. Never go out without a few coins in your pocket. 6. That cake is as hard as a rock. 7. Five pounds a liter is too expensive for me. 8. As a pilot, let me give you this piece of advice: make sure you haven't got a flat tyre. 9. She never swims without a buoy. 10. It's a pity to see a refuse dump in such a beautiful lanscape.

21

1. There is a man waiting outside in a car. 2. An eye for an eye, a tooth for a tooth. 3. An apple a day takes the doctor away. 4. A thing of beauty is a joy forever. 5. Yesterday I bought a pair of trousers, a cardigan and a blouse.

22

1. such a 2. such 3. Such a 4. such an 5. such 6. such a 7. Such 8. such

23

1. You have **such a** beautiful garden! [*dénombrable singulier*]
2. **What a** bunch of liars! [*dénombrable singulier / dénombrable pluriel*]
3. That was **such a** nice evening! [*dénombrable singulier*]
4. You always have **such** heavy luggage! [*collectif*]
5. **Such** refinement is quite uncommon. [*indénombrable*]
6. **What a** bore! [*dénombrable singulier (singularisation d'une "qualité" associée à une personne ou une situation, etc.)*]
7. We've been having **such** stormy weather recently that we keep indoors. [*indénombrable*]
8. **What a** pity you couldn't come! [*singularisation d'une "qualité" associée à une personne ou une situation, etc.)*]
9. **Such** intelligence I have never seen. [*indénombrable*]
10. That was **such** fun! [*indénombrable*]

24

1. It's too incredible a story. / I can't believe so incredible a story. / I can't believe such an incredible story.
2. It's too abstract an explanation. / I can't understand so abstract an explanation. / I can't understand such an abstract explanation.
3. It's too expensive a trip. / I can't afford so expensive a trip. / I can't afford such an expensive trip.
4. It's too hard a loaf of bread. / I can't cut so hard a loaf of bread. / I can't cut such a hard loaf of bread.
5. It's too high a mountain. / I can't climb so high a mountain. / I can't climb such a high mountain.

25

1-2 **few** : peu de gens, nombre insuffisant / **a few** : quelques personnes, vision positive, optimiste des choses
3-4 **few** : constat négatif du nombre peu élevé de gens arrivés ; on en espérait plus / **a few** : les gens commencent à arriver, vision positive
5-6 **a few** : il m'en reste encore quelques-unes, c'est bien / **few** : il ne m'en reste que quelques-unes, c'est dommage
7-8 **little** : mes connaissances sont rares, voire inexistantes / **a little** : vision positive de ce que je sais ; euphémisme modeste peut-être, utilisé par quelqu'un qui sait beaucoup de choses
9-10 **little** : il en reste peu et c'est dommage / **a little** : il en reste encore un peu et c'est bien

26

1. I only know few things about his life. 2. He is no doctor to me. 3. Half a glass of wine (ou : a half glass of wine) is too small a quantity to get drunk. 4. In half an hour, you'll be convinced that you still have a few friends left. 5. Could I have a little cold water in my coffee? It's too hot. 6. She isn't a very good cook. 7. I only have a few things to tell you. 8. She drove me back home in no time. 9. You have a few other alternatives. This is too risky a solution. 10. A little love doesn't hurt.

27

/ðə/ 5. the university 6. the hospital 7. the horrible mistake 8. the historical landmark 11. the C.D. players 12. the hair 14. the ewe 15. the hotel
/ði:/ 1. the honest proposal 2. the honour 3. the expensive clothes 4. the hour 9. the umbrella 10. the I.C.B.M. 13. the M.P.

28

1. the floor (b) 2. the sky (b) 3. the airport (a) / the city (c) 4. the former one (a) 5. the customer (e) 6. the door (b) 7. the piano (b) 8. the school (b) 9. the same one (a) 10. the best of friends (d)

29

1. The President of France is meeting the English Prime Minister today. 2. The man who's playing the cello in the orchestra is my husband. 3. The World cup drew tourists from all over the world to France. 4. All the people who were able to attend the matches were delighted. 5. Your visit has made the letter I had meant to write superfluous. 6. The child hadn't seen the car coming and was run over. 7. The only witness said the car didn't even stop and one of the passers-by immediately phoned the police. 8. The ambulance arrived next and the doctors said the child would recover quickly from the trauma. 9. I like bathing in the Mediterranean and sleeping in the sun. 10. All the people on strike had gathered in the hall of the building in Regent Street and no one could get inside the office-block.

30

The trial had lasted for eighteen days, and from the moment the judge had entered the courtroom the public benches had been crowded. Suddenly there was a buzz in the corridors, and the members of the jury entered one after the other. The press and the public alike began to come back into (the) court. All eyes were on the foreman of the jury, a fat, jolly-looking little man wearing a suit, a striped shirt and a bow-tie. He seemed the sort of fellow with whom, in normal circumstances, I would have enjoyed a pint at the local pub.

Adapted from *Trial and Error* by Jeffrey Archer.

31

I was awakened earlier than usual by an insistent call of nature. Accompanied by my copy of *The Weekly Telegraph*, I was deeply absorbed by home news when a loud rumbling noise alerted my senses. The apartment began to shake, the curtains swayed vigorously and the crockery rattled on the shelves; I was galvanised into action. Spurred on by the dread that like some ancient Pompeian, I might be preserved in volcanic ash to be viewed thus by future generations of tourists, I hurried out. Living in Arequipa, a city in Peru prone to frequent seismic movements, one becomes accustomed to the instability of the environment. However I have taken it as a definitive warning that I shall have to find somewhere else to read the newspaper.

From *The Weekly Telegraph*, issue n° 358.

32

The sun rose up, at first like a yellow ball, then like a disk of polished brass. Trees, cornfields, farms, pastures, horses and workmen in the fields, all appeared instantly bathed in a soft light. Objects a great distance away, little towers, smoking chimneys. Slowly the dew became visible, hanging upon the trees like ladies' ear-rings. Soon everything was under a warm stillness.

33

1. He hoped that his fame and popularity would stop his creditors from asking for their money. 2. "Pleased to meet you! I read your article in *Newsweek* on the plane," I said, and I went on telling him I was fascinated by his style. 3. She took a seat opposite her husband on the other side of his desk. 4. What I like in soldiers is their uniforms. As for their rifles, I'd rather not see them. 5. She was very proud of her house, her furniture, but not much of her husband. 6. She checked her rear-view mirror, but he was still right behind her car. Her petrol gauge was nearly empty. 7. She handed his (ou : her) canvas over to him."It's your (ou : my) best yet! As long as we're sensible about our prices, we should sell at least half of your (ou : my) pictures before the exhibition closes!" 8. I looked at the two women but decided not to make any comment about their make-up or their hair.

34

1. You're the sort of young man we want. 2. By the time she came round to the apartment the following afternoon, he had realised the truth. 3. He disappeared into the bathroom. There he cleaned his teeth, dropped the toothbrush into its mug and brushed his hair. 4. Then he returned to the bedroom and threw himself on the bed. 5. His final words as he closed the door behind him were lost in the noise of traffic. 6. The car skidded across the gravel in front of the house, coming to a halt in the flowerbed just below the kitchen window. 7. A second later the van came crashing into the back of her car, slamming it against the wall of the house and shattering the glass in the kitchen window. 8. When she reached the far end of the gallery, she became aware of an office in which a short, balding man, wearing an old tweed jacket and corduroy trousers, was examining a picture. 9. His occupation, as described in his passport, was banker. 10. He was the branch manager of Barclays Bank in St Albans, Hertfordshire, which in banking circles is about the equivalent of being a captain in the Royal Air Force.

35

I knew Louise before she married. She was then a frail, delicate girl with large and melancholy eyes. Her father and mother loved her with an anxious adoration, because some illness, scarlet fever, I think, left her with a weak heart and she had to take the greatest care of herself. Her boyfriend gave up the games he excelled in because by a coincidence she had a heart attack whenever he proposed to leave her for a day (ou : the day). He could not be such a brute as to leave her alone. She'd been to all the best heart specialists in the world, and they all said that her life hung on a thread. But she had an unconquerable spirit.

3 This / That

1

this/these : ce qui est proche • ce que l'on aime • le présent immédiat • ce qui va être expliqué par la suite

that/those : ce qui est terminé • ce qui vient d'être dit • le passé • ce qui est éloigné dans le temps • ce que l'on n'aime pas du tout • ce qui est éloigné dans l'espace

2

this/these : now • here • admired • imminent • near • loved • I • introduce
that/those : then • there • over there • yesterday • already • hated • before • distant • remember • noise • they • unknown

3

these men • those days • these mice • those geese • this news / these pieces of news • those peoples ("ces peuples" ≠ *those people* : "ces gens") • these leaves • those chiefs

4

1.This coming year will be fantastic. 2. This crossroads is dangerous. 3. This species is rare. 4. This analysis is wrong. 5. This phenomenon seldom happens. 6. This barracks has to disappear. 7. This aircraft is too old. 8. Check this datum, please. 9. This church is magnificent. 10. Where have you put that key?

5

1. <u>these</u> days (D) : unité de temps appartenant au présent de l'énonciateur 2. <u>these</u> tents (D) : désigne un élément proche dans l'espace 3. <u>this</u> climate (D) : élément de la situation dans laquelle se trouve l'énonciateur 4. <u>this</u> Tibetan (D) : rattaché à l'affectif de l'énonciateur de façon positive 5. <u>these</u> mountains (D) : désigne un élément proche dans l'espace 6. <u>this</u> afternoon (D) : unité de temps appartenant au présent de l'énonciateur 7. <u>this</u> (P) : présentation d'une personne 8. <u>this</u> (P) : annonce un segment à droite

6

1. <u>that</u> (P) : renvoie à toute la proposition précédente 2. <u>that</u> (P) : renvoie à la proposition précédente et plus spécialement au sous-entendu : *I am a suspected person* 3. <u>that</u> (P) : renvoie à toute la proposition précédente 4. <u>that</u> (P) : renvoie à tout ce qui a été dit avant / <u>that</u> plane (D) : distance affective, négative 5. <u>that</u> (P) : = *that idea* ; renvoie à ce qui vient d'être dit 6. <u>that</u> face (D) : distance affective, péjorative / <u>that</u> (P) : renvoie à la totalité de l'énoncé prononcé par l'interlocuteur précédent 7. <u>that</u> (P) : renvoie à toute la proposition précédente 8. <u>that</u> (D) : renvoie à une sensation déjà ressentie avant, avec en plus une nuance péjorative

7

1. Those boys are impossible! 2. I can't carry all those books! Help me! 3. Can you really run that fast? 4. In those days there was no electricity. 5. This is Tim Parsons, my best friend. 6. You believe I am a traitor, is that it? 7. Those from London will arrive later. 8. Those we bought last month were perfect. 9. Those in the first row may stand up. 10. I don't like the one you have chosen.

8

1. Avec ce clair de lune, je peux guider mon avion au travers des cols sans problème, ce qui a toujours été avant la partie la plus difficile de l'opération. 2. Personne n'oserait passer une nuit à la belle étoile dans cet endroit. 3. L'homme sortit un paquet de cigarettes. "Goûtez-en une!" 4. Cette petite aventure fera une lecture des plus intéressantes : "Le mystérieux Anglais," si c'est bien là ce que vous êtes, "a atterri de nuit déguisé en Tibétain." 5. Il était difficile de ne pas aimer un tel homme. 6. Je fais une série de reportages sur le bouddhisme et ce monastère est l'un des rares qui fonctionne(nt) encore dans cette partie-ci du Tibet. 7. J'ai entendu parler de cette fameuse cérémonie. Peu de voyageurs ont la chance de la voir. La Chute du Roi de l'Enfer. 8. C'est aussi simple que cela. 9. C'est censé être quoi, ça ? Du whisky ? 10. Les paysans le vénèrent, ce qui joue énormément en faveur de notre cause.

4 Les quantifieurs

1

<u>exprimer une quantité suffisante</u> • <u>exprimer un nombre</u> • <u>désigner une certaine quantité</u> • <u>exprimer la totalité</u> • <u>signaler une quantité nulle</u> • <u>donner une idée d'abondance</u> • <u>impliquer un nombre indéfini</u> • <u>exprimer une petite quantité</u>

2

<u>both</u> (totalité de deux) • the (déterminant, article) • mine (pronom possessif) • <u>some</u> (une certaine quantité, un certain nombre) • such (intensifieur) • <u>few</u> (un nombre insuffisant) • <u>any</u> (une certaine quantité, un certain nombre) • an (déterminant, article) • <u>much</u> (l'abondance) • <u>all</u> (la totalité) • this (démonstratif) • <u>a lot</u> (l'abondance) • <u>a little</u> (une petite quantité) • a (déterminant, article) • <u>one</u> (un nombre) • that (démonstratif) • his (déterminant ou pronom possessif) • <u>enough</u> (quantité ou nombre suffisants) • yours (pronom possessif) • <u>thirty</u> (nombre) • <u>plenty</u> (abondance) • <u>no</u> (quantité,

nombre nuls) • either (choix entre deux) • these (démonstratif) • whole (totalité) • those (démonstratif) • whose (relatif possessif) • each (totalité) • so (intensifieur) • every (totalité)

3

1. Both my friends 2. Both of them 3. Both her sons 4. The two 5. the two of them (ou : both of them) 6. Both of these books 7. the two 8. My two parents 9. Both his parents 10. both

4

1. I can't choose, I love them both.2. Make up your mind! You can't marry the two, it's either one or the other. 3. But they are both so charming! 4. Either you get married or you remain single! 5. Either one would do in fact. 6. You can *not* get married. I am not married either. 7. But both my parents insist. 8. Both of them are wrong. 9. Either I obey them or I leave home. 10. I'm sure you wouldn't like that either.

5

1. Pour sucrer, vous pouvez ajouter soit un, soit deux morceaux de sucre. 2. Vous pouvez prendre l'une ou l'autre route pour aller à l'hôpital. 3. Elle sait écrire des deux mains. 4. C'est le genre d'homme qu'on aime ou qu'on déteste. 5. À vous de choisir : ou c'est elle qui s'en va, ou c'est moi. 6. Il y avait des fleurs à chaque bout de la table. 7. C'est ça ou rien du tout. 8. J'ai vécu à Londres et à Détroit, mais je n'aime pas beaucoup ces deux villes (ni l'une, ni l'autre). 9. Elle était assise à l'arrière de la voiture entre deux hommes. 10. Il y a des cabines téléphoniques à chaque extrémité de la rue.

6

1. both 2. either 3. Both 4. Both 5. either 6. both 7. either 8. both 9. both 10. Both 11.both 12. both 13. either 14. both 15. both

7

all these people • all my friends • all the papers • all those nice things • all day long • all three men • all these new methods • all your life • all the time • all her money
All *est toujours devant le groupe nominal.*

8

1. Tous les chiens sont des animaux, mais tous les animaux ne sont pas des chiens. 2. Tous les gens que vous avez rencontrés sont des amis à moi. 3. Les cinq enfants sont tous bons musiciens. 4. Toute laine tend à rétrécir. 5. Vous avez eu tout le plaisir et eux tout le travail difficile. 6. Toutes ces lettres doivent être postées avant cinq heures ce soir. 7. Ils ont travaillé dur tout l'été. 8. Nous vous avons attendu tout ce temps. 9. Ils étaient absents toute la semaine dernière. 10.Ils sont arrivés en toute hâte.

9

1. Elle ne cuisine pas si bien que cela. 2. Je n'aurais jamais pensé que vous, et surtout vous, l'apprécieriez. 3. Tous mes très bons vins ont été bus. 4. Tous les spectateurs ont applaudi le spectacle. 5. Tout ceci t'appartient désormais. 6. Elle était tout de blanc vêtue. 7. Ma vieille grand-mère habite toute seule. 8. Elle était toute bouleversée par ces mauvaises nouvelles. 9. Le score était de deux partout. 10. Il va vous falloir travailler d'autant plus dur après deux semaines d'absence.

10

1. All things come to those who wait. 2. All's for the best in the best of all possible worlds. 3. All that glitters is not gold. 4. All's well that ends well. 5. It's all or nothing.

11

1. all 2. whole 3. whole 4. all 5. All 6. whole 7. whole 8. All 9. whole 10. whole

12

1. has 2. costs 3. received 4. passes 5. has 6. is 7. is 8. knows 9. brings 10. is

13

each coming day : déterminant • **thirty pound each** : pronom • **each one** : déterminant • **each of you** : pronom • **each of the dogs** : pronom

14

1. They **each** had a suitcase to carry. 2. **Every** one did as they wanted. 3. I saw those two films last week. **Each** of them has a definite appeal. 4. You don't have to pay for **every** *ou* **each** drink. 5. **Every** *ou* **each** time you see her, you feel miserable. 6. **Each** of us knows the truth. 7. They watched her **every** move. 8. Take one **each**. 9. **Each** gave him a coin for Boxing Day. 10. I met her twice. It was **each** time a pleasure.

15

Dans chaque cas, la structure avec **each** permet d'individualiser le repérage (chacun, chacune, chacun d'entre eux) alors que la structure avec **all** crée une globalisation (tous, toutes).

16

1. all day • every day • each day 2. the whole • all 3. all 4. each • every 5. the whole 6. all

17

1. *Remplacement impossible.* 2. He has read every novel I have given him. 3. *Remplacement impossible.* 4. *Remplacement impossible.* 5. I'm sorry, I think I've broken every one of them. 6. Every film I have seen yet is rather disappointing. 7. The policemen wanted to know every detail of her timetable. 8. *Remplacement impossible.* 9. Every fellow-student of hers was present at the meeting. 10. They had left every single dish on the table.

18

1. C'est l'exception qui confirme la règle. 2. On ne peut pas plaire à tout le monde. 3. Toute chose a une fin. 4. Il y a un temps et un lieu pour chaque chose. 5. Tout vient à point à qui sait attendre.

19

1. much 2. many 3. much 4. much 5. enough is enough 6. much 7. many 8. much 9. enough 10. many

20

1. a lot 2. Many 3. enough 4. a lot 5. A good many 6. A good deal of 7. plenty 8. too many 9. enough 10. much 11. enough 12. much

21

<u>exprimer une certaine quantité</u> • <u>montrer que l'énonciateur ne connaît pas exactement le nombre d'éléments</u> • <u>montrer qu'une certaine quantité existe</u> • <u>montrer que tous les éléments ne sont pas concernés</u> • <u>dire que l'on a apprécié particulièrement ce qui suit</u>

22

1. déterminant 2. adverbe 3. déterminant 4. déterminant 5. pronom 6. déterminant 7. déterminant / pronom 8. adverbe 9. pronom 10. pronom

23

1. some 2. Ø 3. some 4. some 5. Ø 6. Some 7. Some 8. some / Ø ou some 9. Some 10. some

24

1. / səm/ 2. /sʌm/ 3. /səm/ 4. /sʌm/ 5. /sʌm/ 6. /sʌm/ 7. /sʌm/ 8. /sʌm/ 9. /sʌm/ 10. /sʌm/

25

1. If you need some (/sʌm/), there's some (/səm/) ice left in the fridge. 2. Do you know you have left some (/səm/) money on the living-room table? 3. Some (/sʌm/) children were playing tennis while others were having a swim in the river. 4. She was reading some (/sʌm/) sort of newspaper. 5. He is some (/sʌm/) chess player!

26

1. déterminant 2. adverbe 3. pronom 4. déterminant 5. pronom 6. déterminant 7. déterminant 8. pronom 9. adverbe 10. déterminant 11. déterminant 12. adverbe

27

1. any 2. some 3. some 4. any 5. some 6. any 7. any 8. some / some

28

1. some 2. some 3. any 4. any 5. Some 6. Any 7. some / any 8. some

29

1.any /*Tu veux des abricots, mais je ne pense pas qu'il en reste.*
2. any /*Dis-moi combien tu en as, si tu en as.*
3. some /*J'ai fait une tarte aux pommes. Tu en veux ?*
4. any /*Je suis désolée mais je ne peux pas aller plus vite.*
5. Some /*Certaines des maisons ont été détruites par l'inondation.*
6. some /*Elle a gagné dans les deux mille livres en pariant sur les (des) chevaux.*
7. any /*Je pense qu'elle n'ira jamais mieux.*
8. some /*Et si vous repreniez un peu de gâteau ?*
9. Some /*Certains de ses amis sont de vrais zonards.*
10. any /*Je ne ferai pas un pas de plus.*

30

a few people • a little water • a few houses • a little wine • a few sheep • a little time • a few times • a little fish • a little faster • a few criteria • a little chicken • a few series • a few mice • a little love • a little help

31

1. I have few reliable friends. 2. I'm a little afraid of him. 3. I have a few good reasons not to like him. 4. Couldn't you drive a little faster? 5. All you will need is a little patience. 6. He gave me too little time to type these few pages. 7. There are a few problems left to solve. 8. Can you leave me alone a little? 9. Give me a few explanations. 10. I'm seeing too few people these days. 11. I have too little time off to spend a few days with you. 12. Very few journalists have reported the event. 13. Few ecologists approve of nuclear power. 14. I know little about her. 15. The minister reportedly had a few love-affairs with a few young women.

32

1. no 2. no 3. none 4. no 5. nothing 6. none 7. nothing 8. no 9. no 10. nothing

33

1. no / no 2. no 3. nothing 4. none 5. none 6. Nothing / nothing 7. none 8. no 9. nothing 10. Nothing / nothing

34

137,000 people : one hundred and thirty seven thousand people • **0.9143** : (nought) point nine one four three • **40,000,000 inhabitants** : forty million inhabitants • **3.7853** : three point seven eight five three • **0.394** : (nought) point three nine four • **2.205** : two point two nought five • **378** : three hundred and seventy-eight • **499** : four hundred and ninety-nine • **219.98** : two hundred and nineteen point nine eight • **29,028** : twenty-nine thousand and twenty-eight

35

an inch : 2.54 cm • **a foot** : 30.48 cm • **a yard** : 0.9143 m • **a mile** : 1.609 km • **an acre** : 40.4672 a • **a pint** : 0.56791 l • **an ounce** : 28.35 g • **a pound** : 453.59 g • **a stone** : 6.350 kg • **a gallon** : 3.7853 l

36

1 cm : 0.394 inch • **1 m** : 3.280 ft • **1 km** : 0.621 mile • **1 l** : 1.1760 pint • **1 kg** : 2.205 lb • **1 cm2** : 0.155 sq.inch • **1 ha** : 2.471 acres • **1 km2** : 0.386 sq.mile • **1cm3** : 0.061 cubic inch • **1 m3** : 219.98 gallons

37

00 44 18187498523 : O O (ou double O) four four (ou double four) one eight one eight seven four nine eight five two three • **00 44 16034556588** : O O four four one six O three four five five (ou double five) six five eight eight (ou double eight) •
00 33 02356065079 : O O three three (ou double three) O two three five six O six five O seven nine • **00 33 02326007057** : O O three three O two three two six O O seven O five seven

38

November the third, nineteen fifty-three • October the seventeenth, nineteen eighty-five • May the twenty-first, nineteen seventy-nine • March the twenty-seventh, nineteen eighty-eight • August the second, nineteen forty

5 La mise en relation des noms

1

1. to 2. for 3. by (ou : to) 4. from 5. on / for 6. to (ou : in) 7. in 8. by 9. on / for 10. on / to 11. from 12. to 13. to 14. from 15. by 16. for 17. on / by 18. in 19. for 20. to

2

France's foreign policy • the children's toys • my parents' friends • the President's men • Jenny and Peter's wedding party • Dickens's novels *ou* Dickens' novels • Ulysses' travels • St Paul's (cathedral) • today's weather report • anyone's guess

3

Groupe nominal 's (adjectif) nom :
France's foreign policy • the children's toys • the President's men • Jenny and Peter's wedding party • Dickens's novels • today's weather report • anyone's guess
Groupe nominal ' (adjectif) nom : my parents' friends • Dickens' novels • Ulysses' travels
Groupe nominal 's : St Paul's (cathedral)

4

1. a man's clothes 2. The man's 3. a woman's hat 4. a year's experience 5. a policeman's six-shooter 6. Ø last week's meeting 7. a woman's footsteps 8. His novels' success 9. a rich man's wife 10. Ø Britain's hooligans

5

Génitifs dits déterminatifs (ils prennent la place du déterminant ; nous avons intégré un adjectif afin de prouver leur rôle déterminatif)
1. a man's (dirty) clothes : his (dirty) clothes 2. The man's (denim) trousers : his (denim) trousers 3. a woman's (pink) hat : her (pink) hat 5. a policeman's (shiny) six-shooter : his (shiny) six-shooter 6. Ø last week's (political) meeting : that (political) meeting 7. a woman's (hurried) footsteps : her (hurried) footsteps 8. His novels' (tremendous) success : their (tremendous) success 9. She was a rich man's (unhappy) wife : she was his (unhappy) wife 10. Ø poor Britain's (shameless) hooligans : its (shameless) hooligans

Génitifs dits classifiants (ils prennent la place d'un adjectif)
3. a woman's hat (a pink hat) 4. a year's experience (a short experience) 5. a policeman's six-shooter (a shiny six-shooter) 9. a rich man's wife (a spoilt wife)
Les génitifs qui sont dans les deux catégories comportent toujours ici le déterminant **a**.

6

1. my brother's yellow eyes 2. today's newspaper 3. Saint Peter's cathedral 4. Merlin's magic 5. Dublin's fair city center 6. my father's eyes 7. John's letter 8. Mary's book 9. Kennedy's murder 10. Manson's murder of Sharon *ou* Sharon's murder by Manson 11. Spielberg's many films 12. his ten years' imprisonment 13. a butcher's knife 14. the train's departure

7

jewels at the jeweller's • flowers at the florist's • chicken at the poulterer's • tomatoes at the greengrocer's • shoes at the shoemaker's • material at the draper's • cigarettes at the tobacconist's • meat at the butcher's • hats at the hatter's • medicine at the chemist's • cream at the dairyman's • thread and needles at the haberdasher's • pans at the ironmonger's • tins at the grocer's • oysters at the oyster seller's (ou : the fishmonger's)

8

1. **Lucy's parents** : répétition inutile à cause du coordonnant 2. **my sister's in-laws** : comparatif, on retrouve forcément in-laws des deux côtés 3. **the MacFarlanes' home** (sous-entendu : home) : connaissance culturelle 4. **her mother's** (sous-entendu : among her mother's cousins) 5. **the dentist's surgery** (sous-entendu : surgery) 6. **St John's hospital** (sous-entendu : hospital) : connaissance culturelle 7. **the jeweller's shop** (sous-entendu : shop) : connaissance culturelle 8. **Ulysses' adventures were incredible adventures** : emploi littéraire, la répétition est évitée par avance 9. **E.T.'s voice** : comparatif, on retrouve forcément voice des deux côtés 10. **the lady's bike** (sous-entendu : bike déjà mentionné)

9

1. Il est maintenant tiré d'affaire. 2. Les deux jeunes enfants de la pauvre femme ont été légèrement blessés dans l'accident. 3. Mieux vaut être la petite chérie d'un vieil homme que l'esclave d'un jeune. 4. Ce monstre avait des pattes de chèvre et des ailes de corbeau. 5. Elles portaient des vêtements de deuil. 6. Il nous a fallu une journée entière de travail. 7. L'activité favorite de ma grand-mère paternelle était de se rendre chez le libraire. 8. Cet ami de Jenny a des yeux de démon et un visage d'ange. 9. Pour l'amour de Dieu, tiens-toi bien ! 10. Es-tu déjà allé(e) à une vente chez Sotheby ?

10

1. Let me introduce **the chieftain's two young children.** 2. I'd been hoping that **that contractor's workers** could help me build my house. 3. The nurse had finished bandaging **the wounded man's head.** 4. non (quantification de joy) 5. non (proverbial) 6. non (qualification de disinfectant) 7. non (relation partie / tout) 8. non (nominalisation de she knew the situation) 9. non (adjectif substantivé) 10. non (relation partie / tout)

11

1. this boy's problem 2. the end of the century 3. last year's wine 4. the leg of the table 5. a mother's duty

12

1. **milk chocolate** : chocolate made with milk 2. **chocolate milk** : milk flavoured with chocolate 3. **malt whisky** : whisky made with malt 4. **whisky malt** : malt used to make whisky 5. **a race horse** : a horse that runs in races 6. **a horse race** : a race for horses 7. **a vegetable garden** : a garden where you grow vegetables 8. **garden vegetables** : vegetables that grow in a garden 9. **bag leather** : leather used to make bags 10. **a leather bag** : a bag made of leather

13

tea-cup : a cup for tea • **address-book** : a book in which you write addresses • **bank account** : an account in a bank • **daydream** : a dream during the day • **fingertip** : the tip of the finger • **handshake** : when you shake hands with someone • **landowner** : someone who owns land • **money box** : a box in which you put money • **vegetable garden** : a garden in which you grow vegetables • **leather coat** : a coat made of leather

14

mouse-traps • on-lookers • corkscrews • grown-ups • race-horses • sit-ins • blood transfusions • after-thoughts • landscape gardeners • oak forests • in-patients • story-tellers • pin-ups • dining-rooms • all-day sessions

6 Les adjectifs

1

1. Vrai 2. Faux 3. Vrai 4. Faux 5. Faux 6. Faux 7. Vrai 8. Vrai 9. Faux 10. Faux

2

1. her crazy ideas 2. her last daughter's last name 3. considerable interest in various circles

4. no conceivable practical application 5. his greatest love 6. a pleasant, white-painted house 7. the great, white peaks 8. A strange, fatalistic calm 9. Her long woollen dress 10. the high grassy bank

3

1. All this is but mere coincidence. 2. Could you say something nice, for a change? 3. This first edition of the novel is quite unique. 4. It's totally impossible, I'm sorry. 5. His face was a little too white. 6. It was far too ambitious a plan. 7. Mind you, I have as good a memory as you. 8. These apricots are not ripe enough to be eaten now. 9. Don't worry, it happened by sheer accident. 10. It's too complicated a question for me.

4

1. **essential** : peut être épithète ou attribut 2. **sheer** : ne peut être qu'épithète 3. **content** : ne peut être qu'attribut 4. **much** : n'est pas un adjectif mais un quantifieur

5

1. un verre à vin plein / un verre rempli de vin 2. la seule pièce disponible (pas de différence entre les deux structures) 3. les gens en question / les gens soucieux 4. l'explication compliquée / l'explication en cause 5. Vous avez rencontré la bonne personne. / Vous avez rencontré la personne proprement dite.

6

1. with / for 2. of 3. about 4. with 5. about 6. to 7. for 8. with 9. to / for 10. with 11. with 12. to 13. with 14. about / about ou on 15. to

7

1. nasty 2. new 3. oblivious 4. open 5. petrified 6. pressed 7. proud 8. quick 9. sure 10. scared

8

1. The handsome tall seventeen-year-old white French boy 2. A rather common tiny wooden cane chair 3. that old-fashioned grey flannel shirt 4. a flashy brand new black sports car 5. a small ice-cold Bloody Mary 6. in the crowded, hot and noisy night club 7. the deadly twenty-year-old African-born virus of Aids 8. a very expensive rather large black leather bag

9

1. all the people present were amused 2. even someone so blasé as my brother looked astonished 3. the two protagonists were speechless, so confused were they 4. the most optimistic of the viewers can't help feeling depressed 5. the council for the defence confessed to being disgusted 6. I still couldn't sleep, so frightened was I 7. I went to see him at the end and told him how interested I was 8. I saw on the doctor's face that he too felt worried 9. anybody listening to him grows interested 10. even the most attentive pupils got bored

10

1. well-fed 2. home-made 3. long-legged 4. well-mannered 5. heart-broken / heart-breaking 6. a corn-producing country 7. an expensive-looking car 8. a never-ending story 9. left-handed

11

1. a ten-minute rest 2. a two-month holiday 3. a fifty-year-old man 4. a forty-page magazine 5. a sixty-litre tank 6. a five-pound book 7. a two-thousand dollar answer 8. a ten-mile walk

12

1. The blind, the deaf, the dumb 2. the Blacks / the Whites 3. the young and the old 4. the under-fourteens 5. The sublime and the beautiful 6. The Welsh / the English 7. the uncanny or the supernatural 8. the difficulties of the disabled

13

1. Some parking spaces are reserved for the use of the disabled. 2. The homeless are more and more numerous nowadays. 3. Have you read *The Naked and the Dead* by Norman Mailer? 4. Three young people out of four like going to the pictures. 5. The difficult is done at once, the impossible takes a little longer. 6. The rich man has his ice in the summer, the poor man gets his in the winter. 7. The dumb can't communicate with the blind through sign language. 8. Darwin exposed his theory of "the survival of the fittest" in a book called *The Origin of Species*.

7 Les comparatifs / Les superlatifs

1

1. His hair was not as black as a raven's wing. 2. My sister works in the same hospital as my father. 3. Her necklace is twice as long as mine. 4. The English teacher is not as funny as the music teacher. 5. I make as many mistakes as my neighbour. 6. I've had a quarter as many sweets as my little sister. 7. American wine is as good as any other wine. (ou : American is as good a wine as any other.) 8. She likes going to the theatre as much as he does (ou : as him).

2

1. Don't buy this book! It is four times as expensive here as in the other bookshop. 2. I have got as many friends as you (have). 3. Unfortunately she is not as clever as she looks. 4. She speaks as good English as a BBC announcer. 5. Could you speak half as quickly so that I understand twice as quickly? 6. In this weather we are as well here as outside. 7. I don't think she is that cross (ou : as cross as that). 8. Stop doing the same as me over and over again.

3

1. happier 2. sadder 3. spicier and tastier (ou : more spicy and more tasty) 4. more intelligent 5. nearer / heavier 6. elder 7. more angry 8. more smashing 9. narrower 10. for better and for worse

4

bigger • fatter • wider • deeper • higher • narrower • feebler • heavier • more handsome • more right • truer • better • more wrong • worse • more real • thinner • more meagre • more acid • fairer • older ou elder

5

Comparatif en **-er** : 1, 2 (en redoublant la consonne finale), 5. Comparatif en **-ier** : 6, 7. Comparatif en **more** : 3, 4, 8, 9, 10, 11, 12. Comparatif en **-r** : 13, 14.

6

1. If you're not more careful in the future, I won't buy anything for you any more. 2. It's far easier than you think. 3. If you ask me, she's more stupid than nasty. 4. I've never known anyone to be richer than him. 5. All this seems more real to me now, I found it difficult to believe. 6. Your insight is more right than you think. 7. I won't go any farther; my legs are more tired than the rest of me. 8. He wouldn't let me read any further. 9. The handicapped arrived later than the others but not last. 10. I saw Tim and Tom last week: the former has grown bigger and the latter thinner.

7

1. It's getting harder and harder to find someone you can really trust. 2. His speech was so long that the audience felt less and less interested. 3. Means of communication are becoming quicker and quicker. 4. It was pouring outside and I was less and less in a hurry to leave. 5. Going on holiday costs more and more money. 6. Village schools have fewer and fewer pupils. 7. She was more and more pleased as she heard the nice speech of the manager. 8. More and more people use the Internet. 9. The imaginary world was getting more and more (ou : less and less) real. 10. There are fewer and fewer hitchickers on the roads these days.

8

1. The more I know you, the less I appreciate your company. 2. The more he earns, the more he spends. 3. The older she gets, the more beautiful she is. 4. The dearer her clothes, the less they suit her. 5. The harder you try, the better it is. 6. The more friends he has, the happier he feels. 7. The earlier you come, the sooner we leave. 8. The more he loves her, the more she loathes him. 9. The more drinks you have, the more dangerous you become. 10. The farther he goes, the fewer chances he has of coming back.

9

1. Les actes en disent plus que les mots. 2. L'attaque est la meilleure forme de défense. 3. Mieux vaut faire envie que pitié. 4. Mieux vaut tard que jamais. 5. L'herbe est toujours plus verte de l'autre côté. 6. Plus on est de fous, plus on rit. 7. La plume est plus puissante que l'épée. 8. Mieux vaut prévenir que guérir. 9. Les choses les plus courtes sont les meilleures. 10. Plus vite ce sera fait, plus vite ce sera fini.

10

1. This is the nicest piece of news of the day. 2. He is the most famous senator in Congress. 3. That's the worst place Ø I know. 4. China is the most populated area in the world. 5. The day I got my divorce was the happiest day of my life. 6. It's the strangest remark Ø I have ever heard. 7. This is the best ever book in the history of literature. 8. Chartres' is the most interesting cathedral in France. 9. Alain Proviste is the most talented player in the French team. 10. What is the highest building in the world?

8 Les pronoms personnels et possessifs

1

1. He used to bring her flowers every other day. 2. The milkman brought them milk every morning. 3. Could you give them my share? 4. All her friends gave her presents for her child's birth. 5. She had promised him a few things so that he would not go. 6. I send them my best regards. 7. They never showed him their holiday photographs. 8. I had to teach them linguistics. 9. He was supposed to tell them the truth. 10. She gave it to him (ou : her).

2

1. She said that all she knew was that they didn't like her. 2. She wondered whether she should go or stay with him (ou : her). 3. She asked the two of them if they could give her a hand. 4. They said to me that I should be more careful because I had hurt my leg again. 5. He said to them to mind their own business from then on. 6. She started by saying that in that novel, she had tried to show what her life was (ou : had been) in those days. 7. She shouted to him that he'd better hurry or they'd be late! 8. How could you say that you were pleased to meet him to such a detestable man!

3

1. Nobody except you knows where she is. So *you* are going to go and fetch her. 2. "Who bought all this?" "I did." "You did!" "Yes, it is I (ou : me) who went shopping (ou : I went shopping)." 3. "I haven't met them yet. Have you?" "I saw them yesterday." 4. I'm fed up with him. He's getting on my nerves. 5. He is three times as big as she is (ou : as her) and yet she eats twice as much as he does (ou : as him). 6. The doorbell's ringing. It must be her. She's always late when she visits us. 7. "What's your cat's name?" "Kitty. She is really independent." 8. It's her father who wants to speak to her on the phone, but she isn't at home and he won't believe me when I tell him. 9. "Who said, 'You never know.' (ou : 'One never knows.')?" "What I know is it isn't me!" 10. "We are arriving from New York." "Pleased to meet you. *We* are arriving from Cuba."

4

1. Il est important que tu le saches. 2. Je ne pourrai pas venir à ton mariage et je te prie de m'en excuser. 3. Il m'a été très difficile de croire que tu ne le savais pas non plus. 4. C'est gentil à toi de le faire à ma place. 5. J'ai pensé qu'il valait mieux t'en parler en premier. 6. Cela ne fait rien, d'ailleurs, je m'en moque. 7. Il était évident que personne ne trouvait essentiel de le vendre. 8. Si c'est si facile à faire, pourquoi ne le fais-tu pas toi-même ? 9. C'est toujours celui qui parle en dernier qui a raison. 10. C'est lui qui l'a cassé !

5

1. mine / mine 2. yours / mine 3. theirs / hers 4. ours 5. Yours / theirs / his

6

1. Ton soi-disant docteur, tu ne penses pas qu'il ressemble étrangement au nôtre ? 2. Elle me regardait avec ce sourire dans les yeux qui n'appartient qu'à elle. 3. Prends-le-leur si tu n'as pas le tien, mais en aucun cas je ne te prêterai le mien. 4. Tu peux amener tes enfants, les miens seront ravis de jouer avec les tiens. 5. Leur maison est une très belle maison, rien à voir avec la sienne à lui. 6. Rien de sérieux ! C'est juste un ami à moi... 7. As-tu dit à ton espèce de mari de se dépêcher ? À cause de sa paresse habituelle, nous allons être en retard ! 8. Mon diamant à moi, comme tu dis, est bien plus authentique que le sien à elle. 9. Ses cheveux à lui sont bouclés naturellement, pas les miens. 10. Entre les tiens, les leurs et les miens, je choisirai toujours mes propres enfants !

7

1. Un jour, tu comprendras qu'il vaut mieux avoir un ami sûr que dix bons copains. 2. Je voudrais une très belle rose rouge, s'il vous plaît. C'est pour la seule femme de ma vie. 3. Tu as dit un million, pas un million deux cents ? Comment as-tu pu faire une telle erreur ? 4. Mon seul et unique loisir, c'est de faire une partie de squash de temps en temps. 5. Elle a eu des jumeaux. L'un est un garçon, l'autre une fille et chacun a un grain de beauté sur la joue droite. 6. J'ai acheté quelques bonnes bouteilles. On en ouvre une ce soir ? 7. Quelles pêches voulez-vous ? Des vertes et des pas mûres, comme d'habitude ? 8. Ma voiture est trop petite, il va me falloir en acheter une plus grande. 9. Un plus un plus un font trois. 10. Tu connais celle-là ? Un jour, un Allemand rencontre un Belge et lui dit...

8

1. these ones 2. these blue ones / those green ones 3. the ones 4. these ones / the ones 5. the ones / those ugly ones

9

1. You should have been told I would be late! 2. Shall we go? Are you ready? Hurry up or we'll miss the beginning of the film! 3. So you're happy with your trip, my boy? 4. What horrible weather we had in July! 5. Someone wants to speak to you, she's waiting outside at the gate. 6. The management say they are going to fire the two secretaries. 7. I was (ou : have been) asked to write this report for tomorrow. 8. You should never trust a second-hand car dealer, you know! 9. We really had fun yesterday, what did *you* do? 10. Three people are reported to have been seriously wounded.

10

1. On essaiera de démontrer que deux et deux ne font pas toujours quatre. 2. On ne dirait jamais qu'il a plu autant l'été dernier.

3. On dit qu' on lui a fait avouer des crimes dont on n'avait jamais trouvé les auteurs. 4. On te l'a volé pendant que tu dormais ! On ne t'a jamais dit de fermer ta porte à clé ? 5. On ne devrait jamais dire ces choses-là à quelqu'un de déprimé ! 6. Tu sais, on ne sait jamais ce que le futur nous réserve ! 7. On t'attend à huit heures devant la gare. 8. Alors on a des choses à me dire ? Par quoi commence-t-on ? 9. On m'avait dit qu'on me couperait les cheveux en brosse mais on me les a laissés tels qu'ils étaient. 10. On dit toujours que c'est dans le besoin que l'on reconnaît ses amis et c'est bien vrai.

9 Les pronoms réfléchis et réciproques

1

1. yourself 2. herself 3. themselves 4. yourself 5. you 6. yourselves 7. him 8. them 9. themselves 10. herself 11. yourself (ou : yourselves) 12. yourself / you 13. you 14. him / himself 15. yourself

2

1. John and Mary kept looking at each other. 2. Brothers and sisters love one another. 3. They congratulated each other for their degrees. 4. We have never met. 5. We send each other letters.

3

1. The more I think of us, the more I think we should see each other less often. 2. They have lost the last match and they are really annoyed with themselves for it. 3. She has been ashamed of herself ever since everybody was told she had cheated. 4. There's nothing like trying to help one another. 5. People were talking to one another and I couldn't make myself heard. 6. Your book sells well, you can be proud of yourselves. 7. Relax, have a ten minute nap and when you wake up, you will feel very well. 8. I'm going to congratulate myself if no one else does. 9. I met the president himself and he showed an interest in what I did. 10. She taught herself the piano. / She learnt to play the piano all by herself.

3 La phrase

1 L'ordre des mots dans la phrase simple

1

1. Hardly had it been raining when the hurricane hit the house. 2. Only then did I understand what he was saying. 3. Never shall we forgive them for what they did. 4. Often have I complained about it, but to no use. 5. Seldom have I seen so much happiness.

2

1. *No sooner* had she left her home than the sun started shining. 2. *Never before* has there been such a disaster. 3. *So angry* was I that I decided to write a letter to the director. 4. *Such* was my anger that I became speechless. 5. *Nowhere* was the boss to be seen. 6. *Not only* did he arrive late *but* he didn't even apologize. 7. *So* absurd was his conduct that they all laughed. 8. *Never before in my life* have I had such an idea. 9. *Well* do I remember your grandmother. 10. *On no account* are you to talk about it.

3

1. So have I. 2. So have you. 3. Nor (ou : neither) can they. 4. So have you. 5. So did his girlfriend. 6. So shall (ou : will) we. 7. So does her mother. 8. Nor (ou : neither) can Pierre. 9. So did the others. 10. Nor (ou : neither) had we.

4

1. Had he arrived earlier... 2. Should she arrive now... 3. Had he had a better idea... 4. Should you change your plan... 5. Should it start raining now... 6. ... had they passed their exams.

5

"Perhaps it is too late to start our meeting."
"So it is indeed. So, we can decide to leave."
"But here comes our boss!"
"I'm sorry. There were so many trucks on the road! Among them was even a tractor! Never shall I forget that nightmare. No sooner had I left home than problems started. Had I known, I wouldn't have left home."
"Nor would we."

6

1. It was Annabel who wrote a love story when she was ten. 2. It was a love story that Annabel wrote when she was ten. 3. It was when she was ten that Annabel wrote a love story. 4. It was him (*plus soutenu* : he) who married his own cousin last year. 5. It was his own cousin that / who (*plus soutenu* : whom) he

married last year. 6. It was last year that he married his own cousin. 7. It's you, Mr President, who are telling us a lie. 8. It's to us that you're telling a lie, Mr President. 9. It's a lie that you're telling us, Mr President.
10. It was us (*très soutenu* : we) who understood what he did at that moment. 11. It was what he did that we understood at that moment. 12. It was at that moment that we understood what he did.

7

1. What Sophie's looking for is a new apartment. 2. What Steve wanted was a cheeseburger. 3. What she broke was a vase. 4. What they will like is Brooklyn Bridge. 5. What she has visited is New York. 6. What I might see is the parade in London. 7. What they want to buy is three copies of that book (ou : What they want is to buy three copies of that book). 8. What he says is that he's never felt that way before. 9. What Errol is sticking to is the idea that life is for living. 10. What I've never understood is what they liked about him. 11. What she'll always feel sorry about is not understanding her daughter. 12. What you just can't understand is how much I loved her.

8

1. Can she speak German? 2. Will he go to New Zealand next year? 3. Are you going out tonight? 4. Has the unemployment rate come down in Britain? 5. Do they prefer tea to coffee? 6. Do your parents never (ou : ever) leave their country? 7. Do they have a nice house? 8. Would they rather stay inside? 9. Does Steve have many brothers and sisters? 10. Did Brenda say she'd be late?

9

1. Yes, she can. No, she can't. 2. Yes, he will. No, he won't. 3. Yes, I am. No, I am not. 4. Yes, it has. No, it hasn't. 5. Yes, they do. No, they don't. 6. Yes, they do (leave their country). No, they don't (ever leave their country). 7. Yes, they do. No, they don't. 8. Yes, they would. No, they wouldn't. 9. Yes, he does. No, he doesn't. 10. Yes, she did. No, she didn't.

10

1. you 2. Who 3. you 4. Who 5. Which one 6. you 7. they 8. What
Le mot interrogatif est sujet du verbe dans Who called?, Who wrote that stupid letter?, Which one said that?, What happened?
Lorsque le mot interrogatif n'est pas le sujet, on a recours à un auxiliaire dans la question (Where **did** you go?, Who **did** you see?, Which letter **did** you write?, What **did** they do?). *On assiste d'autre part à une inversion sujet / auxiliaire.*

11

1. *What* happened? 2. *What* were you doing last night? 3. *Who* rang? 4. *Who* wants some more tea? 5. *Where* did she go? 6. *What* did they look at? 7. *How* did you do it? 8. *When* did they arrive? 9. *Who* left a note on my desk? 10. *When* did Omar live in California?

12

1. Who did you send the flowers to? (*très soutenu* : Whom) 2. Who did he rely on? (*très soutenu* : Whom) 3. Who did they care for? (*très soutenu* : Whom) 4. What was Carey listening to? 5. What was she thinking about? 6. Who did he think of? (*très soutenu* : Whom) 7. What did we both laugh at? 8. Whose doctor did you send for? 9. Whose house did the hooligans break into? 10. When did you say he would be back?

13

1. *Their friends wonder* where they are going. 2. *Laurie wants to know* who called. 3. *I'd like to know* when you will see her again. 4. *Let's ask them* who was on the phone. 5. *Peter wants to know* how old her grandparents are. 6. *I'd be pleased to know* what they bought. 7. *I'm asking you* why you are crying. 8. *I'd be interested to know* what you were listening to. 9. *I'm just asking* how you managed it. 10. *Could you tell me* why she ran away?

14

1. *The policeman asked* what I (ou : he / she / they) had been doing at that time the day before. 2. *The librarian wanted to know* which of these books I (ou : he / she / they) had liked best. 3. *She enquired* why Louise had lied to her (ou : me). 4. *She forced him to tell her* where he would spend his Easter holiday. 5. *He was furious and asked her* who (*très soutenu* : whom) she had been seeing.

15

1. How deep... 2. How old... 3. How high... 4. How often... 5. How many... 6. How much... 7. How long... 8. How far... 9. How long... 10. How wide...

16

1. espace 2. temps 3. temps 4. espace 5. temps 6. temps 7. temps 8. temps 9. temps 10. temps
Phrase 5 : Since when have you been learning Spanish? *Phrase 8* : Since when have they been married?

17

1. De quelle longueur est le lac ? 2. Combien de temps comptez-vous rester ici ? 3. Pendant combien de temps as-tu vécu avec elle ? 6. Est-ce qu'ils t'ont dit combien de temps ils ont passé en Afrique du Sud ? 7. Il y a combien de temps que leur famille est arrivée en Grande-Bretagne ?

18

1. So, how are you today? 2. Do you know what his (ou : her) mother is like? 3. How do you know he won't come? 4. How come he didn't tell you anything? 5. How did you learn about it? 6. How could I get him (ou : her) to understand? 7. How do you want me to know about it? 8. How did she do it? 9. Can you tell me what that guy is like? 10. How shall we do it?

19

1. What 2. What 3. What 4. What 5. Which 6. What 7. What 8. Which 9. Which 10. What

20

Who's that? / Oh, **what** do you want? / **What** do you mean, 'Hi'! Do you know **what** time it is? / **What** does it matter? / **Which** one? / I don't care **which** one. Just call **who** you want. / OK, of John, Peter and Steve, **which** (*lequel*) / **who** (*qui*) should I call? / Talking of **which** (*à ce propos*), Linda, could you lend me your car? / **Which** one? / But **what** happened to your own car?

21

1. What's the weather like? 2. What are his (ou : her) parents like? 3. How are your parents? 4. How long have they been in Germany? 5. Whose book is this? (ou : Whose is this book? / Who does this book belong to?) 6. How long are they in Scotland for? (ou : How long will they stay in Scotland?) 7. When did it last rain? (*moins fréquent* : How long is it since it last rained?) 8. But, didn't you see that car?! 9. Could you tell me whose car this is? (ou : who this car belongs to) 10. I sometimes wonder why he ever did that. 11. I wonder how far (ou : to what extent) he is really determined to succeed. 12. How likely is she to get her driving licence?

22

1. How nice it was to see you! 2. How she has changed over the years! 3. What a sweetheart you are! 4. How nice your cousin is! 5. What a fool he was not to listen to her advice! 6. How hot this tea is! 7. What a relief it was to see them! 8. How stupid this programme is! 9. How strange it feels not to be with my daughter! 10. What a fuss he made about nothing!

23

1. It was so great to see you! 2. I behaved in such a stupid way. 3. I have so much to study (ou : I have to study so much). 4. It hurts so much to listen to you! 5. She was so mad at him! 6. I was such a fool to believe you! 7. He really cares so much for you (ou : cares for you so much). 8. I'm sorry but I am in such a hurry!

24

1. There were so many mistakes that I couldn't read his paper. 2. We had such terrible weather that we decided to leave after an hour. 3. I was in such a hurry that I didn't notice the accident. 4. The book was so funny that I couldn't stop reading. 5. I was so late that it was useless to try to make it. 6. They were given so much wine to drink that they got drunk in less than an hour. 7. It rained so much that we decided to cut short our holiday. 8. It was such a lousy film that we didn't watch it to the end.
Il est possible à l'oral de ne pas utiliser la conjonction **that** *dans ces phrases.*

25

1. What a 2. so much 3. so much 4. How (ou : So) 5. so 6. such a 7. so 8. How 9. so many 10. such an 11. so much 12. so 13. so much 14. so much 15. such

26

1. Don't they speak well! *Ce qu'ils parlent bien!* 2. Didn't they behave badly! *Comme ils se sont mal comportés!* 3. Aren't I smart! *Hein que je suis malin!* 4. Don't I know! *À qui le dites-vous!* 5. Isn't it clever! *Comme c'est intelligent!* 6. Isn't he old now! *Ce qu'il est vieux maintenant!* 7. Doesn't she look sweet! *Comme elle est mignonne!* 8. Doesn't it taste nice! *Ce que c'est bon!* 9. Doesn't time fly! *Comme le temps passe vite !*

2 Les constructions verbe + verbe

1

1. to leave 2. to tell 3. travelling 4. not to talk 5. driving 6. waiting 7. to listen 8. not having (ou : not to have) 9. to give up 10. not to worry

2

When it was too late he decided **to tell** his Mum about his secret love affair. He knew how **not to shock** her and wanted **to be cautious** with her so as **not to cause** any problem. He is very sweet and hates **hurting** (ou : **to hurt**) people's feelings but at the same time he couldn't bear **not to let her** (ou : **not letting her**) **know.** So he asked her **to promise not to talk** while he was speaking. He had to wait **for her to sit up** in her bed and then started **to explain** (ou : **explaining**) that he disliked **her prying** into his affairs and that he enjoyed **leading** his own life. He kept **talking** never daring **to look** at her. When he stopped **speaking** he realized that she was sound asleep.

3

1. I advise you not to write that letter. 2. They swear never to have stolen that bike. 3. They swear never to steal again. 4. My parents have always let me do anything I want. 5. I was listening very carefully. I heard her whisper (ou : whispering) to her husband. 6. I distinctly remember him (ou : his) taking your keys. 7. I would prefer not to see her right now. 8. I like listening (ou : to listen) to opera. 9. I would like to listen to an opera. 10. The government proposed to give money to fund the programme.
11. I promise not to do it again. 12. This time I won't forget to tell them.

4

1. Can you help me (to) fill in this form? 2. If you choose to stay, you will have to cooperate. 3. I like being admired. I would so much like to be admired. 4. I want you to tell me the truth. 5. You refuse to tell me where he is? (ou : Won't you tell me where he is?). 6. You all agreed to see that film, didn't you? 7. In the end, we convinced (ou : persuaded) her to come with us. 8. I am waiting for his (ou : her) friends to arrive. 9. They can't stand being touched. 10. His parents will not (ou : won't) let him go.

5

1. They pretend not to see me. 2. It is no use telling me how it works. 3. I don't mind not going there. 4. It didn't stop raining (ou : it never stopped raining). 5. I heard her sing (ou : singing). 6. I don't know how to tell him (ou : her). 7. The customers intended to boycott that product. 8. Try to concentrate for a change. 9. Taking this train means travelling for fifteen hours. 10. I regret not mentioning it. 11. Be patient, I'll come and help you some day. 12. The roof needs (ou : wants / requires) repairing.

3 Les propositions causatives-résultatives

1

1. get 2. made 3. have 4. had 5. made (ou : had) 6. have (ou : make) 7. get 8. makes 9. make 10. had

2

1. I had my bedroom painted by my brother. 2. Fry the fish in a little oil. 3. I was made to open my suitcase. 4. Don't worry, I'll get a policeman to help you. 5. Did I make myself understood? 6. I tried in vain to make myself obeyed. 7. He had his watch stolen. 8. The traffic was very heavy and the result was that I arrived late (*très soutenu* : this led to my arriving late). 9. The thought made him smile. 10. They made me drink vodka.

3

1. I managed to get him to clear up his mess. 2. Mum has sent for the doctor. 3. I'll let you know as soon as I can. 4. At last, I've had my car repaired! 5. They've had their hair cut. 6. Poor things, they've been had by their lawyer. 7. All these beautiful stories make us dream. 8. The prince had the castle rebuilt. 9. As a child, my father made me make my bed every morning. 10. Don't try to make (ou : have) me believe that he's here.

4

1. She has washed her car clean. *Elle a lavé sa voiture, qui est maintenant propre.*
2. Jo shouted herself hoarse last night. *À force de crier hier soir, elle s'est enrouée.*
3. Steve read himself almost blind. *À force de lire Steve est presque devenu aveugle.*
4. She ran quickly out of the shop. *Elle sortit du magasin en courant.*
5. They starved to death. *Ils sont morts de faim.*
6. They starved themselves to death. *Ils se sont laissé mourir de faim.*

5

1. They blackmailed her **into resigning**. 2. They threatened her **into signing** the document. 3. My mother tricked me **into picking up** my aunt at the airport. 4. Erwin talked Sue **out of accepting** (ou : **into not accepting**) the offer. 5. The President clearly fooled the State Secretary **into supporting** the resolution. 6. Sheila argued Betsy **out of becoming** (ou : **into not becoming**) a nurse. 7. His parents begged him **not to marry** the girl. 8. My dad persuaded me **to do** a degree in maths.

4 La coordination et la subordination

1

• wheat and wine • the wheat and wine route (from north to south) and the salt and silver route (from west to east) • salt and silver • the Duke's son held out against attacks for more than a month, but the castle was finally pillaged and burnt • pillaged and burnt • the Prince of Mornmouth and his young and beautiful wife • young and beautiful • (either) restore it or build a new one (coordonnant en deux parties : either... or) • that he would restore it but that he would do it slowly and meticulously • slowly and meticulously • ten or fifteen • he and the Prince

2

Dear John,
I suppose that you'll be using my bedroom (= sub. 1) while you're in London (sub. 2 dépendante de sub. 1). I'm afraid I've lost the key to the large cabinet (sub. 1) that is next to the bed (relative incluse dans sub. 1). So if you have anything confidential you should keep it under the carpet, as no one will think of looking there. You can use my books, which are all in my bedroom (relative), though I'd appreciate (sub. 1) if you wouldn't lend them to anyone (sub. 2 dépendante de sub. 1), as books are rarely returned (sub. 3 dépendante de sub. 2). I have been told by Carey, who came round last night (relative), that you intend (sub. 1) to give a party during your stay in London (sub. 2 dépendante de sub. 1). It's all right with me but make sure that nothing gets broken and that everything stays clean (sub. coordonnée à la sub. précédente). You know I hate (sub. 1) coming back to a dirty house (sub. 2 dépendante de sub. 1).

5 Les subordonnées relatives

1

The Duke, **who...** • the castle, **which ...** • the wheat and wine route (**which ...**) • salt and silver route (**which...**) • his son, **who...** • attacks, **which...** • the castle, **whose** walls... • the town of Rigmarole, **which...** • an architect, **whom...** • The roof, **whose** tiles...

2

The Duke, **who** = humain / pronom relatif sujet
the castle, **which** = non humain / pronom relatif sujet
the wheat and wine route (**which...**) = non humain / pronom relatif sujet
the salt and silver route (**which...**) = non humain / pronom relatif sujet
his son, **who** = humain / pronom relatif sujet
attacks, **which** = non humain / pronom relatif sujet
the castle, **whose** walls = non humain / pronom relatif génitif
the town of Rigmarole, **which** = non humain / pronom relatif sujet
an architect, **whom** = humain / pronom relatif complément
The roof, **whose** tiles = non humain / pronom relatif génitif

3

1. My mother **who** was a relatively aggressive person pushed her neighbour roughly forward. 2. We lived in a street **which** (ou : that) contained a garage called Ever-Ready. 3. We lived in a street **whose** name was Langdon Park Road. 4. It was a narrow room **which** (ou : that) had two windows between two wings of the building. 5. Once in a while she appeared with something **that** took you by surprise. 6. My uncle, **who** had never married, was always generous. 7. The house (that) we live in (ou : in **which** we live) is old. 8. The man **whose** photograph is in my wallet was on television last night. 9. Brian, **who** is a police inspector, asked me a lot of questions. 10. The shop towards **which** I'm walking (ou : (that) I'm walking towards) belongs to my husband.

4

1. **with whom** 2. **Ø** (ou : who / *soutenu* : whom) 3. **who** 4. **who** 5. with **whom** 6. **Ø** (ou : that / *plus rare* : which) / and **which** 7. none of **which** 8. **whose** 9. **Ø** (ou : that) 10. **that** 11. **whose** / **which** 12. **which** 13. **which** (ou : that) 14. **Ø** (ou : that) 15. **which**

5

1. Pronom relatif : *that* / proposition relative : *that women use regularly* / antécédent : *the same.*
2. Pronom relatif : *that* / proposition relative : *that has been worn and worn for many winters* / antécédent : *some old dress.*
3. Pronom relatif : *who* / proposition relative : *who no longer wanted to live with him* / antécédent : *the woman.*
4. Pronom relatif : *which* / proposition relative : *which she had received as Christmas presents* / antécédent : *two novels.*
5. Pronom relatif : *that* / proposition relative : *that she actually lived with* / antécédent : *one.*
6. Pronom relatif : *that* / proposition relative : *that dated from the 1920s* / antécédent : *records.*

7. Pronom relatif : *who* / proposition relative : *who had a job in a coffee shop* / antécédent : *a poet*
8. Pronom relatif : *whom* / proposition relative : *whom we barely remembered* / antécédent : *a man*.
Pronom relatif : *whose* / proposition relative : *whose name was never mentioned* / antécédent : *a man*.

6

3. Relative **nécessaire** pour savoir de quelle femme il s'agit.
4. Relative **non nécessaire** : *which she had received as Christmas presents* est une information supplémentaire concernant les deux romans.
5. Relative **nécessaire** : si on la supprime, la phrase n'a plus beaucoup de sens.
6. Relative **nécessaire** car l'information importante est la date donnée dans la relative.

7

1. This is the person who I think would be a good candidate. 2. I don't like the way he drives at all. 3. What can we do with these books that nobody wants? 4. This museum owns many paintings, only one of which is from the twentieth century. 5. The story, which I remember very well, is less interesting than the style. 6. Here is a machine whose usefulness is obvious. 7. It's a play whose modernity had surprised everybody. 8. She owns several cars, only one of which can be used (ou : is in working order). 9. What I realize is that it is never too late. 10. What I am proud of is my accent. 11. He's bought a house that is old but the roof of which (ou : but whose roof) is brand new. 12. The friends I'm telling you about do not live here.

8

Dans ces phrases, l'antécédent est une proposition (*He became a drug addict / That was the end of my third section / You've always loved him / My boyfriend has been offered a new job*) et non un nom ou un groupe nominal.

Traductions de ***which***
1. ce qui 2. ce qui 3. ce que 4. ce qui

9

1. What I regret is that he didn't tell me about it. 2. Ruth has always refused to tell me about it, which I regret. 3. What she told me is none of your business. 4. What they want is to be left alone. 5. Can you see what's over there? 6. What is regrettable is that he is not (ou : he should not be) aware of it. 7. Go and see them? That's precisely what I refuse (to do). 8. They all left before the end of the match, which is really incredible. 9. What you need is a new watch. 10. He arrived with (ou : in) what looked like a car.

10

1. Whoever loves me is to come with me. 2. I'll go wherever you go. 3. We can go whenever you want. 4. Whoever can do this exercise has understood it all. 5. He is never pleased, wherever we eat (ou : wherever we may eat / whatever the place where we eat may be). 6. Of all these cars you can choose whichever (one) you want. 7. We'll do whatever you want (us to do). 8. Whichever (one) of you finds the right solution first will be entitled to my respect.

---

6 Les subordonnées nominales en V-ing

1

1. Melvin('s) being late annoyed Michael. 2. Henry('s) passing his exam rejoiced his parents. 3. My failing my exam did not sadden my boyfriend. 4. Their hesitating could have been dangerous. 5. Her ringing five minutes after the accident puzzled the policeman. 6. His leaving a note didn't make things easier.
Dans la phrase 4 : For them to hesitate could have been dangerous.

2

1. I hate being late. 2. Do you mind my (*oral* : me) leaving right now? 3. Jane remembers writing a letter of complaint to her boss. (*avec* her writing, *le sujet de* writing *serait différent de celui de* remembers) 4. We dislike not being invited. 5. He left without saying goodbye. 6. On learning the news she immediately rang her best friends. 7. After failing to convince the prime minister, the minister decided to resign. 8. Don't forget that before taking off you have to fasten your seatbelts. 9. Thank you for listening with so much interest. 10. I don't object to you (ou : your) smoking in here. 11. My students are used to travelling a lot. 12. I prefer his new habit to him (ou : his) waking up very late. 13. We all look forward to Errol('s) visiting us soon. 14. They were caught dreaming of the Mediterranean. 15. They were busy repairing their old car.

3

1. Le fait que Melvin soit en retard a agacé Michael. 2. Le fait que Henry ait réussi ses examens a fait plaisir à ses parents. 3. Mon échec à l'examen n'a pas attristé mon petit ami. 4. Leur hésitation aurait pu être

dangereuse. 5. Le fait qu'elle ait téléphoné cinq minutes après l'accident a intrigué le policier. 6. Le fait qu'il ait laissé un message n'a rien arrangé.

7 Les subordonnées conjonctives

1

1. Ø 2. Ø 3. Ø / that 4. Ø 5. that 6. Ø 7. that 8. Ø 9. Ø 10. that

2

1. She finds it strange that he shouldn't have phoned (*plus oral* : that he didn't phone). 2. I find it worrying that she shouldn't answer (*oral* : that she doesn't answer). 3. Do you find it normal that they should have left (*oral* : that they left) so fast?

3

1. They complained that people didn't listen to them. 2. I doubt (if) I can answer you. 3. They say they want to help you. 4. I think I'll go to Edinburgh tomorrow. 5. You think you'll get away with it just like that? 6. I admit that I don't know how to do it.

4

1. That he should only arrive tomorrow is surprising (*plus oral* : That he's only arriving). 2. That it should only rain once a year (ou : rain only once a year) here seems strange to me (*oral* : That it only rains...). 3. That he should hold it against me is normal (*oral* : That he holds it). 4. That she shouldn't be able to (ou : she can't) make up her mind is understandable. 5. That he shouldn't have phoned (ou : that he didn't phone) worries me. 6. That they should have liked (ou : That they liked) Wagner is not that easy to understand. Les structures en *it is* sont bien plus fréquentes : *it is surprising that he should only arrive tomorrow* (oral : *that he is only arriving*).

5

1. He'll regret it all the more as some day I'll be rich. 2. I don't know how she is. All the more so since she doesn't write to me any more. 3. It's all the more dangerous as you can't drive.
4. This test is all the easier for Sean as it is in English.

6

1. that she should start (ou : that she start)
2. that she should be (*oral* : that she is) 3. that they should be (ou : that they be / *oral* : that they are) 4. that we should go (ou : that we go)
5. that you should remain (ou : that you remain) 6. we should do (ou : we do)

7

1. It's incredible that she should have said that (ou : that she said that). 2. It's surprising that such a thing should have happened (ou : that such a thing happened). 3. It's not normal that they should have behaved like that (ou : that they behaved). 4. It is regrettable that you should have quarrelled (ou : that you quarrelled).

8

1. get / *Je vous téléphonerai dès que je serai rentré.*
2. had driven / *Il a dit qu'il arriverait dès qu'il aurait reconduit Karen chez elle.*
3. breaks down / *Nous achèterons un nouveau téléviseur quand notre vieux poste tombera en panne.*
4. broke down / *Mes parents ont dit que nous achèterions un nouveau téléviseur quand notre vieux poste tomberait en panne.*
5. have finished / *Nous partirons quand tu auras terminé ton travail.*
6. want / *Nous déménageons pour Miami le mois prochain. Venez nous voir quand vous voudrez.*
7. was / *La juge a dit qu'elle inviterait la presse une fois que son enquête serait terminée.*
8. is / *Je sais qu'il arrivera (quand il sera) trop tard.*

9

1. No sooner had I seen her than I stopped my car. Hardly had I seen her when I stopped my car. 2. No sooner had it started raining than we left the beach. Hardly had it started raining when we left the beach. 3. No sooner had she rung than they started laughing. Hardly had she rung when they started laughing. 4. No sooner had we got off the plane than we were gripped by the cold. Hardly had we got off the plane when we were gripped by the cold. 5. No sooner had I begun accelerating than my husband screamed at me. Hardly had I begun accelerating when my husband screamed at me.

10

1. If I had known, I **would not** (ou : wouldn't) **have come.**
2. He **will not** (ou : **won't**) **go** if it starts raining.
3. The examiners **would have cancelled** the exam if they had been told about the cheating.
4. Brenda **wouldn't have talked** to Kevin if she had known the truth.
5. If he comes with his grandparents we **will not** (ou : **won't**) **be able to** go climbing.

6. If you arrived two days earlier you **could** meet my new girlfriend.
7. If you pass your exam **I'll take** you to the restaurant.
8. If you ever passed your exam I **would take** you to the restaurant.

11

1. were 2. made 3. had been 4. had not been 5. behave themselves. 6. applied

12

1. He insisted on trying again even though he knew it was useless. 2. They looked at each other as though they had never met. 3. They'll do it when they can. 4. We'll leave as soon as it stops raining. 5. The government will negotiate if they stop striking. 6. Take my advice: don't get married until you are over 30. 7. The path runs around a corner where it turns out of sight. 8. No sooner had he met her than he offered to marry her. 9. She is so famous that she would never think anyone could be disrespectful to her. 10. They immediately stood up to greet the new mayor. 11. How can he know London since he said he'd never been to England? 12. He took a picture of the monument in case he had to describe it.
13. You may borrow my car provided you bring it back with a full tank. 14. The students enjoy this novel all the more as it is easy to read.
15. You may have any of my books as long as you take good care of them.
Dans les phrases :
1. Even though he knew it was useless, he insisted on trying again. 4. As soon as it stops raining we'll leave. 5. If they stop striking the government will negotiate. 10. To greet the new mayor, they immediately stood up. 12. In case he had to describe it he took a picture of the monument. 13. Provided you bring it back with a full tank you may borrow my car. 15. As long as you take good care of them you may have any of my books.

13

1. **after** you phoned 2. **until** he apologizes
3. **while** the iron is hot 4. **so as** not **to** wake you up 5. **to** know the truth 6. **so that** they wouldn't have to do it again 7. **so that** they won't have to do it again 8. **Since** you really want to know
9. **since** she returned from her holiday in Leeds
10. **even though** I'll never admit it to her
11. **However** intelligent he may be 12. **whereas** her parents would like her to be an actress

14

1. **while** he was trying to rescue his dog
2. Strange **though** it may seem 3. **As** it was dark 4. **as** I was cooking for Dominique
5. **unless** it's a matter of life and death 6. **In case** you didn't know 7. **as long as** your parents don't mind 8. **provided** nobody tells me what to do 9. **for fear that** there might be riots
10. **if** he decided to emigrate to South Africa? (*proposition principale sous-entendue* : What would you do if...?) 11. **for** telling me lies 12. **to** forget that I love him

---

8 Discours direct et discours indirect

1

1. She didn't say anything to me.
2. Unfortunately, they didn't tell their parents anything. 3. He told you lies. (say *impossible*)
4. The headmaster told the assembly that discipline should be encouraged. 5. Stop saying to everyone that you're my boyfriend!
6. They said to their best friends that they did not want to get married. 7. You keep telling the same jokes over and over again! (say *peu envisageable*) 8. Tell the teacher about it before it's too late.

2

1. said 2. told 3. say 4. saying 5. told 6. tell 7. tell 8. say 9. told 10. tell 11. telling 12. say

3

1. *My mother enquired* whether (ou : if) I wanted to marry him or not. 2. *She asked me* if I had had a nice meal. 3. *He wondered* if (ou : whether) I had lost anything. 4. *She wanted to know* if (ou : whether) I was going out that night. 5. *My husband asked* whether the children would be home for dinner. 6. *The neighbour wondered* if (ou : whether) the minister had resigned yet.

4

1. *She asked* where I had met him. 2. *She enquired* when I would be back. 3. *They wanted to know* what he had said to me.
4. *John wondered* why Chris had been late.
5. *They asked* who had gone. 6. *She wondered* how it had happened. 7. *The judge wanted to know* where they were. 8. *Their mother asked* when they were coming back.

5

1. *He ordered* us (ou : me) to shut up. 2. *She asked* us to open our books on page 43. 3. *He advised* us never to say we're (ou : we were) sorry. 4. *He suggested* that we should go (ou : we go) to the cinema. 5. *The guest apologized* that he hadn't warned us (ou : for not warning us). 6. *She told* me not to lie to her. (ou : *She*

forbad(e) me to lie to her. / *She forbad(e)* me from lying to her.) 7. *The policeman warned* us not to park our car there (ou : warned us that we shouldn't park our car there). 8. *She invited* us to come round for tea.

6

1. *The children cried* they wanted to go to Disneyland. 2. *Mr and Mrs Litten complained* that John and William never wrote to them. 3. *He said apologetically* that it was too late to catch the train.

4. *She announced* that she had met the man of her dreams the day before. 5. *Her mother explained* that anyway Liz had never trusted Al. 6. *The Reverend claimed* that he had had a dream about his children. 7. *The policewoman testified* that she had remembered looking at her. 8. *They insisted* that if John came two days earlier it would make things simpler.

9. *The boy said* he had come to say goodbye. 10. *The President's wife cried* that she had decided to get a divorce. 11. *The station master told Kirstie* that he was sorry but that she had just missed her train.

12. *The secretary explained* that Mr Byrd would be here (ou : there) in a moment. 13. *Her former husband exclaimed* that he would not speak to her. 14. *The clairvoyant predicted* that things would get better.

15. *Mother told Thomas* he must (ou : had to) come in at once. 16. *Michele bragged* that she could swim that length in 30 seconds. 17. *The priest then said* we may (ou : might) sit down. 18. *The headmaster shrieked* that we could stand up when he came in.

7

1. *He asserted* that he was going to New York. 2. *She acknowledged* that she had made a mistake. 3. *He admitted* that it was too late to react. 4. *They confirmed* that they had never been invited. 5. *He answered* that he would probably move to London in September. 6. *She objected* that she had (got) no time to lose. 7. *The boss shouted* to Nick that he was too stupid for the job. 8. *Alex accepted* that he hadn't had the courage to talk to her.

8

Nathalie asked Henry if he had found anyone who could help her. Henry replied that he had found a priest who would be able to help her. His name is (ou : was) Father McCrory. He told her to go to him. Father McCrory might be able to tell her something. Nathalie thanked Henry and said that she supposed that would help. Henry asked her if she had any relatives around here / there. She answered she only had an aunt. He exclaimed that that helped a bit. She then said her aunt had had the house in Langdon Park Road. Henry said that anyway he felt sure Father McCrory could help her. He had known everybody in that neighbourhood. He advised her to try not to be too sad. One never knew. Nathalie said she knew, that life went on (ou : goes on).

9

... Why had it happened to her? Did she deserve such a harsh treatment? She had always been kind to everybody and could not understand what was going on in her life. ...
Perhaps he could not pray today because of the pain he felt. In a few days, perhaps next week, he would probably feel differently. He might even break down. That would be terrible. If he broke down, it would take weeks for him to recover...

10

Mrs Litten was feeding the fire. Tears rose to her eyes. She asked herself: "Why has it happened to me? Do I deserve such a harsh treatment? I have always been kind to everybody and cannot understand what is going on in my life. The other women did not say a word but Mrs Litten felt their sympathy (ou : The other women don't say a word but I feel their sympathy). She crept closer to her son and asked him, "Melvin, can you pray?" "No, mother." Mrs Litten could understand her son's feelings. She thought: "Perhaps he cannot pray today because of the pain he feels. In a few days, perhaps next week, he will probably feel differently. He may even break down. That would be terrible. If he breaks down, it will take weeks for him to recover." Outside the wind abated as if it feared to disturb the mother and her son.

1 Les prépositions

1

1. afraid of 2. angry with (ou : at) 3. annoyed with 4. ashamed of 5. aware of 6. bad at / good at 7. bored with 8. close to 9. crazy about 10. disappointed with 11. famous for 12. fond of 13. full of 14. furious with / furious about 15. glad about (ou : of) 16. interested in 17. jealous of 18. kind to 19. nice to 20. pleased with / satisfied with 21. proud of 22. sorry about 23. surprised about (ou : at) 24. tired of 25. worried about

2

1. amazed at (ou : by) 2. annoyed with 3. worried about 4. busy with 5. clever at 6. delighted at (ou : about) (ou : by) 7. dependent on 8. different from 9. disgusted at (ou : by) (ou : with) 10. excited about (ou : by) 11. familiar with 12. fed up with 13. frightened of 14. grateful to you for telling 15. impressed with (ou : by) 16. keen on 17. mad at (ou : with) 18. mad about 19. responsible for / rude to / scared of / sick of 20. terrible at 21. typical of 22. upset about (ou : by)

3

1. think of 2. go to 3. suffers from 4. hide ... from 5. escape from 6. apologize for 7. steal ... from / borrowed ... from 8. separates ... from 9. take part in / participate in 10. succeed in 11. translate ... into 12. divide ... into 13. turned ... into 14. made of 15. depend on 16. live on 17. spend ... on 18. congratulate ... on 19. Fill ... with 20. cover ... with 21. looking for 22. laughing at 23.approve of 24. pay for 25. comment (up)on

4

1. *What* did you reply with? 2. *Where* did you go last summer? (pas de préposition avec *go* interrogatif) 3. *What* did she kill him with? 4. *Who* are you in love with? 5. *Who* are you dependent on? 6. *Whose* house did you sleep in? 7. *Who* is he married to? 8. *Which* story did you feel more interested in?

5

1. This is a (ou : the) book (that) John is keen on. 2. I wrote a story (that) no one is interested in. 3. She is my cousin (who) I have often told you about. 4. They are friends (who) we depend on for food. 5. They are former schoolchildren (who) we are so proud of. 6. Here is a (ou : the) house (that) the three men broke into. 7. These are rare books (that) I've been looking for everywhere. 8. The Smiths are our neighbours (who) passers-by keep looking at.
Dans les phrases 3, 4, 5 et 8, on aurait pu employer whom *dans un style soutenu.* Which *aurait pu être utilisé à la place de* that *dans les autres phrases.*

6

1. The dog brought Peter two bones *ou* two bones to Peter.
2. The magician showed his partner the hat *ou* the hat to his partner.
3. My parents sent me a letter and I left Anny a message *ou* a message for Anny.
4. She wants to book Bob a plane ticket *ou* a plane ticket for Bob.
5. I'll teach her maths and she'll pay me for it.
6. The manager explained the problem to his employees.
7. We'll provide them with enough food.
8. The murderer described his act to the jury.
9. I'd like to remind my friends of the presents I gave them.
10. There is no need to ask him for his help.

7

à travers : across / through • *au-dessus de* : over / above • *le long de* : along • *derrière* : behind • *parmi* : among • *au-dessous de* : below • *près de* : close to / near / by • *en bas de* : down • *à l'intérieur de* : inside • *à côté de* : next to • *au large de /séparé de* : off • *en face de* : opposite • *devant* : in front of • *autour de* : round • *vers* : towards

8

1. across 2. across 3. through 4. across 5. through 6. across 7. through 8. across 9. through 10. through

9

1. at / in 2. at 3. at 4. at / at 5. at 6. in / in 7. in 8. in / in 9. in / at 10. at

10

1. to 2. into 3. on(to) 4. in 5. into 6. on(to) 7. into 8. onto

11

1. between 2. between 3. Among 4. among (between them = deux personnes) 5. between 6. among 7. Between 8. between

12

1. at 2. on 3. Ø / Ø 4. on / Ø 5. at / on 6. at / in 7. On 8. in/ on 9. in / in 10. in / in 11. on / in 12. in / at

13

1. I'll be waiting for you from 3 to 4. 2. Can you finish this work by tomorrow? 3. What were you doing during the summer? 4. I didn't work from June to September. 5. Give me a ring tonight by 6 o'clock. 6. I have been at university since last year. 7. He didn't write to us for five years. 8. I have been seeing her regularly for three years.

14

1. Stop dawdling, because of you we may never be in time for our appointment. 2. Due to a late arrival of the train, the express to London will leave at 10:05. 3. Unlike Ruth I've always liked going to the pub. 4. Given their children's reluctance they decided not to go to New Zealand. 5. Considering what Brenda said we'd better not count on her. 6. Owing to the heatwave the sports event was cancelled.

15

1. Why don't you go out for a walk instead of wasting your time watching TV? 2. They decided to go on foot in spite of the weather conditions. 3. We managed to go to New York thanks to Patty's generosity. 4. What you have done is contrary to the headmaster's orders. 5. The meeting was postponed on account of their being late. 6. She failed despite her parents' encouragement.

16

1. like 2. As 3. As 4. like 5. like 6. like 7. as 8. like 9. like 10. like

17

1. on foot 2. on television 3. in my opinion (ou : to my mind / to me) 4. on the phone 5. on strike 6. on this side of 7. on the dole 8. on the third floor (*américain* : on the fourth floor) 9. in the snow 10. on fire 11. by train 12. on the plane

18

1. from / at 2. On / to / on 3. for 4. of / as 5. As / for 6. by / for

19

1. Who do you wish to speak to? 2. Give it to him. 3. I have already explained to you how it works. 4. Louise has asked Karim for some money. 5. I asked the shop assistant the price. 6. It reminds me of my first driving lesson. 7. This famous actor lives down the road. 8. She doesn't like dancing any more. She is now into computers. 9. When he went back to his parents' home, he no longer felt at home. 10. To me it's the only way of going about it.

20

In my opinion singing **in the rain** is a bad habit. If you sing alone **in the street** or **at work** people will think you're strange. **For example** the other day I wanted to go home **on foot** rather than **by bus**. I live **in the suburbs**, five kilometres **from the city centre**. I was not **in a hurry**. I just had to be (at) home **by eight o'clock**. I felt like I was **on holiday**. As I was walking **through the park** which is **opposite the town hall**, I started singing an operatic aria. Everybody **was looking me up and down**. They were even **turning round** as I went by. **In the end**, I had to stop, so **scared** was I **of** these people.

To me it sets a **limit to** my freedom. All the more so as I have a beautiful voice. I've been taking singing lessons **for sixteen years, in fact since my childhood. As a child**, I wanted to sing **as a tenor, like Pavarotti**. True, **I'm far from it** (ou : I'm not nearly there), **despite all my effort**. But **between you and me**, does it really matter?

When we are **among friends**, it does not matter. By the way I am ready, my dear colleague, **to sing to you** the great tenor aria **from** *Turandot*, just **for you**. What do you mean **"Out of** the question"? You don't want to **listen to me**? It's **because of people like you** that freedom is trampled. I'd be better off **on a desert island** than **among** ignorant people. **At Easter**, that is **in two months**, I'll tender my resignation. I'd rather be **on the dole** than with you all. **On your arrival in September** I thought you were better than the others. How wrong I was!

---

2 Les adverbes

1

1. Quite frankly, I have other things to worry about. *[modifie la phrase entière]*
2. You're too good to be true. [*modifie l'adjectif*]
3. Honestly I didn't say anything against you. [*phrase entière*]
4. I'll always love you. [*verbe*]
5. This film is incredibly long – and dull. [*adjectifs coordonnés*]
6. He's still looking for his keys. [*verbe*]
7. I read it quite recently. [recently *modifie la phrase et* quite *modifie* recently*]*
8. He expressed his opinion convincingly. [*verbe*]

2

1. He is often away. 2. She does not always answer her mail. 3. I'll never write to them. 4. It hardly ever rains here. 5. He's always complaining about the service. 6. We've really enjoyed the show. 7. It can't possibly be true. 8. I certainly will. / I certainly will not.

3

1. *No sooner* had she opened her mouth than I recognized her voice. 2. *Never before* had they seen such a beautiful show. 3. *Hardly* had he said a few words when he began crying. 4. *No sooner* had the children closed their eyes than they fell asleep.

4

1. We've all decided to move to Chicago.
2. They are all lodging a complaint against their boss. 3. We are both properly married. 4. They have each of them returned to their parents' home. 5. We will all write soon. 6. They can both be quite tiresome. 7. We each had cucumber sandwiches for lunch. 8. ... "We all are."

5

1. He explained his role unexpectedly.
2. She sang her aria well.
3. They answered angrily.
4. If you've already seen that film, we can see another one.
5. It's beautifully (ou : nicely) said.
6. Suddenly it started raining (ou : It started raining suddenly).
7. I'll soon go and see her in Glasgow.
8. He finally passed away at the age of 92.
9. If you go upstairs don't forget to switch off the light.
10. When did you last talk to the victim?

6

1. still 2. yet 3. still 4. yet 5. still 6. yet

7

1. He hasn't bought his new car yet.
2. The baby still doesn't talk.
3. I think they are still in bed.
4. Jonathan hasn't finished his work yet.
5. The defendant hasn't spoken yet.
6. The defendant is still not speaking.

8

1. The warmth of friendship seldom mellowed her contacts. 2. Only one or two of the club women had called on her. 3. Mrs Briggs always believed in keeping her distance, too. 4. Has she ever been to Denmark? 5. They are not often ready on time. 6. On Sunday evenings she sometimes went to a lecture on philosophy. 7. You can just never tell when he is happy. 8. He had never seen Mrs Briggs so generous before. 9. She never wanted to see him again. 10. It's the worst concert I've ever heard. 11. It doesn't often rain here. 12. ... "No, I never have."

9

1. It's a little better. 2. I really thought she had gone. 3. I think Ives is a little drunk. 4. They really liked it (ou : It really appealed to them). 5. This place is so much better now. 6. Look! It's been snowing a little. 7. I hardly talked to them. 8. Almost (ou : nearly) 80,000 people attended this concert. 9. Peter's friends are completely (ou : totally) hopeless. 10. I'm not rich enough to be able to afford this hotel.
11. I'm not really hungry. I'm really not hungry.
12. She almost felt like resigning.

10

1. Unfortunately I'm not nearly finished (ou : I'm far from having finished). 2. I barely (ou : hardly / scarcely) counted twenty people.
3. My young brother can hardly talk, let alone write. 4. It was even hotter than last year. 5. It's a rather rich country (ou : it's rather a rich country). 6. They are rather (ou : pretty / fairly) lazy. 7. I don't even want to talk to him (ou : her) on the phone. 8. Even Kevin wouldn't agree with you.

11

1. Don't walk so fast. 2. This book is far too difficult to read. 3. He eats so much. He eats too much. 4. He is a far too dangerous neighbour (ou : he is far too dangerous a neighbour). 5. He has eaten so much that it has made him ill. 6. I have too much to do, I'm overworked. 7. It's too much. I won't be able to eat it all. 8. It's so clean that we no longer want to use it.

12

1. They also speak German and Italian.
2. What else could we do?
3. I too want to be a musician (ou : I want to be a musician too).
4. We also have laptop computers if you want.
5. Anything else for you, Madam?
6. Also, we are not allowed to sell them.
7. She not only plays well, but also composes music.
8. My alarm clock didn't go off. Also, I had trouble starting the car.

13

1. Tom ne se sentait pas bien, mais il est quand même allé travailler. Cependant il n'a pas réussi à se concentrer.
2. Je n'ai jamais aimé Harry et pourtant j'ai décidé de l'aider.
3. Il est vrai néanmoins que j'ai été un peu dur avec lui.
4. Je sais que tu n'aimes pas recevoir des invités. Néanmoins tu pourrais faire un effort.
5. Arrête de tricher, autrement je te dénoncerai.
6. En fait (ou : à vrai dire), je ne peux pas te parler maintenant. Je te rappellerai.
7. À propos, puis-je te suggérer de réécrire le premier paragraphe?
8. "Ne t'en fais pas, on y arrivera d'une manière ou d'une autre. – Je ne sais pas pourquoi, mais j'en doute."
9. Ces chiffres ne prouvent rien. Et d'ailleurs qui les a calculés ?
10. Nous avons de plus en plus de clients et c'est pourquoi il nous faut davantage d'ouvriers.
11. C'est la fille aînée et donc l'héritière du titre.
12. Ce n'est pas très utile. C'est beau, pourtant, non ?

14

1. probably (ou : presumably) 2. frankly 3. arguably 4. most certainly (ou : assuredly) 5. maybe (ou : perhaps) 6. fortunately 7. undoubtedly 8. personally 9. hopefully 10. surely 11. of course 12. admittedly 13. obviously 14. surprisingly 15. certainly 16. clearly 17. probably (ou : very likely) 18. naturally

3 La formation des mots

1

counter-clockwise (dans le sens inverse des aiguilles d'une montre) • asymmetry (asymétrie) • incoherence (incohérence) • re-evaluate (réévaluer) • forearm (avant-bras) • disconnected (débranché) • undo (défaire) • irreproachable (irréprochable) • mistrust (méfiance, se méfier de) • amoral (amoral) • foreground (premier plan) • illegal (illégal) • forecast (prévisions, prévoir) • rebuild (reconstruire) • misspell (mal orthographier) • undoubtedly (indubitablement) • immature (immature) • non-smoker (non fumeur) • ex-husband (ex-mari)

2

• **waitress** = nom formé de : nom (waiter, lui-même formé sur wait = servir) + suffixe -ess (= féminin) ▷ *serveuse*
• **boyhood** = nom formé de : nom (boy) + suffixe -hood (= statut) ▷ *enfance*
• **stardom** = nom formé de : nom (star) + suffixe -dom (= condition) ▷ *célébrité*
• **useful** = adjectif formé de : nom (use) + suffixe -ful (= plein de) ▷ *utile*
• **sadden** = verbe formé de : adjectif (sad) + suffixe -en (= pour former des verbes) ▷ *attrister*
• **driver** = nom formé de : verbe (drive) + suffixe -er (= agent) ▷ *conducteur*
• **hairy** = adjectif formé de : nom (hair) + suffixe -y (= pour former des adjectifs) ▷ *poilu*
• **refusal** = nom formé de : verbe (refuse) + suffixe -al (= action de) ▷ *refus*
• **friendliness** = nom formé de : adjectif (friendly ◀ friend + ly) + -ness (= condition) ▷ *gentillesse*
• **catastrophic** = adjectif formé de : nom (catastrophe) + suffixe -ic (= pour former des adjectifs) ▷ *catastrophique*
• **childless** = adjectif formé de : nom (child) + suffixe -less (= qui exprime une absence de) ▷ *sans enfants*
• **foolish** = adjectif formé de : nom (fool) + suffixe -ish (= qualités négatives) ▷ *stupide*
• **laughable** = adjectif formé de : verbe (laugh) + suffixe -able (= que l'on peut...) ▷ *ridicule*
• **strangely** = adverbe formé de : adjectif (strange) + suffixe -ly (= pour former des adverbes) ▷ *étrangement*
• **violonist** = nom formé de : nom (violin) + suffixe -ist (= agent) ▷ *violoniste*
• **catholicism** = nom formé de : adjectif (catholic) + suffixe -ism (= comportement) ▷ *catholicisme*
• **backwards** = adverbe formé de : adverbe (back) + suffixe -wards (= en direction de) ▷ *en arrière*
• **childlike** = adjectif formé de : nom (child) + suffixe -like (= comme) ▷ *enfantin*
• **popularize** = verbe formé de : adjectif (popular) + suffixe -ize (= rendre) ▷ *populariser / vulgariser*
• **symbolical** = adjectif formé de : nom (symbol) + suffixe -ical (= pour former des adjectifs) ▷ *symbolique*

3

• **underpaid** = adjectif ◀ particule under (= sous) + participe passé de pay : *sous-payé*
• **undercooked** = adjectif ◀ under + participe passé de cook : *pas assez cui*
• **outrun** = verbe ◀ particule out (= dépassement) + verbe run : *distancer, dépasser*
• **overeat** = verbe ◀ particule over (= excès) + verbe eat : *trop manger*
• **overdressed** = participe passé ◀ over + participe passé de dress : *trop habillé*

• **upgrade** = verbe ◀ particule up (= vers le haut) + verbe grade : *améliorer, mettre à jour*
• **outgrow** = verbe ◀ out + verbe grow : *devenir trop grand pour*
• **uplifting** = adjectif ◀ up + verbe lift + suffixe -ing : *édifiant, inspirant*
• **overreact** = verbe ◀ over + verbe act : *réagir de manière exagérée*
• **overlap** = verbe ◀ over + verbe lap : *se chevaucher*
• **underrate** = verbe ◀ under + verbe rate : *sous-estimer*
• **overrate** = verbe ◀ over + verbe rate : *surestimer*
• **outdistance** = verbe ◀ out + verbe distance : *distancer*
• **upstage** = verbe ◀ up + verbe stage : *éclipser, souffler la vedette à*

4

Le verbe *out-Herod* est formé sur le nom *Herod* (Hérode, personnage de la Bible, responsable du massacre des Innocents) et la particule *out*, qui exprime un dépassement. L'expression, créée par Shakespeare, signifie donc littéralement "être plus Hérode qu'Hérode", c'est-à-dire le dépasser en cruauté. Elle traduit parfois la tournure française "être plus royaliste que le roi".

Imprimé en France par I.M.E. - 25110 Baume-les-Dames
Dépôt légal : Mars 2004 - Édit. 18389 - N° Imprimeur : 18005